INTERNATIONAL DISPUTE RESOLUTION
Volume 2

INTERNATIONAL DISPUTE RESOLUTION
Volume 2

Dialogue Between Courts in Times of Globalization and Regionalization

CARL BAUDENBACHER (ED.)

German Law Publishers
www.germanlawpublishers.com
International Law Edition

ISBN 978-3-941389-06-9

The Deutsche Nationalbibliothek lists this publication in the Deutsche Nationalbibliografie; detailed bibliographic data are available on the Internet at http://dnb.d-nb.de.

Typesetting: GreenTomato GmbH, Stuttgart
Printing and binding: Druckhaus "Thomas Müntzer", Neustädter Straße 1–4,
99947 Bad Langensalza

Table of Contents

Preface

In times of a globalized economy arbitration tribunals and courts have become powerful players in a globalized economy. Among them "Judicial Dialogue" has become a vital feature. Thus, this topic was chosen as the overall topic of the 2nd St. Gallen International Dispute Resolution Conference IDRC-HSG.

In October 2009, experts in the field of international dispute resolution from Europe and the U.S. gathered in the historic Parliament Hall of the Canton of St. Gallen. Distinguished judges and arbitrators, well-known scholars and practitioners elaborated on the overall topic in four keynote speeches ("Judicial Dialogue – Contextualized"/"Arbitrators and Judges – Opponents or Collaborators"/"Judicial Dialogue – Challenges for Counsels"/"Judicial Ping Pong – Conflicts of Jurisdiction") and four panels ("Dialogue Between the ECJ, the ECHR and the WTO Judiciary"/"Arbitration Tribunals"/"The Application of Uniform Law"/"International Bankruptcy Law"). In line with the "famous St. Gallen" spirit each keynote and panel was followed by animated debates.

After my introduction into the subject the conference was opened by ULRICH HALTERN, who spoke about "Judicial Dialogue – Contextualized." After I had the pleasure to give an introduction to the panel "Dialogue between the ECJ, the ECHR and the WTO Judiciary", ALBERTO ALEMANNO shared his thoughts and opinions on the "Tale of Judicial Dialogue: The Genesis of One of the Most Celebrated European Judicially-made principles – the Precautionary Principle." LARS BAY LARSEN dealt with the topic from the ECJ's point of view. The focus was concluded by the contribution of PEER LORENZEN who referred to the dialogue between the ECJ and the ECHR on a vertical and horizontal level. Then, ALAN RAU, BEN STEINBRÜCK and PER RUNELAND contributed to the topic of "Arbitration Tribunals". PIERRE TERCIER delivered the second keynote speech of the first conference day and focused on the topic of "Arbitrators and Judges – Opponents or Collaborators?", whereas he preferred the subtitle "Competitors or Co-Operators". The second conference day started with the keynote speech by MARCO BRONCKERS. He spoke about "Judicial Dialogue – Challenges for Counsels". ACHIM BENDER, ALASTAIR MULLIS and ERICH SCHANZE then examined the topic of "The Application of Uniform Law". The last panel was dedicated to judicial dialogue in the area of "International Bankruptcy Law". First, ADAM GOODISON discussed the topic from a British perspective. CHRISTOPH PAULUS then described a German's thoughts on a dialogue between courts in border crossing insolvency proceedings. The focus was concluded with the contribution by JAY WESTBROOK. The second St. Gallen

International Dispute Resolution Conference ended with a keynote speech by CHRISTELLE CHALAS on “Judicial Ping Pong – Conflicts of Jurisdiction”.

The editor of this book is deeply indebted to the eminent speakers and moderators whose contributions and personal support are the backbone of the IDRC. I would like to thank all those who assisted in the planning, organization, and coordination, namely BENJAMIN RHYNER, PHILIPP SPEITLER, SEBASTIAN MORITZ HEIDECKER, FELIPE PÉREZ POSE, FRANK BREMER and MICHAEL HOFMANN. In particular, I would like to mention SIMON PLANZER, who was in charge of preparing this conference, not only with regard to organization. He was also heavily involved in the substance of the conference. Furthermore, I would also like to express my warmest thanks to SEBASTIAN MORITZ HEIDECKER for the valuable help in editing and preparing this book.

St. Gallen/Luxembourg, August 2010 *Carl Baudenbacher*

Authors

PROF. DR. ALBERTO ALEMANNO, LL.M., Associate Professor at HEC Paris, Lecturer at the University of St. Gallen

PROF. DR. CARL BAUDENBACHER, President of the EFTA Court, Luxembourg, Professor at the University of St. Gallen, Director of the Institute of European and International Business Law, St. Gallen

LARS BAY LARSEN, Judge at the European Court of Justice

ACHIM BENDER, Presiding Judge at the German Federal Patent Court, Munich, Lecturer at the Universities of Düsseldorf, Dresden and St. Gallen

PROF. DR. MARCO BRONCKERS, Professor at the University of Leiden, Partner at Vermulst Verhaeghe Graafsma & Bronckers, Brussels

DR. CHRISTELLE CHALAS, Lecturer at the University Paris 8

ADAM GOODISON, Barrister, Gray's Inn, London

PROF. DR. ULRICH HALTERN, LL.M., Professor at the Leibniz University of Hanover

DR. DANIEL HUNKELER, LL.M., Partner at Schumacher Baur Huerlimann, Zurich

DR. H.C. PEER LORENZEN, Section President and Judge at the European Court of Human Rights

PROF. ALASTAIR MULLIS, Professor at the University of East Anglia

PROF. DR. PETER NOBEL, Professor at the Universities of St. Gallen and Zurich, Judge at the Commercial Court of Zurich, Partner at Nobel & Hug, Zurich

PROF. DR. CHRISTOPH PAULUS, LL.M., Professor at Humboldt University, Berlin

PROF. ALAN RAU, Burg Family Professor at the University of Texas at Austin School of Law

PER RUNELAND, Consultant with the International Arbitration Group of SJ Berwin, London

PROF. DR. DR. H.C. ERICH SCHANZE, LL.M., Professor emeritus at the Philipps University of Marburg, Professor at the University of Bergen, Permanent Guest Professor at the University of St. Gallen

DR. BEN STEINBRÜCK, M.Jur., Research Fellow at the Max Planck Institute for Comparative and International Private Law, Hamburg

PROF. DR. DR. H.C. PIERRE TERCIER, Professor emeritus at the University of Fribourg, Honorary Chairman of the International Court of Arbitration of the ICC, Paris

PROF. DR. FRANZ WERRO, LL.M., Professor at the University of Fribourg and Georgetown University

PROF. JAY WESTBROOK, Benno C. Schmidt Chair of Business Law Professor at the University of Texas at Austin School of Law

Moderators

PROF. DR. CARL BAUDENBACHER, President of the EFTA Court, Luxembourg, Professor at the University of St. Gallen, Director of the Institute of European and International Business Law, St. Gallen

PROF. DR. PETER NOBEL, Professor at the Universities of St. Gallen and Zurich, Judge at the Commercial Court of Zurich, Partner at Nobel & Hug, Zurich

PROF. DR. FRANZ WERRO, LL.M., Professor at the University of Fribourg and Georgetown University

DR. DANIEL HUNKELER, LL.M., Partner at Schumacher Baur Huerlimann, Zurich

Welcome

PROF. DR. CARL BAUDENBACHER[1]

Good morning ladies and gentlemen, distinguished speakers. It is my pleasure to welcome you to the 2nd St. Gallen International Dispute Resolution Conference. Our topic will be judicial dialogue from various perspectives. The notion of dialogue seems appealing throughout the world. If proof was needed, it was furnished a few days ago. In these post-neo conservative times, the mere readiness to enter into a dialogue may win you a Nobel Prize. But coming back to judicial dialogue: the notion relates to the practice of national, international and supranational courts to refer to each other. A sign of its current popularity is the fact that American authors have started not to speak of international judicial dialogue anymore, they created an acronym in order to save time, I think. They call it simply IJD. I am looking forward to two days which will offer us excellence in more than one respect.

As you see from the programme, the conference features outstanding speakers with rich experience in their respective fields. They will share their views on judicial dialogue from a wide array of professional backgrounds, be it as academics, counsel, judges or arbitrators. And we have speakers from two continents.

But I also wish to mention our participants. From a brief glance at the list, I understand that many of you have a strong academic or professional background and I am particularly pleased to see that even very long journeys were no obstacles to your coming here. The conference takes place in the Kantonsratsaal, a unique setting, the Parliament Hall of St. Gallen where in the old days the local prince abbot used to sit on his throne and in 1803 the independent Canton of St. Gallen was proclaimed. We will have lunch in the Hofkeller, a historic cellar which is also located in the heart of St. Gallen's monastery district.

Let me make a few introductory remarks on this year's overall topic. Judicial dialogue is not a brand new phenomenon. It has existed for a long time and I may recall here that the Swiss Supreme Court has always been a front runner in this. However, as a consequence of globalization and the judicialization of international law, judicial dialogue has been intensified and commentators have tried to put it on new grounds. Hence courts may quote judgments of other courts. Judges also meet each other. There is the saying of the "wanderlust" of judges. And they build regional and global networks. The main focus is on supreme and international courts, but during a recent visit in Japan

---

1 President of the EFTA Court, Luxembourg, Professor at the University of St. Gallen, Director of the Institute of European and International Business Law, St. Gallen.

I learned that in this country the Supreme Court is very reluctant to make reference to foreign judgments, whereas lower courts do that almost as a routine. Yet, proper cross-fertilisation of courts may only be feasible if certain framework conditions exist. One may say that a market economy and a system of separation of powers are indispensable. I have suggested that three basic constellations can be distinguished: prescribed, necessary and voluntary dialogue.

Prescribed dialogue may be laid down in a legally binding document. To give an example, under the Agreement on the European Economic Area, the EFTA Court when interpreting EEA Law is bound to pay due account to the case law of the European Court of Justice, rendered after the date of the signature of this agreement.

Second, dialogue may constitute an objective necessity in situations where there is uniform law, but no common court. I may mention the Paris Convention for the Protection of Industrial Property, the Bern Convention for the Protection of Literary and Artistic Works and the European Patent Convention as examples. Further illustrations would be the Vienna Sales Convention or the Convention Relating to the Status of Refugees. ECJ Judge Allen Rosas is even of the opinion that the longstanding practice of the European Court of Justice to make reference to rulings of the European Court of Human Rights when dealing with fundamental rights is an example of necessary cooperation. We will come back to that. It is probably not the only issue which is at stake with regard to the relationship between these two European Courts.

Third, maybe the sole real form of dialogue is voluntary dialogue, dialogue by choice. Courts may choose to reference other court's rulings without there being any legal obligation or uniform law in the strict sense. This would for instance apply to the relationship between the European Court of Human Rights and the United States Supreme Court. I remind you of the famous judgement in Lawrence v Texas, which has caused quite some debate in particular on the other side of the Atlantic Ocean.

We will have four panels and four keynotes. The first panel will address the dialogue between the European Court of Human Rights in Strasbourg and the Court of Justice of the European Communities in Luxembourg, certainly not a new topic but a fascinating one. Both courts are major exporters of ideas. But we also have seen important developments in their relationship. I may just mention the Bosphorus judgment of the Strasbourg Court or the ongoing discussion whether the way European Competition Law is being enforced is compatible with Article 6 of the Convention. I will chair this panel and I am pleased to welcome Lars Bay Larsen and Dr. Peer Lorenzen, two prominent judges from these courts. Peer Lorenzen has been awarded his Doctor Honoris Causa just one month ago. Furthermore, Professor Alberto Alemanno from HEC in Paris, a former legal secretary at the Court of Justice and at the Court of First Instance of the European Communities will include a view on the WTO judiciary.

The second panel will deal with questions of dialogue in the field of arbitration. As far as I can see, this has been neglected in the academic debate on judicial dialogue. This debate has so far mainly focused on state courts and on international courts, which are set up by states, too. And this is unfortunate because arbitration seems to be a particularly fertile soil for dialogue because it is characterized by delocalization and flexibility. My friend and colleague Prof. Dr. Peter Nobel, who has decades of experience as an academic, as a counsel, judge and arbitrator, will chair this panel. A special welcome goes to Professor Alan Rau, a specialist in alternative dispute resolution and in international arbitration, who has come all the way from Austin, Texas; and to Dr. Ben Steinbrück from the Max Planck Institute in Hamburg. Per Runeland, the highly experienced consultant from London, will offer us some practical insight.

The third panel will be dedicated to the application of uniform law. It will be chaired by Prof. Dr. Franz Werro who is the academic director of the Centre of Trans-National Legal Studies in London. There are constellations, I have said it, where dialogue is not prescribed but necessary, wherever we have uniform law but no common court. Prof. Alastair Mullis from the University of East Anglia and Prof. Dr. Dr. h.c. HSG Erich Schanze who teaches at Marburg, Germany, and Bergen, Norway, and here in St. Gallen will focus on the Vienna Sales Convention. I am also particularly glad to welcome Judge Achim Bender from the German Federal Patent Court, an old friend of St. Gallen.

The fourth panel will address judicial dialogue in the context of bankruptcy law. Here, dialogue is not only a necessity, it is also a reality. This panel will be chaired by Dr. Daniel Hunkeler, a leading Swiss insolvency lawyer. We are very proud to have gathered an outstanding group of experts consisting of, if I may say so, the grand old man of international bankruptcy law, my good friend Prof. Jay Westbrook from the University of Texas, Humboldt University Professor Dr. Christoph Paulus and Adam Goodison, a London based barrister specializing in insolvency law.

We are finally looking forward to four keynotes. Prof. Dr. Dr. h.c. Pierre Tercier, Honorary Chairman of the International Court of Arbitration in Paris, will close up the first day with a presentation on the subject of whether arbitrators and judges appear as opponents or rather as collaborators. Prof. Dr. Marco Bronckers from the University of Leiden will launch the second day with a speech on the challenges that judicial dialogue may involve for practicing counsel and finally, Dr. Christelle Chalas will illustrate, in the light of the Flash Airlines case, how conflicts of jurisdiction may end in a judicial ping pong. I recall in this context Lord Denning's well-known statement in the Court of Appeal's 1983 Smith Kline judgement: "As a moth is drawn to the light, so is a litigant to the United States of America. If he only can get his case into their courts, he stands to win a fortune. At no cost to himself, and at no risk of having to pay anything to the side."

Let me conclude by introducing our first keynote speaker, Prof. Dr. Ulrich Haltern, Professor at Leibniz University of Hanover and Director of the Institute of National and Trans-National Integration Research. When Juliane Kokott was appointed Advocate General of the European Court of Justice in the fall of 2003, Ulrich Haltern became a member of this faculty for three semesters, if I am not mistaken. And he is unforgotten here in St. Gallen. Ulrich Haltern was, if I may say so, infected with the virus called law in context during his studies at Yale and at Harvard, and it is from this perspective that he will introduce us to the aspects which surround judicial dialogue. Please, Ulrich, the floor is yours.

Keynote

Judicial dialogue – Contextualized

ULRICH HALTERN[1]

Ladies and gentlemen, it is a pleasure to be back in beautiful St. Gallen. I feel very honoured to be invited to give the first keynote. Carl Baudenbacher has managed, again, to put together an impressive group of scholars and practitioners. Stepping up to the podium, one feels truly humbled. So thank you so much for having me. The task Carl has set me is to introduce and to contextualize the concept of judicial dialogue. There is no way I can do justice to the rich phenomenology of judicial dialogue and the learned and lively debates surrounding it. However, let me try and make a few observations, meant as an effort to structure our discussions to come, as well as to provide a theoretical backdrop – perhaps a sobering backdrop as well to something that seems overwhelmingly promising.

My first remark is purely academic, and on top of it, it is a remark that I must ask forgiveness for, being a German academic. German legal academia still all to often engages in what Martin Shapiro almost 30 years ago famously described as "Constitutional Law without politics, the written constitution was a sacred text, the professional commissary as legal truth, the case law as the inevitable working out of the correct implications of the constitutional text and the constitutional court as the disembodied voice of right reason and constitutional teleology." To be sure, I do not mean to disparage doctrinal work, quite on the contrary. Doctrine is the first intellectual stratum of judicial developments, and as such it is neither intellectually empty nor without systemic significance. Doctrinal work is the foundation of everything that comes after. However, in doctrinal work, political institutions (like governments, international interests, organisations and, of course, other courts) are objects of a court's jurisprudence. This is not the world of judicial dialogue. Speaking of judicial dialogue means to adopt an actor-centred approach to law. Here, other courts are subjects, interlocutors, partners to a dialogue. Doctrine alone can only take us so far, although we can, from studying some court's jurisprudence, learn something about what that court believes itself to be or claims to believe itself to be. We learn nothing, however, about the power and the compliance pull of its decisions. That, of course, is a matter not of logical deduction from doctrine but of empirical observation and social and political explanation. We must therefore go beyond the self-referential legal universe. The question of the legal content of a court decision is only part of the whole picture.

There is also the question of persuasion, or, we might say, of a decision's compliance pull, which adds an institutional layer to our inquiry. As Carl has already pointed

1 Professor at the Leibniz University of Hanover.

out, it is a truism to state that courts all over the world are talking to one another. National, supranational, transnational, and international courts increasingly, and at length, cite and discuss foreign and international precedent on a wide range of issues. Over time, this cross-citation among the world's courts has developed into a kind of informal dialogue. Courts use judicial dialogue in a way that seems to cross-fertilize ideas. This development is not at all limited to constitutional law. We see it in areas such as bankruptcy, antitrust, intellectual property, and defamation law. We should not be surprised because the increasingly globalized nature of trade relations and the Internet drive the world's legal systems into closer contact with each other, and judges respond by participating in various forms of dialogue. While this may not be entirely unexpected – it is, after all, a truism –, for a German legal academic, it is a happy and almost miraculous development that we are able to theoretically frame these developments as "judicial dialogue", and even call it a truism. Because to recognise judicial dialogue as such means to leave behind Shapiro's disembodied voice of reason that we Germans hold so dear. Judicial dialogue drives German positivism towards recognizing the severe limitations of purely doctrinal legal thought.

My second remark concerns different forms and levels of judicial dialogue. I have neither the intention nor the time to establish an exhaustive taxonomy of judicial dialogue. Others will do so; Carl has already begun, and today and tomorrow, we will continue to hear about the details of very different forms of dialogue. Still, let me point out at least some categories.

There is, of course, the sort of institutionalized judicial dialogue between the European Court of Justice and its Member State counterparts. Judicial review on the Community level, as you all know, is a tandem system of justice; one leg being located at the Community level, the other at the Member State level. The largest number of cases reaches the ECJ by way of preliminary references through national courts according Article 267 TFEU. The importance of this procedure cannot be overestimated. It has become the principle vehicle for imposition of judicially driven Community discipline. The results have been quite extraordinary. National judicial hierarchies have been torn apart. Sacred cows have been slaughtered. British Courts overturned the doctrine of parliamentary sovereignty, and issued an injunction blocking the effect of a British law pending judicial review at the European level. The French Cours de Cassation accepted the supremacy of EC law in the face of threats from the French legislature which distributes jurisdiction under the age old charges of Gouvernement de Juge.

Outside of this procedure, ECJ national courts keep talking to each other no less intensely than under Article 267. The prime example, of course, is the German Constitutional Court. Noting that its power was being eroded, it fought back. And the result is what the Court calls the "cooperative relationship" between the ECJ and national highest courts. We have seen the last instance of that cooperation in the recent decision on the Lisbon Treaty. Yes, we do have a tug of war between the ECJ and the German Court, which of course gathers support from the Italian, Belgian, Spanish, and

Polish highest courts. Still, the tug of war is incredibly fertilizing. For instance, there would be no, or less, human rights jurisprudence at the EU level had it not been for threats and demands from Karlsruhe. And sometimes those highest courts even look to each other and come out with integration-friendly (and sometimes not so integration-friendly) decisions in support of each other.

Then, there is an external dimension as well. The European Court is partner in the dialogue with many other non-national courts as well. Unsurprisingly, it has close relations with the EFTA Court; they cite each other frequently. Also, the relationship between the ECJ and the Strasbourg Human Rights Court has become more and more intense. Suffice it to mention the European Court of Human Rights decisions in Matthews, Cantoni and, of course, Bosphorus. In Yusuf and Kadi, Segi and Gestoras Pro Amnistía, the ECJ made its decision with a view to talking to the Strasbourg Court. In MOX Plant the ECJ talked to international tribunals, perhaps in less fortunate words than it did when it talked to the European Court of Human Rights or to the national courts. Finally, the WTO panels and Appellate Body are never quite happy with how their conversation with the ECJ turns out.

There is, alas, not always convergence. Sometimes there is resistance. Invariably, however, there is engagement. Judicial dialogue can be understood as a site of engagement between domestic law and international or foreign legal sources and practices. Courts do not treat foreign legal material as binding, but neither do they put on blinders that exclude foreign legal sources and experience. Foreign sources are seen as a way of testing the understanding of one's own traditions. How does that help judicial discourse, or facilitate the decision? First, to the extent legal systems perform similar functions, similar concerns may arise about interpretive choices. Approaches taken in other countries may be helpful information in deciding what interpretation works best. Secondly, comparisons shed light on difference. Considering the questions that other systems pose can sharpen our understanding of how different our own system is. To understand yourself, it is helpful to step out of yourself and look from the outside. Thirdly, there may be something universal, trans-national and perhaps natural about some rights. While they are enshrined in specific constitutions, perhaps they reflect something like essentialia humana, the ubiquity the idea that human beings are the central concern for any legal system. That, at least, is the hope.

My third remark, finally, is less disjointed and less cheerful. I would like to address an issue that is widely discussed in the United States, but seems less plausible in Europe. It happens more often than not, even under President Obama's administration, that Americans and Europeans are facing each other in a curious mixture of fascination and total bewilderment. This is true in politics as it is in law. Judicial dialogue has become a matter of intense discussion in the United States as well. However, we hear many more critical voices than, in the light of our European integration experience, we would expect. I will try to make sense of that critique. I believe it points to a deepstructure of law that is perhaps readily overlooked in Europe – if you will, the law's dark underside. The case that sparked off the heated debate in the United States was Roper v Simmons. Of course, there have been others, like Atkins v Virginia and Lawrence v Texas, where the Supreme Court has considered foreign and international law, causing considerable praise and also criticism from the academy. Roper, however, was a new dimension. The United States Supreme Court granted a motion against juvenile execution, holding it cruel and unusual punishment. Justice Kennedy, writing for the majority, observed that international opinion had turned against juvenile death penalty, and he cited foreign courts. Unsurprisingly, Justice Anthony Scalia dissented. He bristled at the notion that foreign and international law might be used by the United States Supreme Court and argued that "either America's principles are its own, or they follow the world; one cannot have it both ways". Scalia acidly continued that "[t]hough the views of our own citizens are essentially irrelevant to the Court's decision today, the views of other countries and the so-called international community take center stage." Justice Scalia concluded that "the basic premise of the Court's argument – that American law should conform to the laws of the rest of the world – ought to be rejected out of hand."

You might think: This is, well, Scalia. But no, members of both the House and the Senate introduced resolutions declaring that "judicial determinations regarding the meaning of the Constitution of the United States should not be based on foreign precedent, unless such foreign precedent informs an understanding of the original meaning of the Constitution." At the confirmation hearings of both Chief Justice Roberts and Justice Alito, US senators expressed the view that a judge's citation of foreign precedent constituted an impeachable offence. Prominent scholars called for a constitutional amendment banning that practice.

What is going on? What happened to the idea, also voiced by some members of the United States Supreme Court, that American judges are participating in an emerging world community of courts? Are those who believe that reliance on foreign authority to interpret constitutional rights represents a dramatic departure from American traditions, crazy nationalists? To be sure, there is some truth to the notion of American exceptionalism. While I have no time to explore it more deeply here, I am sure you all know examples. It is fair to assume, then, that there is more to the matter than simple starry-eyed nationalism.

Here is what the European experience suggests. Legal scholars understand constitutional courts to be working on a common set of problems, dealing primarily with rights and legitimacy. They look to the variety of national constitutional courts in order to learn from the experience and arguments of others. Every modern liberal state confronts the same set of constitutional issues (rights to privacy, speech, due process and welfare) on the one hand, and issues of legitimate institutional design on the other. Since courts address these issues in an order that is entirely accidental, one constitutional court can make use of the research and reasoning of another constitutional court that may have confronted a similar problem earlier. Comparative materials thus come to compete with precedents as a substantial source of legal reasoning. If the authority of the court decision rests upon its appeal to reason, then this approach appears not only natural but essential. It draws upon the model of inquiry of other sciences. No research programme can fetishise its own past; rather it must be open to new discoveries wherever they are made. Universal constitutionalism rests on two familiar and intertwined discourses: on a doctrine of rights, and on a theory of political legitimacy. The former locates constitutionalism in a discourse of human rights, the latter in a discourse of the social contract tradition. Both are based on reason, both know no boundaries. Human rights, social contract and, alas, reason do not end at national borders. That is precisely what our European experience suggests.

This experience speaks to most, if not all of us. It does not speak, however, to all Americans, and I wish to suggest why that is. Based on the borderless discourse of rights, interests, and reason, universal constitutionalism misses much of what is essential to law and democracy. It fails to understand how law is deeply embedded in beliefs about the rule of law. The rule of law is not merely about justice. It is a shorthand expression for the imaginative construction of a complete social political order. It is a way of perceiving events. It is a framework for our understanding that makes it possible to perceive legal meaning in every single event. Finally, it provides a geographical and temporal shape to events, a normative foundation for claims of authority and understanding of the self and others as subjects of rights and responsibilities. Law has its own imaginative universe. It is the imagination that constructs the past and the future of the polity just as it constructs, at the same time, the political identity of the citizen. For example, in the political imagination of citizens of Germany, the rule of law echoes with the memory of World War II and Auschwitz. American citizen's political imagination of the rule of law echoes with the memory of the Revolution and the Civil War, with a continuity between the citizens and the founders. In other words, the rule of law is a structure of beliefs about the meaning of the polity. Its value lies not in objective facts, but in the deployment of power to sustain these beliefs. What we must investigate, then, is the structure of meaning within our experience of public order as the rule of law occurs.

National law usually has a richly textured cushion of cultural resources that it can rely on. It is a symbolic form which establishes the world of pre-existing rules to which individuals appeal in order to make sense of their lives. That means it serves as a community's memory, as a storing space that preserves existing meaning. In other words, there is a deep-structure underneath law's smooth, liberal surface design. There is also myth and memory, not only rationality and principle. There is also sacrifice, not merely contract. There is also will, and not just reason and interest. A nation state's legal system exerts a tremendous normative pull, not because of the threat of punishment or some sort of basic consensus. Rather, the legal regime expresses in traditional terms the sovereign will of the community. To disconnect law from the idea of sovereignty fails to see the crucial connection of the rule of law to self-rule. In a democratic regime sovereignty and law are tightly linked. The sovereign people governs through the rule of law; by following the law, citizens participate in popular sovereignty and achieve self-government. Law, then, is not simply about the promise of order. It is about identity. And as such, as any identity question, it is incredibly political, erratic and also a little dangerous.

I believe that if we really want to understand what is at stake in law and in sovereignty, we need to turn from the discourse of justice and liberty to that of love. Certainly in the United States, popular sovereignty in and through the rule of law constitutes a civic religion of ultimate meanings, which is love. How can we doubt for a single second that as soon as Justice Kennedy cites European Court of Human Rights decisions as precedent, there will be a call for impeaching him?

If you want another analogy, here it is. There is a theological conundrum, thousands of years old. Why do we accord ultimate value to God's words? Do we because they are true and right, or because they were spoken by God? We see the same conundrum with regard to law. Do we value the law, and follow it, because it is good and just, or because it was spoken by the popular sovereign? Both questions are hard to answer; perhaps it is both. Perhaps it is impossible for theology and for democratic theory to separate one from the other. But at a closer look, in Europe, with its progressive understanding of global constitutionalism, we do separate these two. We value the law because it is good and just, not because it was spoken by the sovereign. In Europe we have begun to liquidate, to fragment or at least to invisibilise the sovereign. We like to think of our political order as post-sovereign if not even post-political. Law is what it is, whoever spoke it into existence. Different from the United States, in Europe there is no law that is more authentic or more valuable than other forms of law simply because it was brought into existence by our sovereign, our Founding Fathers. On the contrary, EU law trumps national law. In Europe law is law. Not so in the United States.

We need to remember that this European way of seeing things is a social construction, no less mythical or metaphorical than the American myth of popular sovereignty and authentic law spoken into existence by the Founding Fathers. We also need to remember that a post-sovereign order has consequences far beyond the law. It is an order stripped of its attachment to the popular sovereign, a world of economic transactions, consumption and markets. A world, that is, in the words of the Schumann declaration, where war becomes unthinkable. The political seems widely replaced by the market ideas. Identity is as fluid as money flows. Citizenship becomes more a matter of consumption than of political rights and duties. And in such a world, with the political and the market largely conflated, the citizen and the consumer become essentially one and the same thing. There is a flattening of identity and experience. But still, this may be progress, because we are leaving behind a heritage of sacrifice, of collective sovereignty with all its dangers, and calls for pro patria mori. Maybe this is what we want? It comes at a cost, but it may be worth it. It is not up to me to decide. But let me be crystal clear: the European model is not the model of the world. Judicial dialogue is but a manifestation of an entire mindset that marginalises sovereignty, history, authenticity and identity. This mindset holds a lot of promise, but also means loss. There is a reason why President Obama can seriously speak of sacrifice and love in the political realm while we cannot. None of this means we have turned the wrong corner. But it does mean that we need to be aware of where we are going.

Thank you very much.

Discussion

CARL BAUDENBACHER

Thank you very much Professor Haltern for this fascinating opening speech on judicial dialogue in context. You rightly focused on the transatlantic relationship and tried to explain why there are these differences in approach. Now, we have two American speakers here and I wonder whether they would like to say something not on the US position, but on how they see the position of the United States Supreme Court, and even the Supreme Court is not unanimous.

JAY WESTBROOK

Carl you have already introduced me as old so I speak hesitantly. I am only an expert in insolvency law and not in these larger questions. It was a wonderful talk and a very informed one and very good at capturing a lot that is the essence of the American difficulty with this issue. Periods of transition are always very difficult and we are in a period of transition. One thing that your talk addressed a little bit less than perhaps an American might think of: If there is to be this transition to a more internationalized view, in so far as that transition is simply among a sort of elite dialogue that someone like Ann-Marie Slaughter has talked about in her book, then that loses the *foundation* of popular sovereignty. Popular sovereignty lies at the heart of our experience and our beliefs in America, so unless, although this is a cliché I suppose, unless there is some elevation of popular sovereignty to another level internationally, then internationalization will be greatly resisted no matter how attractive it is in many, many other ways. So, I think that is maybe one comment that an American would make on this excellent talk.

ALAN RAU

I wish I had a half hour to reflect on the talk and then a half hour to write out some comments on it because I am not very good at thinking on the floor. But, the notion that the elaboration of the law is rooted in legislative sovereignty – an idea rooted in positivism – is a critical notion in American legal development, and a notion which is very hard for me to get away from, it is a notion that is almost second nature to me. I remember when I first went to Europe and I spoke to a student from France and he was talking about his experience in America with windows that opened from the bottom and you would raise them up and he thought that this is a very American way of opening the window – and my reaction was, "Well, good grief, that is the way all windows have to be, right? That is the natural way a window is. That is what a necessarily is." So, as an alternative to this curiously American way of looking at the law – is the alternative, which I take to be a kind of a natural law approach – the approach that you were suggesting? Perhaps this is merely an artificial dichotomy, but it does seem that the notion that you were criticizing – the Scalia approach – is in essence the very positivistic notion, that what we think of as our American law is rooted in our legislative sovereignty and there is nothing else to American law other than that.

ULRICH HALTERN

Maybe I need to clarify two things. One is, I have not really positioned myself normatively. I do not mean to say that this or that way is the right way to go – Scalia is wrong, Kennedy is right, or the other way around. What I was trying to do is to describe.

ALAN RAU

Maybe I gathered that from your tone.

ULRICH HALTERN

Well, I have certain sympathy for Justice Scalia – not because I believe he is right. But, he does phrase things in a way that gives voice to a strain of thought that is deeply embedded in American legal thought and that makes me believe that Europeans and Americans stand to each other as two different systems of belief. We do share a lot; we do have common values. But, we also remain within what German philosopher Ernst Cassirer would call different symbolic forms, or different universes of thought – precisely your window example. Americans look to Europe and see confusion, no phone number, not one single face, no hierarchy, little or weak belief, fragmented political identities. Europeans look to America and see different things: hierarchy, strong belief, and strong political identity. If you want an analogy, this is precisely how Catholics and Protestants view each other. They have a lot in common, but they are also bewildered by each other. When it comes to the imagination of the political, Europe is Protestant: Lacking hierarchies, lacking a single identity, fragmented, and believing in the word rather than the ritual. The US imagination of the political seems more Catholic: Strong identity and authority, believing in miracles and rituals rather than the word, and so on. Protestants sometimes believe themselves more enlightened and disparage Catholicism as "smells and bells". Europeans are sometimes prone to do the same with regard to the American imagination of the political.

There is no way of saying that Protestantism is "better" than Catholicism. There is now way of saying that Europeanization is better than Americanization. All I am trying to do is to point out where the differences are; that these are different universes of thought, universes of life. So, that is the normative status of what I am trying to do.

Secondly, I believe America goes even further in its symbolic form of thinking about the law. It is not just rooted in legislative sovereignty; it is actually rooted in violence. We have different perspectives on the world. One is through law. We put on the "glasses of the law", look through its lenses, and see the whole world through the rule of law. We take off those glasses and put on different glasses, let us say the lenses of political action. The world looks different. Those two perspectives are always separated (law needs to invisibilize political action, while political action marginalizes the law). At one point, however, these two perspectives are not separated and in competition with each other, but inseparably linked. That point is the foundation of the law. That foundation is, of course, entirely mythical. In the US it is the Revolution which gave rise to the constitutional state and its law. A revolution is two things coming together: Ideas, and people who fight for them, violently. So, there is blood, there are bodies being harmed and mauled – at the very foundation of the state and its law. It was Abraham Lincoln who used those mauled and mangled bodies of the revolutionary generation in order to transfer their perceived authenticity (because what is more authentic than the body itself?) on to the Constitution. He did so as early as in 1838, in his speech about "The Perpetuation of Our Political Institutions", and completed the picture in his world famous Gettysburg speech 1863. He called that a "political religion" of the United States, the essence of which was to follow the law. President Obama, by the way, does the same thing. In other words, law in the United States of America has a corporeal aspect to it, a deep connection to the body and to violence, something that is very much amiss in Europe. Again, I am not offering any normative position on that. It stands to reason, however, that after 1945, there is no way we Europeans, especially we Germans, would enter that universe of thought again. That universe of thought is that of deep sovereignty: A conception of the sovereign as a body whose part the citizens want to be. There is, actually, much metaphysical promise to this imagination. Being part of the body of the state means to be able to transubstantiate into the sovereign. Not only do you know your place in the world. You can also become one with the sovereign and partake in its metaphysical qualities. For instance, you become immortal. Even if you die for the state, the sovereign will live. Sacrifice is, in its imaginative or symbolic form, the opposite of death. You die so that the collective body can live. There is no way we Europeans can go there again. That is the difference in thinking about the law between Europe and America. It is more than legislative sovereignty.

ERICH SCHANZE
It is breathtaking what you say, and I like it a lot. A footnote: The current phenomenon of "constitutionalization of law" seems to me a new version of a perennial problem which was treated in Roman times under the heading of "law and rhetorics". The "locus classicus" is the causa Curiana, a litigation in the Republican era reported by Cicero in De inventione. Mucius Scaevola, the most distinguished lawyer of his time, presented the "literal" legal view on a clause in a testament. Before the tribunal of 40 men he was derided by the prominent rhetor Crassus who pointed at the inequity and inconsistency of the consequences of the literal view. Scaevola lost the case. Scalia's literalism is easily misunderstood from the rather freewheeling style of interpretation of European constitutional courts. The deeper, unanswered question seems to be: What are the "constitutional" rules of organizing the conflict between "original" legal texts and its changing context with reference to ageing statutes. It is a well known problem, but a most difficult one.

ULRICH HALTERN

It is indeed an old problem. I am not sure, however, how much the old tradition can help today. The reason is the concept of will. I believe the American notion of popular sovereignty and law as embodied in popular sovereignty has a lot to do with will – the collective will of the sovereign. The Greeks had no concept of the will. It was St. Augustine of Hippo who introduced the will as a whole new concept. The American concept owes a lot to early Christianity.

On Scalia, I think there is something extraordinary about his notion that in order to find constitutional truth you have to show forth the founding. That, after all, is Scalia's originalism: You show forth the moment of the founding, nothing more. If you do that, you will arrive at truth. There is an institutional part to this argument: It is up to political institutions, not to courts, to adjust the law to the necessities of today's reality. If law does not fit today's problems, it needs to be adjusted by parliament, not by courts. Courts, in other words, abandon the quest for justice – something that Chief Justice Taney, who also was an originalist, explicitly spelled out in his infamous and racist Dred Scott decision of 1857. To Europeans, such an approach seems utterly counterintuitive. It is not what we think judges should do. They should not be historians who find out the original meaning of constitutional phrases at the time of the Founding; rather, they should be scientists who apply principles like proportionality and balancing. Truth is something courts arrive at through rational reasoning and through the power of the better argument. In contrast, Scalia conceives of truth as something that needs to be historically tested: Truth is history, history is truth. That, too, is more than a mere theory of constitutional interpretation. It is a complete world view, and it shapes much of the American imagination of the political, the state, and the nation.

ALBERTO ALEMANNO

A very quick comment. You refer in your talk about the fact that judicial dialogue is often accidental, circumstantial, and unpredictable and as such it does not seem to fit with the law's permanent aspiration towards legal certainty. So, what about the other side of the story? What about introducing a statutory provision mandating the judges to look outside of the legal border? Instead of prohibiting them to do something, you inject perhaps a sort of new ethics of adjudication. Frankly speaking, this kind of provision really speaks loudly to new generations, people who have this reflex every time they look at a fresh case at looking at what has been decided somewhere else. This comparative perspective is embedded in a lot of young lawyers' mindsets nowadays. So, to what extent this might be normatively construed, exactly in the opposite way as in the US is envisaged today?

PETER NOBEL

I like your description of law as a body full of will, of violence, this pragmatist approach. But, the other side is that you have a very strong judiciary as a controlling means. We are seeing, in Europe it is true, we see law rather as a structure, a rational structure. But, the judges on the other side, they are very often bloodless followers and executing much more than in the United States, the tiny little bits of the rules of law. I prefer actually this strong American judiciary, a scene full of life than trying to hide and disguise things behind a so called rationalism. The evil spirits, I prefer them.

ALASTAIR MULLIS

I just wonder where you would put the English courts in that. In this debate you talk generally about Europe being very different from the United States. But, I am not terribly happy with discussions of Europe as though everything in Europe is happening at the same pace. Because it seems to me if you look at everything, in many respects we are much closer to the United States in the way that we approach many of the questions.

ULRICH HALTERN

I agree. Of course, it is a blatant oversimplification to talk of "Europe". At the same time, it is probably just as oversimplifying to talk of "America" – west coast, east coast, the south-west, they are all very different. (And the south west is breath-takingly beautiful, too.) England is a case on point. United States law is begotten by violence – that is the American myth. In England, law begets more law begets more law begets more law. Common law reaches down into the invisible depths of history, and we do not know how deep to reach because once we pull up one judgement, it points to another precedent. Germany is very different from that – history plays a small role only in legal or constitutional interpretation, science or pseudoscience plays a much bigger role. Of course, France is different again from Germany, and Spain is very different from Great Britain. So, yes, I agree, I am oversimplifying. You can deconstruct the whole thing. But then, you can always deconstruct anything. It is always possible to take an even closer look. I believe that my oversimplifications may be excused by the fact that the varying legal traditions within Europe are coming together in a way that may justify a look that is less hard than that of Alastair Mullis. Think of the holy cows slaughtered by the European Convention of Human Rights or, even more so, by EU law. There has been talk of an emerging single European legal sociology already. What I suggest is a fundamental divide between Europe and the United States, visible to every European visitor entering the United States. That divide mirrors a split imagination of the political and, at the end of the day, a different universe of legal thought.

Like Peter Nobel, I too like American legal discourse, which to my mind attests to a vibrant democracy. There is something to be said for the European paradigm of rationality though. A democracy is not a machine for creating consensus – and yet, a democracy may suffer from a law caught in the crossfire of the two political camps. Also, the anaemic and bloodless legal and, sometimes, political discourses have not been adopted out of the blue. They are path-dependent, just like the American discourses are, and the European path used to be extremely mythical, violent, and bloody. Against the collective will, we have set institutions; against sovereign power, a system of rights. Europe wanted to be anaemic in order to leave the divisive political past behind. Part of that bloodlessness is management by experts (think of the EU Commission), and lawyers are always part of that expert cohort. The Union's finality is not deep politics, but output-legitimacy because its aim is to be a counter-weight to unfettered nationalism. Nationstates after World War II tied themselves, like Odysseus, to the European integration mast so they would not be able to follow the sirens' song of nationalism. The bonds were, and still are, made of reason, rationality, and expertise. They may be bloodless, but after so much blood in European history, that may actually be a relief. Perhaps there is more ethos to expertise than we are ready to acknowledge.

ALAN RAU

I do not want to use this term in too much of a pejorative sense but there is something profoundly Cartesian in what you are saying and that is very troubling to me because it is so terribly ahistorical. When you are looking at the American experience, you are really not taking into account at all the fact that you are looking at a political compromise at a particular moment in history where an attempt was made to limit, in a written document, political power for the future, by compromising among various political interests to lay down limits on political power for the next several hundred years. This is not an exercise in rationality because politics is not an exercise in rationality. This is an exercise in conflict of interest. To impose some sort of truth-telling rational enterprise on that, is a very European enterprise which seems to miss or risks missing the essential; it is a bloodless enterprise which seems to miss the essential, the guts of the entire enterprise. That is a risk, I think, with that kind of analysis.

ULRICH HALTERN

I am not sure I agree. American constitution, I think the founders conceived of themselves as political artisans. The Federalist Papers testify to their self-understanding as scientists: They tried, as a first step, to find the truth of political science, and, as a second step, thought of their task as connecting the historical state to the timeless truths of political science. They tried to work these ideals through in the newly founded American state. The Founders were political scientists and also political artisans – builders, really. That did take a lot of guts, I agree. But, it was also an effort to find reason in politics. There was, I might add, one exception, slavery. Slavery was not governed by political republican theory. The Federalist Papers actually acknowledge that much, by indicating it was a bad, albeit necessary compromise between the north and the south. Slavery seems, at the Founding, the exception – a political margin outside the center of republican thought. But, then it came back to haunt the United States by leaving the margins and entering center-stage, threatening to collapse the whole republican construct. The response to that threat, as you all know, was violence; no theory, no political science, and certainly no law could resolve the crises, only Civil War. Law, it had turned out, had only fuelled the flames; and again we speak of the infamous Dred Scott decision. Now, to say that the Framers thought of themselves as political artisans does not mean that that kind of political imagination could in any way be stabilized. On the contrary: At some point the revolution ends, the founding generation dies, and you need to turn the American people from artisans, revolutionaries and builders into a people that engages in maintenance. This, precisely, is what Lincoln did – he turned the whole political imagination around. He successfully established a political imagination which placed the maintenance of existing political meanings of the polity at its center: His "political religion" of following the law.

ALAN RAU
I do not agree, but I think we are engaged on the right level.

BEN STEINBRÜCK
I liked your point that a US Supreme Court Justice might face impeachment proceedings if he would start quoting case law of the European Court of Human Rights in Strasbourg. Would these impeachment proceedings be successful? There is not only Scalia, there is also the movement of dynamic interpretation of the constitution. The second question is: In which direction are we going? Towards a more dynamic interpretation of the law? How will the situation be in ten years, in twenty years? Is there, despite the differences today, an emerging trend or are the two groups going into opposite directions?

ULRICH HALTERN
As to your first question, I am sure impeachment procedures would be unsuccessful. But, they were suggested, and I used that example to show how strongly many people feel about this issue – perhaps more strongly than we do – and how outraged they are.

As to your second question, Oxford University Press has just published a book on "The Constitution in 2020". Of course, its authors have been writing what they usually write, so it is not really about the constitution in 2020. But, I loved the title. I am not sure where constitutional discourse in the United States is going. With more democratic appointees on the Supreme Court, my hunch is there will be more Kennedy-like justices, quoting and citing to the European Court of Human Rights, the German Federal Constitution Court etc. On the other hand, we see President Obama who is deeply steeped in the myth of the American Founding, of Lincoln's new way of thinking about the law as a maintenance project, as somebody who is showing forth the founding to reach the truth. The American myth – just like the European myth – has a very strong hold on people, Presidents and Justices alike. I do not believe this to be an automatism, or an easy triumph for universal constitutionalism.

So, I am not sure where we are going. It is hard to predict.

CHRISTOPH PAULUS
Just as a footnote: You are talking about the constitution, that is one thing; insolvency law is another. In this down to earth area, for instance, you find a countervailing tendency. My dear teacher and then friend, Steve Riesenfeld: When he came to the United States, he was advised by Dworkin in New York: Never quote any foreign source because that is "a kiss of death". In contrast, it is now three years ago that Chapter 15 of the Bankruptcy Code has been enacted which is modelled after the UNCITRAL

model law on cross-border-insolvency. There, you find a rule which explicitly states: Look around in the world, and search for foreign decisions in order to keep global uniformity of this law! You see, there are countervailing developments. That is all I wanted to say.

ULRICH HALTERN
Thank you, I think that is an important point. Of course, if there is a rule that says you have to do it, there is an easy prediction of what is going to happen. But then, I just read an empirical study of what federal courts in America quote and cite to. There is no suggestion whatsoever that they quote or that they cite to more to foreign national courts than decades ago.

CARL BAUDENBACHER
We are at the end of this first session. Thank you very much once more for a stimulating speech, Ulrich. Let me conclude with three remarks. The former president of the European Court of Human Rights, Luzius Wildhaber, used to say when he spoke about the attitude of certain US Supreme Court Justices vis-à-vis judicial dialogue; if they do not want to, they do not want to. Just let them, it is going to be a matter of time. That is probably a good approach. Second point; the former Canadian Supreme Court Justice Claire L'Heureux-Dubé wrote some eleven years ago that in the long run, those Americans who do not participate in this global dialogue, will face a problem. They will not be referred to the same extent as they used to be in the past. I mean, let us not forget that after 1945 the US Supreme Court was the main exporter of ideas to the whole world. There was a notion of "trade in human rights", all coming from the US Supreme Court. The third point, you mentioned it yourself Ulrich, is that judges realize that dialogue gives them power. If they can make reference to a foreign source with a reputation, that gives them strength. This is in particular so in Europe, because as a European judge your "opponent" is often a national government or a number of national governments. National governments do not necessarily like that judges get additional support.

Focus:
Dialogue Between the ECJ, the ECHR and the WTO Judiciary

Introduction

CARL BAUDENBACHER[1]

Now, we come to the first panel on Dialogue between the European Court of Justice, the European Court of Human Rights and the WTO judiciary. The first focus will be on the relationship between the Court in Strasbourg and the ECJ in Luxembourg. But, we will also hear about the WTO dispute settlement mechanism and there is, if I am not mistaken, a citation by the European Court of Justice in Luxembourg of a WTO decision. To a certain extent, I think that also the EFTA Court will be mentioned.

As far as the players are concerned, we have two Danish judges, it is Danish dynamite this morning; Judge Peer Lorenzen from the Human Rights Court and Judge Lars Bay Larsen from the Court of Justice of the European Communities. We also have an Italian voice, Professor Alberto Alemanno, originally from the Università Commerciale Luigi Bocconi in Milan, a university which is a close cooperation partner of St. Gallen. He is a pupil of the WTO Chairman Giorgio Sacerdoti and now a professor at HEC in Paris.

The relationship between the Human Rights Court in Strasbourg and the ECJ is certainly an interesting one. You will remember that EEC integration started as a pure economic undertaking and it was only under the pressure of national courts that the ECJ started to recognize what it called fundamental rights, not human rights, but it is probably the same. In the meantime, there is a codified full-fledged fundamental rights system in Community Law. With this I mean not only the protection of fundamental rights in substance, but also the procedural aspects which are commonly referred to as access to justice. The Charter of Fundamental Rights will become binding under the Lisbon Treaty and dealing with fundamental rights and making reference to the Convention and the case law of the Human Rights Courts has become routine for the ECJ. I may remind you that in the cases *Schmidberger* and *Omega* the ECJ balanced fundamental rights versus fundamental freedoms and the fundamental rights prevailed. I doubt, whether this would have been possible some twenty years ago. But, there is another development. Not only has ECJ case law been loaded, if I may use this expression, with fundamental rights, the other side of the coin is that the court in Strasbourg is more and more dealing with cases that involve essential questions of economic law. I may just mention a few: The right to freedom of expression, which is guaranteed in Article 10 of the Convention is highly relevant for the whole sector of advertising; the interpretation right to respect for private and family life laid down in Article 8 of the

---

1 President of the EFTA Court, Luxembourg, Professor at the University of St. Gallen, Director of the Institute of European and International Business Law, St. Gallen.

Convention may have certain consequences for the way the European Commission has to conduct its dawn raids in cases of suspected antitrust infringements. Both courts have finally been called upon to rule on the fundamental economic law issue of collective bargaining. Some three years ago the court in Strasbourg in the case *Soerensen & Rasmussen vs Denmark* ruled on a so-called closed shop agreement in Danish law. A closed shop agreement provides that if you want to be employed in a certain firm, you have to become a union member and the court in Strasbourg found this to constitute a violation of the Convention.

The European Court of Human Rights makes reference to ECJ case law when interpreting notions of the Convention. The ECJ, as I said, quotes as a matter of routine. This kind of dialogue is characterized by an equal status of both courts. Most observers are stunned that there has been so little judicial conflict over the years and decades, but there are diverging judgments. I will give you a recent example: On 12 November 2008 and on 21 April 2009 the Human Rights Court delivered two judgments concerning the right to collective bargaining and the right to take industrial action, to strike, in two Turkish cases. The right to strike was also allowed in the public sector. Commentators see a conflict with the ECJ's landmark decisions in the Laval case and in the Viking Line case. They see the Strasbourg Court as more union friendly than the court in Luxembourg. Now, talking about the possibility of a judicial conflict, I would like to raise the question of whether there is some sort of a soft mechanism between the two courts. Do we have a committee that meets on a regular basis in order to discuss pending cases involving similar legal questions? At any rate, the relationship between Strasbourg and Luxembourg is not limited to this horizontal dimension. Individuals have brought cases before the Human Rights Court in which they challenged decisions of Member States of the Convention which were taken on the basis of Community Law or of decisions of Community organs including the ECJ. They alleged violation of the Convention. I know that Judge Lorenzen will address this issue.

There is finally the WTO dimension. I mentioned that the European Court of Justice has made reference to WTO case law at least once, but also in the Court of Human Rights WTO decisions have played a major role. I will just mention the Biret case, which concerned the well-known EC legislation imposing a ban on import of hormone treated beef from the US and from Canada. That is one of the reasons that prompts me to go back to my old law school at Texas at least once a year that I can get a decent piece of beef, because here in Europe it is hardly sold anymore. Both community courts dismissed an action for compensation by one of the firms and at the end one of these firms took the case to the Human Rights Court. There seems to be a type of constellation in the case law of the Court of Human Rights which probably gives it the upper hand vis-à-vis the European Court of Justice. But, the role of the WTO in dialogue matters goes beyond that and Alberto Alemanno will address it.

I give the floor to Judge Peer Lorenzen from the European Court of Human Rights as the first speaker.

A Tale of Inter-judicial Dialogue and Jurisprudential Cross-fertilization: the Precautionary principle in EU, EEA and WTO Law

ALBERTO ALEMANNO[1]

Good morning, Mr President, Ladies and gentlemen.

I am very honoured (although somehow intimidated) to be here today surrounded by several giants not only in their disciplines but – what makes things even more worryingly – also in the specific theme of our conference: The dialogue among courts.

In order to overcome this initial emotional barrier, I propose to immediately start telling my favourite "tale of judicial dialogue": The genesis of one of the most celebrated European judicially-made principle – the precautionary principle.

As you may know, this principle enables public authorities to act also in situation of scientific uncertainty. Its vocation is to strike a balance between the imperative of free trade and the interest in individuals' public health and against the backdrop of both scientific and behavioural uncertainty.

This story does not involve the "classic" ECJ/ECHR dialogue, but rather the other form, perhaps less sensitive but of equal significance, of European horizontal judicial dialogue: The one existing between the Community courts and the EFTA Court, the Court established in 1994 to ensure the application of the EEA to the EFTA countries. Being this a very well-known story which has been successfully analyzed by the giants who I previously referred to[2], I will try to add a further twist in the reconstruction of this successful exercise of "judicial dialogue", by also listening to the voice of the WTO adjudicatory bodies.

---

1 Associate Professor at HEC Paris, Lecturer at the University of St. Gallen.

2 C. Baudenbacher, *The EFTA Court: An Actor in the European Judicial Dialogue*, 28 Fordham International Law Journal, 353–391 (2005) and also C. Baudenbacher, The EFTA Court, the ECJ, and the Latter's Advocates General – a Tale of Judicial Dialogue, in: Continuity and Change in EU Law. Essays in Honour of Sir Francis Jacobs, edited by Anthony Arnull, Piet Eckhout and Takis Tridimas, Oxford 2008, 90 et seqq. and M. Bronckers, Exceptions to Liberal Trade in Foodstuffs: The Precautionary Approach and Collective Preferences, in the EFTA Court 10 Years On, 105–114 (Baudenbacher, Tresselt & Orlygsson eds., Hart Publishing, 2005).

With your permission, having had the good fortune to spot this story before its unfolding and to follow it along my first hesitant steps in my legal career, I will take the liberty to take a narrative path.

Exactly nine years ago, after having spent a few months in Paris as a Summer Associate in a very French(y) law firm, doing research on how to enable European producers to obtain damages suffered as a result of the EC non-compliance with the AB Hormones decision, I embarked on my master's degree studies in Bruges. I had no choice but to pick the fanciest available topic for my LLM paper: The precautionary principle (PP). Ironically, this was the principle that somehow enlightened the Community legislator when adopting its ban on the use of hormones in beef that kept me so busy the previous summer.

It was a great responsibility – as my supervisor kept telling me – to write about a principle which had not been recognized as such neither by the EU legislator (who merely codified it, though without defining it, in the Treaty with reference to the environmental policy) nor by the Courts. No surprise that I was facing so much resistance from my supervisor: Being him universally considered the father of the mutual recognition principle, he felt uneasy with the emergence of a legal tool that would have defied the Commission's efforts to build a common market by enabling Member States to restrict trade even in the absence of scientific proof. Also, behind that principle there was an interesting dialogue, this time involving the administrative branch, the European Commission, who prepared the ground for the establishment of this principle via the 1970 directive, and the judicial branch, the ECJ, who decided the legendary Cassis de Dijon.

It was against this backdrop that in the year 2000 I have began working on what no court dared yet to call the precautionary principle. Yet, there were some embryonic forms of 'precautionary thinking' in the air.

This was the time of the mad cow disease which led the Commission to adopt a ban on the export of beef from the UK fearing a possible transmission of the disease from animals to humans. The ECJ upheld the EC measure by referring to the "uncertainty as to the existence or extent of risks to human health".

Would the ECJ have taken the same stance, if the entity acting in a situation of scientific uncertainty were a Member State and not a European institution? This was the 6 million dollar question keeping my brain warm during the cold Bruges winter.

It was at that time that I learned two interesting developments:

- the EFTA court had a pending case addressing exactly this question (Norway had banned the import and marketing of Kellogg's cornflakes fortified with vitamins and iron in the absence of a nutritional need of the population and this notwithstanding the fact that these cereals had been legally produced and marketed in another MS)[3];

- the European Commission had been working for some time on a draft communication devoted to this principle in the aftermath of the Hormones dispute, which it had just lost against the US[4].

Surprisingly enough, amid my previous EU law studies in Switzerland, I knew what the EFTA Court was, but had no clue to what extent its case law might have bound the ECJ in future cases involving the application of the corresponding provisions of the ECT. In other words, in the utilitarian approach typical of students, was there any compelling reason for which I should have paid attention to this relatively new Court in my analysis? Probably because of lack of talent, I could not find any book providing an answer to this question and – in order to play it safe – I began speculating on the issue by dwelling into the homogeneity principle as enshrined in Art. 6 EEA. According to this provision the EFTA Court is supposed to interpret provisions of the EEA agreement that are identical in substance to corresponding EC rules (as it was the case here) in conformity with the ECJ case law, but quid iuris when the EFTA Court was analyzing a fresh legal case? Could it be bound by the European courts' case law? My attempted answer at the time was: Yes, provided that it was persuasive enough …

The premise for an interesting and unusual judicial dialogue between European courts belonging to two separate legal orders and applying substantial identical law were laid down. Yet, this outcome could have not been taken for granted.

The judgment of the EFTA Court came on April 5, 2001. Although judicially recognizing a MS' right to act in situations of scientific uncertainty, it concluded, by relying on previous ECJ case law, that Norway could not maintain its restrictive approach to fortified foods: Its practice not only was scientifically flawed, but was also inconsistent with other policies (some domestically produced cheese was indeed fortified). By borrowing the expression of Judge Timmermans, there was some clear sign of "creative homogeneity" in that judgment as the EFTA Court did not hesitate to advance the relevant existing ECJ case law which originated in the area of additives.

This judgment came just 2 months after the publication of the Commission Communication on the precautionary principle. This temporal circumstance produced a very intriguing phenomenon of "indirect" judicial dialogue (par ricochet): The EFTA Court, by borrowing some of the language of the Commission Communication which, in turn, was largely influenced by the WTO adjudicatory body's decisions in Hormones, happened to inject into its legal reasoning ideas and concepts which had more to do

---

3 Case E-3/00 EFTA Surveillance Authority v Norway (so called Kellogg's judgment); 2000–2001 EFTA Court Report, 73.

4 European Commission Communication on the precautionary principle, COM (2000) 1.

with WTO law (notably the SPS Agreement) than with the EEA and EC legal orders. Some examples?

The conditions under which the principle may be invoked largely overlap with those established by the SPS Agreement. The adopted measures must be proportionate, non-discriminatory, transparent and consistent[5] and, in any event, cannot be supported by mere hypothetical risk because they must be based on a risk assessment. Although, the Commission Communication was not cited in the judgment, it was quoted in the Judge Rapporteur's Report.

The Commission Communication, acting as a soft law gateway, succeeded in connecting two autonomous legal orders, the EEA and the WTO, and their respective courts, at a very crucial moment: The birth of the precautionary principle.

But to what extent the judicially recognition and framing of the principle by the EFTA court would have been followed by the EU Courts? Would the dialogue being kept alive by the ECJ?

Although some relevant judgments intervened in the meantime in which the EFTA ruling had been quoted by the EC Courts (Pfizer and Alpharma, Monsanto, etc.), we had to wait until 2003 before the introduction of a Kellogg-like case before the ECJ. The facts of the case largely reminded those of the original Kellogg's case: This time it was Denmark instead of Norway subjecting the marketing of fortified foodstuffs (cranberry juice instead of cereals) to the proof of specific need of the population[6].

Although the AG Mischo took as a starting point the EFTA Court's judgment, he came to the conclusion that the Danish practice was justified by the need to protect public health in the name of the PP. The fact that my LLM paper, then turned into an article, had been quoted several times in that conclusion, does not bear the sole responsibility for this very debatable conclusion[7].

The ECJ instead followed entirely the approach taken by the EFTA Court, thus materializing the judicial dialogue engaged earlier on. Although, recognizing the existence of the precautionary principle, under the same conditions listed by the EFTA Court, it condemned the Danish practice for failing to satisfy these conditions.

The dialogue between the Luxembourg sisters' Courts over the principle was not over though. Indeed, the precautionary principle after having been shaped further by both the CFI and the ECJ along the lines sketched out by the EFTA Court – in judgments

5 A. Alemanno, Trade in Food: *Regulatory and Judicial Approaches in the EC and the WTO*, Cameron May, 2007 and A. Alemanno, *The shaping of risk regulation by Community Courts*, Jean Monnet Working Paper 1/18, 2008.

6 Case C-192/01, Commission v Denmark [2003] ECR I–9693.

7 Opinion of AG Mischo in case C-192/01, Commission v Denmark [2003] ECR I–9693.

like the Vitamin line of cases and Bellio, crossed the JFK road in Kirchberg and went back to the EFTA Court. This was the Pedicel case, or the EFTA's Gourmet[8]. To what extent Norway could justify its ban on advertising alcoholic beverages in the name of the precautionary principle?

The EFTA Court, by relying on its Kellogg's judgment as well as the EU Courts' relevant case law developed subsequently, seized this opportunity to square the circle: Since the effect of excessive alcoholic consumption are well-known, the PP "does not apply". The dialogue came full circled.

This is still good law today as recently proven by its extension by the ECJ from the sector of fortified food to herbal medicinal products in Commission v Spain (C-88/07 [2009]).

The EFTA Court's judgment in Kellogg's went down in history, not only as the first judicial recognition of the precautionary principle within the EEA (what eventually led the ECJ and CFI to accept, and shape, this principle within the Community legal order), but also as a sign that EFTA Court's case law may influence, by virtue of its persuasive strength and not because of statutory requirements, the EU case law.

I argued somewhere else that the outcome of the judicial dialogue triggered by the Kellogg's judgment went far beyond the identification of the precautionary principle[9]. The language employed by the EFTA's Court in that judgment laid down the foundations for the emergence of a EU regulatory model for risk regulation. Most of the features that render the EU approach to risk regulation different than other models around the world, can be identified in that judgment: The language of risk analysis, the functional and institutional separation between risk assessment and risk management, the insistence on the consistency precept in the chosen level of protection, the precautionary principle and, finally, the idea that science is necessary, but not sufficient to legitimate action vis-à-vis risks.

Risk regulation seems indeed an area where courts have a further incentive to cooperate by engaging into learning processes, mutual comparison and experimentation.

But to what extent this tale of judicial dialogue has been enriched by the voice of the WTO adjudicatory body? Would it be correct to depict the PP the son of a "ménage à trois", instead of that of a "European judicial affair"?

As mentioned earlier, the first interpretations of the SPS Agreement made it through the EEA and EC legal orders via the Commission Communication on the PP indirectly influenced by the EU judicial interpretation of the PP.

---

8 Case E-4/04 – Pedicel AS v Sosial- og helsedirektoratet.

9 A. Alemanno, *The shaping of risk regulation by Community Courts*, Jean Monnet Working Paper 1/18, 2008.

However, neither the panels nor the AB have referred to the European courts in their judgments in relation to the PF. This is due to several factors, but the most important one, undoubtedly, relates to the rules of interpretation employed by the Geneva courts. Being them "textualment obsedés", they seldom move on along the list of interpretative criteria in Article 32 of the Vienna Convention. Besides this, being their mission bound to the interpretation of the "covered agreements", this statutory requirement limits further their interpretative horizon. Article 3.2 of the DSU, authorizes the use of other sources of law to the extent they may assist the panel in "clarifying the existing provisions of the [covered] agreements in accordance with customary rules of interpretation of public international law".

While they do not seem too prone to engage into a judge-to-judge dialogue, the WTO adjudicatory bodies have systematically shown their readiness to engage into another kind of epistemic dialogue of no less importance: The dialogue with the experts.

In virtually all SPS disputes, the panels have relied on individual experts and engaged into a serious discussion with them. In one of its latest reports, Hormones II, the AB has indeed stressed the importance of this dialogue and even incorporated it within the newly-drafted standard of review[10].

Unlike the WTO adjudicatory bodies, the European courts have shown their reticence in relying on external advice and prefer to engage into a dialogue with their peers rather than with other kind of experts. Although the rules of procedure allow both the EC and the EFTA Courts to appoint experts, their members prefer to avoid this.

We have reasons to suspect, that in today's world the principle iura novit curia, the court knows the law, and probably more than that, lies on shaky grounds.

We, therefore, venture to suggest that the fruitful judicial dialogue among courts will soon be supplemented by an equally fascinating and promising epistemic dialogue: The one between the lawyers and the experts[11].

I thank you for your attention.

10 US-Continued Suspension of Obligations in the EC Hormones Dispute, WT/DS320 and WT/DS321, AB Report, para 591. For a review of this decision, A. Alemanno, Risk Assessment Under WTO Law: Workable Requirement or Probatio Diabolica?, Working Paper presented at the ASIL-ESIL conference on Science and International Law, Helsinki, November 2009.

11 For more on this point, A. Alemanno, *The Dialogue between Judges and Experts in the EU and WTO, in Shaping the Rule of Law through Dialogue: International and Supranational Experiences*, 2009, P. Carrozza, F. Fontanelli, G. Martinico (eds.), Europa Law Publishing.

Dialogue Between the ECJ and the ECHR

LARS BAY LARSEN[1]

A. Introduction

Time is generally a rather limited resource and today's occasion is certainly not an exception to that rule.

I will then try to make my introductory remarks very short, also given the fact as *Carl* has rightfully pointed out, my colleague Peer Lorenzen has already described the general outline of the relations and the cooperation between our two courts very well.

And, I can certainly confirm, what he has already said, in particular concerning the regular and very fruitful meetings of the two courts. It is not, to answer more specifically Carl's question, a case of in-depth discussion of pending cases, but of the background of judgments of the past, current and future problems facing the two courts, and a fruitful exchange of views and experiences.

I would like to stress that judicial dialogue is found not only where we are confronted with a smoking gun in the form of an explicit reference in a judgment of one or the other court. The fact that there is no such quotation in one or another piece of jurisprudence, does certainly not exclude that judgments from other courts, be it national or international courts, have served as a source of inspiration for the judges deciding a particular case.

Peer Lorenzen has tried to present some of the situations where the practices of our two courts overlap one another in a framework of horizontal judicial dialogue and judicial dialogue at the vertical level. It is my intention – in a strictly non-violent fashion – to add further bits and pieces of flesh and blood to the list of examples that *Peer Lorenzen* has already provided us with.

B. A few general remarks

Before I do that, I would like to make one or two general remarks. It is no longer absolutely uncommon or unusual for the ECJ to identify and eventually interpret and apply international legal norms in addition to those already contained in the European

1 Judge at the European Court of Justice.

Convention on Human Rights. This is particularly the case concerning fundamental rights. In the early days of the ECJ, this was certainly done more rarely and much more reluctantly than today, where we find ourselves in a more globalized world. Time does not allow me to dwell on the long evolutionary road which has led the ECJ thus far to settle on the formula which was used in Point 283 of the Kadi judgment, where, "fundamental rights form an integral part of the general principles of law whose observance the Court ensures. For that purpose, the Court draws inspiration from the constitutional traditions common to the Member States and from the guidelines supplied by international instruments for the protection of human rights, on which the Member States have collaborated or to which they are signatories. In that regard, the ECHR has special significance."

This judgment of principle, in Paragraph 278 and for the next approximately 50 paragraphs, addresses a number of fundamental questions of admissibility and access to justice concerning the rather complex relationship between on the one hand, international law, in this case United Nations Security Council Resolutions, which are binding upon the EU member states, but are implemented jointly by the Member States through secondary EC Law although the EC or the European Union is not in itself bound by the UN norms in question; and on the other hand fundamental rights including the European Convention on Human Rights as well as the EC and EU treaty obligations to secure access to judicial control. The conclusion to be found in Paragraph 326 of the Kadi judgment, which reversed the ruling of the CFI, states and again I quote, "[i]t follows from the foregoing that the Community judicature must, in accordance with the powers conferred on it by the EC Treaty, ensure the review, in principle the full review, of the lawfulness of all Community acts in the light of the fundamental rights forming an integral part of the general principles of Community law, including review of Community measures which, like the contested regulations, are designed to give effect to the resolutions adopted by the Security Council under Chapter VII of the Charter of the United Nations."

So, consequently, in this case the ECJ could not agree with the CFI that the contested regulation in the Kadi Case, although it was designed to give effect to a binding resolution adopted by the Security Council, and afforded no latitude in that respect, should enjoy complete immunity from jurisdiction at the CFI and the ECJ.

Much more could be said on the Kadi judgment and on the difficulties linked to this Bermuda Triangle of international law, and I'm sure that both my Court and the European Court of Human Rights in Strasbourg will no doubt further develop their respective jurisprudence in this area further in the years to come.

For me, today, it is sufficient to highlight the current ECJ formula concerning the protection of fundamental rights, and to stress the fact that the principle task for the ECJ is to give judicial review, that validates, interprets and applies EC and EU law. This is our task.

But more and more often, we find ourselves in a situation where we cannot fulfil this task without taking into account notably fundamental rights as they are found in international law, including the European Convention on Human Rights and the constitutional practices of our Member States. Inevitably, this latter taking into account implies that we also have to interpret these fundamental rights, even when they are found in international law.

In fact, sometimes the ECJ is even faced with the task of identifying whether such an international norm exists at all. This was the case in the Advocaten voor de Wereld-affair (Case C-303/05), where the Belgian Arbitragehof asked the ECJ, under a preliminary ruling pursuant to Article 35, to rule on the validity of the Council framework decision on the European Arrest Warrant. Among the questions asked by the referring court, one concerned the fact that, in certain circumstances, the Framework decision on the European Arrest Warrant prohibits making the execution of the European Arrest Warrant subject to the condition, that the acts on which it is based must also constitute a criminal offence in the state of execution. The Arbitragehof asked whether that innovation is compatible with the principle of equality and with the principle of legality in criminal proceedings and, accordingly, whether it complies with Art. 6 (2) of the Union Treaty.

By its answer to this question of substance, the ECJ indirectly made it clear that there is no international principle of a superior nature that requires dual criminality as a precondition for extradition of a suspected or convicted criminal. It is correct that dual criminality is very often found as a precondition for extradition in international extradition arrangements, but that is not as a consequence of the existence of a superior legal principle, rather it reflects the fact that mutual recognition of decisions and judgments politically often depend on a high degree of harmonization or at least approximation of the respective national laws. This is particularly the case when it comes to criminal proceedings.

C. A non-exhaustive list of "crossroads" for judicial dialogue

After these general points, I would like to turn to what could be described perhaps as a non-exhaustive list of crossroads for judicial dialogue; especially between the ECJ in Luxembourg and the Court in Strasbourg.

1. Situation. Of course, the first classical situation which comes to mind, is when a national court has asked my Court for a preliminary ruling under Art. 234 EC and it is argued that a provision, be it Art. 8 on the respect of a person's private and family life, of the European Convention on Human Rights, might be of importance to or even decisive for the ECJ's interpretation of the relevant EC or EU instrument. Here, of course, in this typical, classical situation, we nowadays often find that such references to the European Convention coincide with references to the EU Charter. Although it is not as yet of a binding legal nature, the presumption is that whatever interpretation is given by our Court should be in conformity, not only with the hard law of the Strasbourg Convention and the Strasbourg jurisprudence, but equally with the softer law of the Charter. This is a well-known situation; I will not dwell further on it.

2. Situation. Similarly the ECJ might be forced to interpret and apply the ECHR in a direct action, i.e. when a private party is asking the Community for compensation under Art. 235 EC and 288(2) EC and are arguing that a provision of the ECHR is relevant to the CFI or – in the case of an appeal – to the ECJ, when deciding the case. Equally, in an action for annulment under Art. 230 EC it may be argued i.e. by the European Parliament that the Council while adopting a piece of secondary legislation has violated a fundamental right or principle such as Art. 8 ECHR on the right to respect of family life. This was precisely the situation in Case 540/03, Parliament v. Council, where the Parliament unsuccessfully challenged the validity of Directive 2003/86/EC on the right to family reunification. This situation is in a sense equally classical as the first horizontal situation I mentioned.

3. Situation. Sometimes, and that is the third situation, we have before us an affair where the fundamental rights are argued as the basis for admitting the case.

The underlying idea is that not only should the specific articles of the EC and EU Treaties giving (private) parties access to the Community courts not be interpreted narrowly because of Art. 6 of the Strasbourg Convention, but that even where it is clear that the Treaties have not conferred a competence for the CFI and the ECJ, such competence should nevertheless flow from Art. 6 of the Strasbourg Convention and the general provision of Art. 6(2), EU stating that

> *"[t]he Union shall respect fundamental rights, as guaranteed by the European Convention for the Protection of Human Rights and Fundamental Freedoms signed in Rome on 4 November 1950 and as they result from the constitutional traditions common to the Member States, as general principles of Community law."*

This was argued with force in the two cases, Segi and Gestoras Pro Amnistia in which the said organizations had filed actions against the Council before the CFI, seeking compensation for damages they claimed to have suffered as a result of being included on the list of persons and organizations involved in terrorist acts pursuant to Council Common Position 2001/931/CFSP.

The Council Common Position constitutes one element of the EU implementation of the United Nations' measures taken after the terrorist attacks on 11 September 2001. Other elements – such as those taken with a view to freezing assets related to the financing of terrorist acts – have their legal basis in the first pillar, and are thus subject to the fuller judicial controls at Community level.

[The Council Common Position, which was adopted on the basis of Art. 15 EU and Art. 34 EU, implements the United Nations Security Council Resolution 1373 (2001), which requires all States to cooperate in criminal investigations or criminal proceedings related to the financing or support of terrorist acts. The plaintiffs alleged that their inclusion on the list harmed their presumption of innocence, freedom of expression, freedom of association, and the right to respect of private life. However, the Court of First Instance ruled that it has no jurisdiction over the award of damages under Title VI EU and no jurisdiction to assess the legality of an act within the scope of the common foreign and security policy and judicial and home affairs pillars. Consequently, the Court of First Instance dismissed the actions for compensation as inadmissible.]

In its judgments of 27 February 2007, which upheld the decisions of inadmissibility by the Court of First Instance, the Court of Justice confirmed that under Art. 35 EU the Court of First Instance is not entitled to rule on damages and that the Community Courts – that rely solely on the competences conferred to them by the Treaties – have no jurisdiction to review an action for damages, as it is under the jurisdiction of national courts to review such actions.

The ECJ thus plainly rejected the idea that Art. 6 (2) of the Union Treaty, which states in general terms that we are a Community of law and justice, can in itself provide a jurisdiction for the ECJ or the CFI that goes beyond the specific competences conferred on them by the Treaties.

Consequently, in this area it is the responsibility of the Member States of the Union to assure at national level and, if necessary, at the EU level by amending the Treaties, the judicial controls which are necessary to comply fully with the obligations following from Art. 6 (2) EU and Art. 6 and 13 of the Strasbourg Convention, which were the Articles argued by the parties who were seeking to present their case of compensation before the CFI.

This seems in a sense to go rather well with the logic underlying the jurisprudence of the Strasbourg Court that the member states of the Council of Europe cannot escape their obligations according to the Strasbourg Convention by transferring their legislative powers to other international or multinational organs, which does not live up to the minimum standards of the Strasbourg Convention; or at least offers a level of protection which can be considered equivalent, that is, as *Peer Lorenzen* stressed, comparable to the European Convention of Human Rights as stated in the Bosphorus Judgment. So, here we have in a sense a mixture of a horizontal situation and a vertical situation.

4. Situation. A clearer case of vertical dialogue is the discussion on the role of the Advocate General at the ECJ as introduced by Peer Lorenzen in his presentation and specifically with the reference to the Kokkelvisserij-judgement of 20 January 2009 in which the majority of judges at the Strasbourg Court decided that the publication of the opinion of the Advocate General without a further subsequent contradictory phase did not imply a violation of Art. 6 of the European Convention of Human Rights.

I have been specifically asked for a personal remark on the role of the Advocate General at the ECJ and in spite of the very wise general recommendation that lawyers should normally not plead their own more or less personal cases, I have overcome most of my hesitations and have decided to make at least a very brief, and I stress, personal comment.

It is perhaps not so surprising that I will argue that the system of the Advocate Generals does not violate Art. 6 of the European Convention of Human Rights. The introduction of the Advocate Generals at the ECJ was made as a political compromise and their role is one that is certainly not found in the legal systems of quite a few Member States. Of course, one might well have considered a number of other alternative systems or one might do that in the future. But given the system as it is, I have to confess that I have great difficulties understanding that the publication of an opinion by an independent member of the ECJ, who by the way never takes part in the subsequent deliberation of the judges of the formation, should constitute a violation of Art. 6 ECHR. Is it the fact that this piece of individual inspiration is delivered in a completely transparent fashion that poses the problem? If not, why not also challenge the first draft of the judgment by the Reporting Judge, delivered without any external transparency to the other members of the formation? It is my experience that this first draft of the judgment may well serve as just a strong a piece of inspiration as the opinion of the Advocate General.

I am personally all in favour of respect for the principle of contradiction, but I am equally in favour of applying law, including international law, in such a way that common sense and law, whenever possible, go hand in hand. And I am so far not at all convinced that the current system of the Advocate Generals at the ECJ should not be able to go hand in hand with Art. 6 ECHR also in the future.

5. Situation. Finally, I would like to mention a special case of horizontal dialogue, which can be identified when law-makers in Brussels decide in secondary EC legislation to make reference to, build upon or transpose basic rights found in the European Convention on Human Rights, which are subject to a dynamic interpretation by the Court in Strasbourg. This may pose a certain challenge for my Court as it did in the Elgafaji Case (C-465/07) rather recently. In this case the ECJ was asked by the referring Dutch court, it was the State Council, to interpret Art. 15 (c) of the directive on minimum standards for the qualification of and status of third country nationals or stateless persons as refugees or as persons who otherwise need international protection (subsidiary protection).

The problem – on which the member States did not agree – was more specifically whether Art. 15 (c) of the Directive intended to give a protection that went further than Art. 3 of the European Convention – as it is currently being interpreted in the jurisprudence of the Court in Strasbourg.

In this case the ECJ, handled the relationship between our Court and the task in front of US and the Strasbourg jurisprudence by saying in point 28,

> *"[i]n that regard while the fundamental right guaranteed under Article 3 of the ECHR forms part of the general principles of Community Law, observance of which is ensured by the Court, and while the case law of the European Court of Human Rights is taken into consideration in interpreting the scope of that right in the Community legal order, it is, however, Article 15(b) of the Directive which corresponds in essence to Article 3 of the ECHR. By contrast Article 15(c) of the Directive is a provision, the content of which is different from that of Article 3 of the ECHR and the interpretation of which must, therefore, be carried out independently, although with due regard for fundamental rights, as they are guaranteed under the ECHR."*

This does not exclude that Art. 15 (c) of the Directive might be subject also to a dynamic interpretation in the future. Such a dynamic interpretation may well be inspired by developments in the dynamic jurisprudence from Strasbourg, but it is then for the ECJ and all the law-makers in Brussels to decide, whether it is by dynamic interpretation of my Court or by amending the Directive in Brussels that coherence with an eventual further dynamic interpretation in Strasbourg of Art. 3 ECHR shall be secured.

D. Final and brief comments on the post Lisbon situation

Time does not allow me to go much further, but I will just make three or four very brief comments on the post Lisbon situation, which will imply, eventually, that we will have three more complete legal systems for Fundamental Rights, that is the European Convention on Human Rights, we will have the EU system and we will have the Constitutional practices of the member states.

We will have an EU Charter for Fundamental Rights that is to a large extent inspired by the European Convention, but goes further in scope and will be legally binding.

We will also have an EU which will, eventually, become a member to the European Convention on Human Rights.

Equally, we will have an ECJ with a more complete jurisdiction, not only as concerns the third pillar of the Union Treaty which will be integrated in the first pillar, but also to a limited extent as concerns the common security and defence policy, the present second pillar.

These developments and adjustments of the "judicial polycentrism", which will continue to exist concerning the protection of Fundamental Rights, will no doubt imply new further challenges for both my Court in Luxembourg and for the Court in Strasbourg, but, personally, I see no reason why we should not be able to handle both individually and collectively these new and modified challenges in a constructive dialogue.

Thank you very much for your patience and attention.

Dialogue Between the ECJ and the ECHR and the WTO Judiciary

PEER LORENZEN[1]

A. Introduction

Ladies and Gentlemen, dear colleagues, being the fourth speaker in a row of three eminent speakers before me, at the same time facilitates and complicates matters as one has to adapt to what has already been said. I will do my best. A lot has already been said about the notion "dialogue" between courts and I have no intention to repeat any of it. But allow me a few supplementary comments in this special context.

The first one concerns what is meant by "dialogue"? In the literal sense it simply refers to direct contacts between courts in order to discuss questions concerning their functioning – in particular the application in their case-law of common legal statutes or principles. Such contacts in the form of meetings are today to a large extent institutionalized between various types of courts at the national as well as at the international level. The ECJ and the ECHR are no exceptions: For a long time such meetings have been held with regular intervals and with great success. They are now a firmly rooted pillar in the relations between the two courts.

But in our context "dialogue" is obviously meant in a much wider sense: Without trying to be very precise I think one can simply put it as a question whether courts in their case-law should seek inspiration from case-law of other courts – not only in order to reach similar results, but also in respect of interpretation principles (for example the use of a dynamic interpretation style) or principles for drafting the reasons in a judgment.

However, "dialogue" does not necessarily mean the same in respect of various types of courts. In my opinion a distinction should be made not only between national and international courts, but also – and maybe more important – between courts at different levels in the judicial hierarchy. Thus, the relevant elements in a dialogue may be different between courts performing the same functions (for instance between national supreme or constitutional courts or at the international level between regional human rights courts) compared to courts where one has controlling or supervisory functions in respect of others (for instance between supreme courts and lower national courts or the ECJ and the ECHR in respect of national courts). One could speak respectively of a dialogue at a "horizontal" and a "vertical" level. When it comes to the relations

1 Section President and judge at the European Court of Human Rights.

between ECJ and ECHR the situation is far from clear and in fact rather complicated, but I think it is useful to consider it under both aspects.

B. Dialogue between the ECJ and the ECHR at a "vertical level"

Let me make it very clear that by using the words "vertical level" I have no intention to allege that the ECJ is in any way subordinated to the ECHR when dealing with human rights issues. It follows from the mere fact that the EU is not a Contracting Party to the Convention on Human Rights to which – so far – only states have acceded. The situation might change if the EU becomes a party to the Convention which is foreseen in the European Constitution as well as in Protocol 14 to the Convention on Human Rights. However, none of the instruments have entered into force.

Despite the fact that the ECJ is not as such under the jurisdiction of the ECHR, actions or omissions by community authorities, including the ECJ, may nonetheless be part of the ECHR's examination whether there has been a violation of the Convention in a case. The ECHR has thus held that Article 1 of the Convention implies that a Contracting Party by transferring sovereignty to an international organization is not absolved completely from their Convention responsibility – which would be incompatible with the purpose and object of the Convention. However, state action taken in compliance with international treaty obligations is justified as the Court said in Bosphorus v Ireland judgment 30/6 2005 "as long as the relevant organization is considered to protect fundamental rights as regards both the substantive guarantees offered and the mechanisms controlling their observance in a manner which can be considered at least equivalent to that for which the Convention provides", cf. § 155. The Court further stated that "equivalent" means "comparable" – not "identical". Equivalent protection creates a presumption that a State has not departed from the requirements of the Convention – a presumption which however can be rebuffed if in the circumstances of a particular case, it is considered that the protection of Convention rights was "manifestly deficient". In the Bosphorus-case the Court concluded that the protection of fundamental rights by EC-law was "equivalent" – focusing primarily on the functions of the ECJ – and that the presumption was not rebutted as it could not be said that the protection of the applicant's Convention rights was "manifestly deficient".

The principle of "equivalent protection" has been maintained in the Court's later case-law and the protection offered by the EU-system has not been found "manifestly deficient" in any case. However, only few such cases have been decided so far. Examples are Connolly v 15 Member States of the EU decided 9/12 2008, Biret Cie S.A. and others against the same States and decided the same day, and Kokkelvisserij v the Netherlands decided 20/1 2009. The latter case concerned a preliminary ruling by the ECJ on the interpretation of EC-rules relevant to a lawsuit about the lawfulness of a permission to catch cockles in a part of the North Sea. The ruling of the ECJ was negative to the applicant whose permission was later annulled by a national court. Before the ECHR the applicant alleged a violation of Article 6 of the Convention as it had not been allowed to submit a response to the opinion of the Advocate General before the ECJ gave judgment, cf. the ECJ's decision of 4/2 2000 in the Emesa *Sugar-case*, where the ECJ rejected that the ECHR's case-law on the Belgian Advocate General could be transferred to the ECJ system. In so far as the complaint was directed against the ECJ, it was rejected *ratione personae*. On the other hand, the complaint could be considered against the Netherlands as the intervention of the ECJ was sought by a domestic court in proceedings before it. However, – contrary to Bosphorus – it did not concern action taken by a State, but the procedure before the ECJ. The question was whether this procedure had been "manifestly deficient" in the particular case. A majority of the judges found that this was not the case and referred in particular to the possibility offered by the ECJ Rules on Procedure to order a reopening of the oral proceedings after the Advocate Generals opinion had been read out, and that the national court could have submitted a further request for a preliminary ruling.

The decisions just mentioned all concern the "equivalent" protection of fundamental rights which – even if not limited to that – primarily points to procedural issues, in particular whether the procedure before the EC courts has been at variance with Article 6 of the Convention. Other examples than those mentioned could be the right not to incriminate oneself, cf. the ECHR-judgments in *Funke v France 25/2 1993* and *Saunders v the U.K. 17/12 1996* compared to the CFI-judgment in *Mannesmannröhren-Werke A.G. 20/2 2001* and *Limburgse Vinyl Maatschappij 15/10 2002*. But a conflict could also arise in respect of different interpretation of substantial provisions in the Convention. The classic example is the question whether the notion "home" in Article 8 also protects business premises, cf. the ECHR-judgment *Niemietz v Germany 16/12 1992* compared to the ECJ-judgment *Hoechst 21/9 1989* revised in the later judgment *Roquette Frères 22/10 2002* in the light of the Strasbourg case-law. A further example may be the recent judgment against Turkey just mentioned by professor Baudenbacher about the right to strike. Time does not allow me to go into details, but let me just state that most of these examples are old and none of them points to a deliberate conflict between the two Courts – on the contrary the ECJ has shown a clear willingness to adapt its case-law to the developing case-law of the ECHR.

What conclusions can be drawn? The fact that the ECHR has no jurisdiction in respect of the EU or any of its institutions does not mean that a "vertical problem" can be disregarded right away. The ECHR has maintained that even if Member States have transferred jurisdiction to an international organization, they are still responsible under the Convention not only for acts taken by their authorities in order to comply with their obligations towards that organization, but also under certain circumstances for acts of that organization itself. The ECHR is fully aware that a too rigid application of the Convention in such situations may complicate international cooperation and has accordingly accepted that the protection of fundamental rights by international organizations must not necessarily be identical to that of the Convention. It satisfies that it is "equivalent" (comparable) and if that is so there is a presumption that the Convention has been respected. However, the Court has constantly maintained that a violation might be found if the protection in an individual case has been "manifestly deficient". So far, the Court has not found that to be the case in respect of any international organization. Even if the Court in Bosphorus concluded that the protection of fundamental rights within the EU in general is "equivalent", and even if the risk of a deliberate conflict of interpretation seems rather theoretical, I do not consider it safe to rely on that it is totally excluded that a violation can be found in a future case where action has been taken by Community organs. Only few such cases have been decided so far, but the number is growing and the Court's case-law is still developing. In recent cases where (other) international organizations had been involved, the Court made rather detailed analyses of the level of protection before concluding that the complaint was inadmissible. And in the Kokkelvisserij case the ECHR's reasoning was rather concrete, and the decision was not unanimous.

To manage this difficult situation in a satisfactory way mutual understanding and cooperation between the two Courts is needed. As President Skouris put it in his speech in a seminar in the ECHR in January 2009: "The Bosphorus Airways case-law ought to encourage the Community bodies not to abandon their efforts and to ensure the real and effective protection of fundamental rights in all spheres falling within the powers of the EU." On the other hand, the ECHR must continue to acknowledge that "equivalent" protection does not mean "identical" protection and that there must be room for a flexible approach taking into account the special circumstances under which international organizations operate. "Dialogue" is a very important tool in that respect.

C. Dialogue between the ECJ and the ECHR at a "horizontal level"

The importance of a dialogue between international courts is definitely not limited to avoid conflicts about jurisprudence as described above, but has a much larger scope of application. Drawing inspiration from case-law of other courts – international as well as national – is not less important. Let me briefly explain why this is of a crucial and growing importance for the Strasbourg-Court.

It is well-known that many of the Articles of the Convention are phrased in vague and imprecise terms. Clear examples are notions like "fair trial" in Article 6, "private and family life" in Article 8 and "necessary in a democratic society" in § 2 of Articles 8–11. If the Convention shall not lose its importance as a cornerstone for protection of human rights in Europe, it must be applied in accordance with the developments of the European societies. As there is no real legislator within the Council of Europe (COE) to develop the standards, it is for the Court to assume this task and it has done so constantly in its case-law. As the Court put it in a recent GC-judgment: The Convention has to be interpreted "as a living instrument in the light of present day conditions and in accordance with developments in international law so as to reflect the increasingly high standards being required in the area of protection of human rights", cf. *Saadi v U.K. 29/1 2008 § 55*. The Court has often indicated that one of the most important aims it has to pursue is to secure a minimum protection of human rights in the Contracting States.

In order to accomplish this task the Court to an increasing extent relies on case-law from other international courts as well as case-law from Constitutional and Supreme Courts all over the world. The ECJ is playing an important and growing role in this context. Let me illustrate it with just two examples:

One of the questions that has caused the Convention organs most difficulties when determining the scope of Article 6 § 1 is whether or rather to what extent the expression "civil rights and obligations" covers disputes between States and their servants. The case-law has changed several times, and in the *Pellegrin-case judgment of 8/12 1999* the Court decided to put an end to the uncertainty. It was decided to apply a functional criteria based on the nature of the employee's duties and responsibilities ("exercise of powers conferred by public law"), and in doing so the Court found guidance not least in the case-law of the ECJ, in particular the *ECJ judgment 2/7 1996 European Commission v Grand Duchy of Luxembourg*. Unfortunately, this criteria did not totally solve the problems, and in the *Eskelinen and others judgment of 19/4 2007* it was supplemented – but not abandoned – with a further criteria – whether access to court is excluded in the domestic law and if so whether the exclusion is justified on objective grounds in the State's interest. It is worth noting that when making this extension of the criteria the Court also made reference to Community law as applied by the ECJ and expressly stated that "European law generally provides useful guidance", § 60.

The second example is *Stec and others v the United Kingdom, judgment of 12/4 2006*. In that case the Court had to rule on whether it was in breach of the discrimination clause in Article 14 of the Convention that a legislative decision to stop paying an earnings-related benefit for work accidents and work-related illnesses was linked to the general retirement age which in the United Kingdom is different for men and women. The Court noted that a similar issue had been put before the ECJ in *Hepple v Chief Adjudication Officer judgment of 23/5 2000* in relation to Article 7(1)(a) of a Council Directive of 1978 where it was found that the link to the age-limits was necessary in order to preserve coherence with the old-age pension scheme. The ECHR found no violation of Article 14 and relied inter alia on the findings of the ECJ. I quote from § 58 of the judgment: "In reaching a conclusion on this issue which, while not determinative of the issue under Article 14 of the Convention, is nonetheless of central importance, particular regard should be had to the strong persuasive value of the ECJ's findings on this point."

Other examples are *Christine Goodwin v the United Kingdom judgment 11/7 2002*, *Post and Rahko v Finland judgment of 24/9 2002* and *Maslov v Austria judgment of 23/6 2008*, but as time is limited I just refer to them.

In certain situations not only inspiration to confirm or develop a jurisprudence can be found in the case-law of other courts, but courts can assist each other in carrying out their functions. Let me just illustrate this with a few examples:

The first concerns the relationship between the right to a fair trial according to Article 6 § 1 of the Convention and the obligation of courts in EU-countries to seek a preliminary ruling under Article 234 of the EC-Treaty. The ECHR has in a number of cases stated that even if the Convention does not as such guarantee any right to have a case referred to the ECJ for a preliminary ruling, a refusal of a request may nevertheless infringe the fairness of the proceedings if it appears to be arbitrary, cf. most recently *John v Germany decision 13/2 2007*. So far, the ECHR has found no violation in this respect. It goes without saying that the Court must be very careful when dealing with the issue. It is neither for the ECHR to impose a preliminary rule on the ECJ, nor to justify decisions by national courts not to seek such a ruling. It is only for the ECJ to decide whether a preliminary ruling was required and the ECHR has no possibility to consult the ECJ on the matter.

The second example concerns criminal cases where an applicant alleges that his conviction has been contrary to Community law as applied by the ECJ. As an illustration can serve the decision of 8/7 2008 of the ECHR in *Tolgyesi v Germany*, where a Hungarian lorry driver was convicted for carrying out transports for a Netherlands company without a work permit. The applicant alleged that the conviction was contrary to the ECJ-judgment of 9/8 1994 in *Vander Elst v Office des Migrations internationales* and alleged a violation of Article 7 of the Convention. The argument was rejected by the ECHR, but only because the case was found to be different from the ECJ-case.

The last example is related to several articles of the Convention where it is a condition for an interference that it is "lawful", "prescribed by law" or "in accordance with law", cf. Articles 5, 8–11. It is primarily for national courts to determine whether there is a legal basis for an interference in domestic law, but the ECHR has to supervise that the application of national law has not been arbitrary and that certain conditions as to accessibility and foresee ability are fulfilled. Does the notion "law" in this respect also cover Community law and if so is it for the ECHR to rule on whether a Community regulation has been complied with, or for that matter to rule on an alleged conflict between national law and Community law? There is no doubt under the ECHR case-law that Community law can constitute a sufficient legal basis for an interference, but also that it can only serve as that under the same conditions as national law, cf. for example *Cantoni v France judgment 15/11 1996*. It is clear that if a question of interpretation of Community law has been brought before the ECJ, the ECHR can only take note of the result. It is, however, less clear whether it is also for the ECHR to supervise the way national courts have applied Community law or even rule on an alleged conflict between national law and Community law which has not been brought before the ECJ. To my knowledge there is no case-law, so far, on these issues which are part of a more general question on the relations between national and international law where the latter is granted preference under the Constitution of a country. In a recent chamber judgment the ECHR even noting "an apparent inconsistence" between a Moldovan law and the European Convention on Nationality and that "a question may accordingly arise as to the overall lawfulness of the disputed restriction" nevertheless found that "it is not for the Court to resolve this perceived conflict of norms", cf. *Tanase v Moldova judgment 18/11 2008 § 106*. The case is currently pending before the Grand Chamber. In these circumstances I will not pursue the question any further.

D. Let me finally make some brief conclusions

Even if dialogue between international and superior national judges is not a new phenomenon, it has gained significant importance in recent years – no doubt as a consequence of the growing globalization and facilitated by a computerized world which has given easy access to each others case-law.

Dialogue is important for many reasons. As the International Law Commission said in 2006 with reference to the growing number of international courts "a principle of harmonization" is important in order to avoid "the danger of conflicting and incompatible rules, principles, rule-systems and institutional practices". But its scope is much wider: Its importance as a source of inspiration – a tool for the judicial decision-making process – should not be underestimated. A crucial question is what weight international and superior national courts should attach to each others case-law? The answer is not quite easy to give and depends on many elements. When it comes to a legal instrument like the Convention national courts are obliged to follow the case-law of the ECHR, if they want to avoid a conviction in Strasbourg. It is desirable that international courts applying the Convention – even if not bound to follow the ECHR's case-law – nevertheless do it if a different interpretation would create a difficult situation for the Contracting States bound by the Convention. This is also the clear intention of the ECJ. But apart from this special situation, should courts strive to obtain the same interpretation of identical or at least closely related rules? My answer would be: Not necessarily. There may be many elements for example of a historical, cultural, social or political character which call for a different solution. And when it comes to a human rights instrument like the Convention nothing prevents other courts from going further than the ECHR. Its case-law aims only at establishing minimum standards.

Discussion

CARL BAUDENBACHER

Well then, according to common understanding, it is probably for me to raise a question here. Let me start with Alberto's presentation and his question, why the WTO Appellate Body is so reluctant to enter any kind of dialogue with another court. I take it that the Appellate Body does constitute a court, although this is controversial. They do not, e.g., have the insignia of a court, their president cannot be called president, he must be referred to as chairman in order to give the appearance that it is not a true court.

But there is now a development going on which shows that things may be changing. A couple of weeks ago the EU Court of First Instance in Luxembourg celebrated its 20th Anniversary and for the first time three members of the seven of the WTO Appellate Body were there attending this event. Half a year before, for the first time, the WTO Appellate Body paid an official visit to the European Court of Justice. So, that may also change their attitude. In addition to that, and I'd like to hear your opinion on this: Is there also a development going on in the WTO due to the fact that there is now a second generation of judges? I mean the first ones were obviously a little bit scared in particular by the threats from Washington D. C. not to go too far in interpretation, to faithfully stick to the interpretation rules of the Vienna Convention and not to engage in any kind of dynamic interpretation. But in the meantime there is a second and third generation of Appellate Body members. What do you think?

ALBERTO ALEMANNO

Thanks a lot for your question, Professor. It is true that there is a controversy over the nature of the WTO adjudicatory bodies, whether they are courts, real courts or something else. Usually, scholars define them as entities having a quasi judicial nature. It is indeed true that formally they do not adopt judgments, but they draft the reports that will subsequently be adopted by the DSB. Yet, if one looks at the dispute settlement body mechanism itself I would say, yes, there has been a judicialization in the whole process. An Appellate Body report reads very differently than a GATT report written in the 80s. So, the language is different, the texts are different, we have provisions and technical agreements like the TBT and the SBS. These agreements injected a sort of positive integration into the multilateral trade regime so that WTO Members are no longer subject to the sole principle of non-discrimination, but also to other (positive) obligations. They have to phase out, of course, tariffs, they cannot enforce quantitative restrictions, but they also have to do something else, they have to ensure a scientific basis for the measures they adopt, they have to conduct a risk assessment as we just have heard, and have to be sure that whenever they come up with a new standard setting this would be evidence-based. So, we have some positive integration getting in. This is inevitably imposing a very demanding task to be exercised by the WTO adjudicatory bodies.

It is true that things are changing. There is a second generation of judges who have joined the Appellate Body. Some of them have previously been involved at the panel level, in several panels in the first instance, so they are familiar with the mechanism. There seems to be some interesting sign of the willingness for instance, yes, to stick to the rules of interpretation as suggested by the Vienna Convention but without mentioning anything anymore. So the Vienna Convention of the Law of the Treaty which was a kind of text law bible for the judges is still applied, of course, with a lot of emphasis on the text rather than object and purpose of the agreement. That is true, it is no longer mentioned. So, there might be some opening in that sense and in terms of epistemic community, it is true that there has been a first official visit in 2008 by some members of the Appellate Body to the European courts. It was not a very solemn meeting, it was rather informal. And then as you mentioned, only two weeks ago, we witnessed for the first time some Appellate Body judges assisting an ECJ meeting, which, of course, really makes a difference. But, in general, we should add probably a further twist, we also have to take into account that the WTO adjudicatory bodies operate from a hierarchical perspective in a different world than the European courts. We know that since EU Member States are bound by the WTO, there is an inevitable hierarchical nature in their relationship. This hierarchical dimension should not be overlooked when discussing a possible judicial dialogue between these two courts.

CARL BAUDENBACHER

Thank you. If I may take up your remark that the WTO Appellate Body judges do not quote the Vienna Convention anymore; your court does. You quote the Vienna Convention, but you do not follow it. It is just a lip service you are paying. Would you like to say something on that? He does not want to say anything on that. Ok then, Professor Larsen.

ALASTAIR MULLIS

Just a couple of questions, I was interested in the extent to which the European Court of Human Rights and also the European Court of Justice refers to decisions of domestic courts.

I would also like to know to what extent there is ever any reference to courts from different legal tradition, for example, from the Islamic world.

PEER LORENZEN

I can try to answer for the Strasbourg Court. We do make reference to decisions from both types of courts, but not necessarily in the same way. When it comes to relevant domestic case law, it is often quoted in the part of our judgment called "domestic law and practice". And of course, if the case law is directly part of our examination of an alleged breach of the Convention we normally quote extensively what the national courts have said. To what extent we rely on case law from national courts as a source of inspiration for the interpretation of the Convention depends on what we can find. We have done so for many years, but it is my impression that we do it now to a growing extent. It is normally limited to the highest courts – supreme courts or constitutional courts – but not only to courts in the member states. Quite often, we have references to case law from the Supreme Court of the United States. References are also to some extent made to, for example, Canadian or South African Supreme Court judgments depending on what we can find. They are of course not decisive, but they are taken into account as a source of inspiration when we consider how the Convention should be applied. As I said in my introduction, many of the Articles in the Convention are formulated in a vague and imprecise manner so that they are more like legal standards than statutes in the classic sense. Obviously, the implementation of the Convention in 2009 cannot be limited to the situation as it stood in 1950. We have to apply it in the context of the situation of today. This has been the very firm case law of the Strasbourg Court for many years. When we have to decide, what is the standard of protection of today, it is only natural to be inspired by judgments of Supreme courts as well as by case-law of other international courts.

CARL BAUDENBACHER

Just a practical side question – you said several times, as far as we can find these domestic judgments or foreign materials. How is this done technically? Do you have a research department?

PEER LORENZEN

Yes, we have a research division within the court which is staffed with about 10 lawyers. Our court is consisting now of 47 judges, one for each of the Member States of the Council of Europe, and we are assisted by a registry staffed with more than 600 people. Lawyers from the registry serve in the research division for a certain period of time. For performing our functions it is considered to be absolutely necessary today, to have such a division which is used to a growing extent. Thus, in respect of almost every Grand Chamber case pending before the Court, the division prepares a report – often very detailed 30–40 pages or more – with an analysis of international law, references to legal doctrine, to the case law of various courts, to the laws of the Member States and sometimes also other countries. It has become an indispensable tool for our deliberations.

CARL BAUDENBACHER

Now, your court, Lars, has a very famous departement of research and documentation. How is this handled? How do you deal with judgments from the Bundesverfassungsgericht, for instance?

LARS BAY LARSEN

Well that is quite a number of questions. In my view we are a court that is in general quite happy about quoting other judgments – and of course in particular our own judgments. Although there are quite a few women among us, I think this is perhaps what happens to old men eventually. Nevertheless we do also quote other courts; in particular other international courts including notably the EFTA Court and the court in Strasbourg, and we may also include a reference to national jurisprudence. When it comes to the common constitutional practices of the member states, it will normally be more of a general reference, because otherwise it would be a very extensive list of judgments that we should have to refer to, and that could give rise to perhaps unfruitful discussion whether or not we had a sufficiently complete understanding of each of every one of these individual judgments. But even where we do not quote, we quite often have, through our research department, analyzed how a certain piece of EU legislation has been transposed and applied nationally. What are the national administrative practices in different member states? Is there a national jurisprudence on a specific issue? Such comparative analytic work may also take place in the field of fundamental rights. And when it comes to fundamental rights it is of course of the utmost interest for us to look at the Strasbourg jurisprudence to see if this particular question has been addressed there, because then that is the most authoritative source. But to the extent that it has not been addressed in Strasbourg, it becomes even more interesting to study the national jurisprudence in individual member states.

And from the EU side I could say that in particular in a new area such as the third pillar where the Court in Luxembourg has not yet fully developed its jurisprudence and where its competence is limited by the treaties and by the fact that only 17 out of the 27 member states have granted permission for their national courts to make a preliminary reference to our court to interpret instruments of this third pillar; national jurisprudence may be of particular interest to us. What does it mean, when member states like my own and like the United Kingdom do not permit national courts to make a preliminary reference? It does not mean that the European law will not be applied, but it would mean that it ultimately for i.e. the House of Lords to apply it – as it did in the Dabbas case. In the Dabbas case the House of Lords had to interpret the framework decision on the European Arrest Warrant and decide whether or not the United Kingdom transposition was in conformity with the framework decision. Such a case, whether it is quoted or not, may well take part of the stuff we go through when preparing and forming our individual and collective opinion on a certain case later pending before our Court.

Equally what is presented by formal reports from our research department on the national practices on a specific topic, normally never goes into the judgment. It is internal, preparatory work. But it may well, although it does not lead to a quotation, be of quite significant importance to our work.

CARL BAUDENBACHER
There was Professor Schanze and then Professor Westbrook.

ERICH SCHANZE
A short question: You probably know that the theory of understanding or "verstehen" (as it is still called in English), works with the distinction between the "context of

discovery" and the "context of justification". Would you rather address the matter of judicial dialogue as one of "discovery" or one of "justification"?

LARS BAY LARSEN

Well if I understand your question correctly, it perhaps goes to the heart of the relationship between our two courts. In the present circumstances where the EU is not legally bound neither by the EU Charter, nor by the European Convention on Human Rights, it has nevertheless since a long time been the firm judicial policy of my court to act as if we were legally bound by the European Convention on Human Rights. So, as I think I also stressed in the examples I quoted during my presentation, we apply European Law and we interpret European Law, but we make our best efforts to do it in a way so as to comply with the minimum requirements following from the European Convention on Human Rights as interpreted by our colleagues in Strasbourg. And sometimes we are able to identify the minimum requirement in a specific case of our decision making by a specific piece of jurisprudence from the Strasbourg court. Sometimes we have to interpret the European Convention on Human Rights ourselves as we cannot make a preliminary request for clarification to Strasbourg: When a similar problem is later presented to Strasbourg, we may only then realize that we were too timid or that we went even further than necessary. Depending on the occasion, we may then either feel obliged to or have the possibility to modify our jurisprudence at the next convenient opportunity. So, although we may not be legally bound in the current circumstances, we, I believe, act as if we were. In fact we would create enormous problems for the member states that are bound by the European Convention, if we applied it any other way. There has to be a coherent application of the fundamental rights. It is not that one system for fundamental rights is a good thing and consequently that two different systems are twice as good.

PEER LORENZEN

If I have understood the question correctly, my answer would be both: Discovery and justification, depending on the situation. If you are faced with a totally novel issue where the court has developed no case law, it is often discovery. An example which can illustrate this is Article 8 of the Convention which is very open in so far as it grants protection of private life and family life without any further specification. If you have to apply such an article in the context of, let us say, new biological technology – for example artificial procreation – then it is natural to look around and see what you can find in order to seek inspiration. Have other courts addressed a similar question? What have they done? This would be a clear example of the discovery element.

But it might very well also be a justification. It is the same for all judges whether they are at the national level or the international level: You may have a case where you consider a certain result to be the right one, but need arguments in favour of it in order to justify the result. I can give a recent example from the case-law of the Strasbourg Court. In an Italian case – *Scoppola* which was decided by a Grand Chamber a few weeks ago – one of the issues was whether Article 7 of the Convention, which grants protection against retroactive application of criminal law, also grants a right to have a more lenient law concerning the crime or the sanction, which was adopted after the offence was committed, applied. Such a right is granted expressly in some other international instruments but not in the Convention according to the wording of Article 7. It has always been the case-law of the Strasbourg organs that this protection is therefore not granted in the Convention, but a majority of the Grand Chamber – to which I admit I did not belong – wanted to abandon this practice and did so. The justification for this change of case-law was found not only in other international instruments, but also – and not least – in the case-law from various international organs.

CARL BAUDENBACHER
I add a question here. I spoke about these two Turkish cases which have been decided on industrial action. One was on strike and the other one was on collective bargaining and there have been criticisms that this is a judicial conflict as compared to the ECJ two famous rulings in Laval and the Viking Line. You have not made reference to the ECJ in these cases.

PEER LORENZEN
I must admit that I have no detailed knowledge of the cases in which I have not taken part, but if you are right that there is no reference to the ECJ-cases and that there is a jurisprudential conflict, it would have been relevant to have the cases before a Grand Chamber. But this is probably too late, now, in respect of those cases.

LARS BAY LARSEN
Just a small remark on the possible conflict between the jurisprudence of the European Court in Strasbourg and the Laval and Viking cases decided by the ECJ. Without going deeply into this recent jurisprudence of the ECJ, I would just like to stress that neither Laval nor Viking implies that the right to strike or the right to take action is not a fundamental right. However, in the ECJ we had to balance two sets of fundamental rights, the right to take action against another set of fundamental rights, the four fundamental freedoms of the internal market. We had to balance these two sets of rights against each other and I think it stems from our judgments that we believe that the fact that we have a fundamental right does not in itself imply that there cannot be exceptions. I think this is well recognized also in the practice from Strasbourg and even in the Convention itself. It is the concrete application that may give rise to differences.

CARL BAUDENBACHER
Thank you for this clarification. I just referred to commentaries in literature; I did not take a position on this. Are there any further questions? Ok, then I thank these three gentlemen very much and we have come to the end of the first panel.

Focus:
Arbitration Tribunals

Introduction

PETER NOBEL[1]

Ladies and gentlemen: I welcome you to this afternoon session and hope that the substantial lunch we have enjoyed will not affect your attention – although, granted, this may well be a human right.

In this second session, we will deal with aspects of arbitration, more specifically with dialogue within arbitration proceedings. The distinguished participants of this second panel are as follows: Alan Rau from the University of Texas, Ben Steinbrück from the Max Planck Institute in Hamburg and Per Runeland from Berwin London. I would like to extend a warm welcome to them as well and to thank them for joining us today.

To begin with, I draw your attention to the fact that the root of the word dialogue is traceable to the Greek "dia" and "logos," which translates as "through meaning". Its current definition is an exchange of ideas or opinions on a particular issue, with a view to reaching an amicable agreement or settlement. It is, thus, a word that is seemingly compatible with arbitration and there is room for dialogue.

I will only mention a few points in this introduction – some critical ones, but all of which concern real, physical dialogue. Parties customarily select their "party" arbitrator. Candidates are usually approached by counsel. By experience the requests and subsequent discussions vary to a considerable extent. They can go from a neutral request to an explanation of the case and the parties' positions. Here, in my view, clear rules are lacking and the essential question is whether a subsequent neutrality declaration is sufficient. Then, the party arbitrators endeavor to find a Chairman (umpire); this is also a moment of dialogue, and it seems to be a wide practice for the party-named arbitrators to discuss the proposals for the Chairperson with the parties. The goal is to find a suitable person in the view of both parties, their counsel and the named arbitrators, as well as for the nature of the case. The next phase will be the so-called constitution of the arbitration panel and the discussion about the procedural rules. This is also a phase with quite extensive dialogue, not only with the parties but also amongst the arbitrators. I recall an instance when a panel in which I participated spent hours discussing whether we should accept a party's request that settlement discussions would need the consent of both parties. (In the end, the request was denied. The panel wanted to be free.)

---

1 Professor at the Universities of St. Gallen and Zurich, Judge at the Commercial Court of Zurich, Partner at Nobel & Hug, Zurich.

I will now turn to aspects of the proceedings and look at the kind of behavior arbitrators' exhibit in relation to the parties and eventual settlement discussions. Of relevance here is also the dialogue between the arbitrators themselves. I will not address another chapter here, the relationship between an arbitration tribunal and state courts. The latter is still needed for all kinds of coercive measures as well as for the challenges in relation to an arbitration tribunal and its awards. Also this interplay may be seen as a dialogue, but more in theory than in practice. I think that the keynote speaker or the panelists will come back to this.

I hope that we also take up aspects of institutional arbitration, like the ICC, which can also lead to unhappy types of dialogue over changes in the sentence required.

Now, with regard to the role of the arbitrator, among the more outstanding differences in arbitration is the role played by the arbitrator, in particular the extent to which he or she participates in the proceedings. In Switzerland, arbitrators are more dialogue-oriented and less decision-oriented in comparison to many other countries. Generally, in my view, Swiss arbitrators do not hesitate to discuss findings along the way and as they develop. In other jurisdictions arbitrators may conduct themselves differently, sitting stoically through proceedings and then rendering a decision without any discussion. Indeed, a major distinction in approach, frequently alluded to in international arbitration practice today, is still that between the Anglo-American and civil law traditions. The adversarial Anglo-American tradition is in contrast to the inquisitorial civil law tradition, which is followed in most of continental Europe, where both judges and arbitrators, also the ICC arbitrators, play a more active role in the proceedings. Within the framework of the arbitration, this means that civil law arbitrators draw the facts and law from both witnesses and lawyers, and they are in full charge of witness questioning; here, the party that wishes to question a witness must, in principle, submit the question to the tribunal. On the other hand, the US adversarial approach encompasses a zealous form of advocacy on the side of the lawyers calling for (inter alia) argumentation on legal interpretation, witness preparation (sometimes even coaching), aggressive cross-examination of witnesses, disclosures of party appointed experts, etc. Also noteworthy are the many evidentiary rule differences in the proceedings (e.g., in relation to lawyer-client privilege, protected communications, duty of loyalty and independence, etc.).

I will now turn to the subject of arbitrator assistance in settlement negotiations. Once upon a time, arbitration settlement efforts encompassed the so-called "Method Spartan", which although lacking in dialogue may well have had an effective and expeditious result:

"[The method was first described] by the Greek biographer and philosopher Plutarch who told the story of two men who wanted to avoid the rigors of a trial, but who made the mistake of submitting their dispute to the Spartan king, Archidamus IT (469–427 BC), for arbitration. The king took the disputants to the temple of Athene of the Brazen House and asked them to swear to abide by his award. They agreed. Then the arbitrator said: "You both stay here till you have made up your quarrel."[2]

Today, arbitrator assistance in settlement negotiations is somewhat more sophisticated, and its utility is subject to differing opinions. In the US, as well as in some European countries, it is not favored and may even be considered as improper. There is a view that the arbitrator's role in settlement negotiations should be minimal with maybe only a suggestion of settlement, and basically no mediation. The rational is that the proceedings could be tainted by the information gained during mediation efforts if the settlement efforts fail. In contrast, arbitrators in other countries, in particular civil law countries, are more involved in settlement efforts. Such participation is seen in a positive light, in that it is in the interest of a rapid and efficient solution for the parties. The problem of tainted information is overcome by procedural measures preventing its use should settlement fail. Thus, e.g., in Switzerland and Germany, arbitrators are very often actively involved in settlement efforts. Not only do they propose settlements at the request of a party (or parties), but they also participate in settlement negotiations and even meet with each of the parties separately to discuss settlement possibilities. Interestingly, also many Asian countries seem to favor the fostering of agreements.[3]

Judge participation in and fostering of the settlement process has a long tradition in the European Commercial Courts, in Switzerland, the so-called "Handelsgerichte" (where I was educated and am still active). These courts have historical roots that trace back to arbitration-like proceedings held during the Middle Ages between merchants or traders seeking quick and purposeful means of resolving their disputes at the market place. Such proceedings utilized a set structure that bore a close relation to the trades at hand; they were the forerunners of today's commercial courts, which are often tailored to the special needs of the parties.[4] Nowadays, however, they act strictly according to the rule of law. The commercial court is a particularly well preserved tradition in Switzerland. It is generally composed of judges who are experts in different fields or trades and is reputed to be quick, cost efficient and fair.[5] The Zurich Commercial Court

---

2 Cindy Fazzi, *Tales of Arbitration from Ancient Literature*, *Dispute Resolution Journal*, Aug–Oct 2000, http://findarticles.com/p/articles/mi_qa3923/is_200008/ai_n8905522/, p. 1.

3 Jeswald W. Salacuse, *Is There a Better Way? Alternative Methods of Treaty-Based Investor-State Dispute Resolution*, 31 Fordham International Law Journal 138, December, 2007, p.183, citing from Christian Bühring-Uhle, *Arbitration and Mediation in International Business: Designing Procedures for Effective Conflict Management* (1996) pp. 198 ff.

4 A. Brunner, *Handelsgerichte*, FS *25 Jahre juristische Abschlüsse and der Universität St. Gallen (HSG)*, Zurich 2007, pp. 613 ff. Today commercial courts are found, inter alia, in Germany, Austria, France, Belgium and Switzerland (Zurich, Aargau, Bern and St. Gallen).

5 Peter Nobel, *Vergleich und Urteil – Konkurrenz zweier Erledigungsformen*, in: Mélanges en l'honneur de Pierre Tercier, Zurich 2008, p. 952.

practices the so-called "méthode Zurichoise", according to which parties and lawyers are, at an early stage, invited to a consultation where clarification and substantiation of the problem and of the issues take place and the general legal standpoint of the tribunal at this stage is already presented. This is then followed by an open settlement discussion, which is not recorded. Roughly 60% of the cases going through this court are settled. If not settled, the case can go on as it did before without the possibility of either party using any part of these settlement discussions in a further proceeding. The discussions can thus be conducted in an open manner and maintain the purpose of achieving a compromise.[6]

The aforementioned benefits deriving from arbitrator-assisted settlement efforts are equally applicable to the possibilities for dialogue among arbitrators. An open, comprehensive and thoughtful dialogue is also a useful means of filtering information, weeding out what is relevant and thereby helping to streamline proceedings. Dialogue has the added advantage of increasing an understanding of other perspectives and as such can lead to resolving misunderstandings and reducing or even avoiding conflict. It can and should be encouraged. The flexibility of the arbitral forum compared to the judicial setting lends itself to dialogue. The broader discretion granted to arbitrators confers a natural discourse power.[7] But all of this requires a high degree of the arbitrator independence.

With this brief introduction, I hope to have set the stage for our panelists and would now like to open the floor and invite Alan Rau to begin with his presentation.

---

6 Peter Nobel, *„Handelsgerichte und Schiedsgerichte" in Europäische Handelsgerichtsbarkeit*, Alexander Brunner ed.; Schriftenreihe, Europäische Gerichte in Handels- und Schiedssachen, Band 1, Stämpfli Verlag AG (Bern, 2009), p. 201. (A number of arbitration tribunals – in particular in Germany and other cantons of Switzerland – participate in settlement negotiations in a manner similar to the Zurich Commercial Court. Also the ICC has discussed the merits of the Zurich procedure and called for efficient case handling via the "Early Case Management Conference". See Techniques for Controlling Time and Costs in Arbitration, Report from the ICC Commission on Arbitration, Ziff 31, http://www.linexlegal.com/content.php?content_id=48679.).

7 Michael Hunter Schwartz, *Power Outage, Amplifying the Analysis of Power in Legal Relations* (With Special Application to Unconscionability and Arbitration), 33 Willamette L. Rev. 67 (1997), pp. 140–141.

Arbitral Tribunals and the "Rule of Law"

ALAN RAU[1]

One of the things that makes arbitration such a fascinating subject to me – what encourages me to talk about it endlessly even at the risk of boring to death my closest, most intimate friends – is its Janus-like (or schizophrenic) quality – at the same time containing opposite qualities, and looking in opposite directions – in other words, it is two things at the same time. From one perspective arbitration is private ordering. It is formed by private agreement. The shape it takes is a result of conscious private choice. But at the same time, from another angle, arbitration is an exercise in adjudication. It is the presentation of proof and argument to a neutral decision maker, resulting in a final and binding decision that has the force of a judgment of a public tribunal. So, it is two things at the same time and there is a tension and a balance between these two models of arbitration. Do we see it as an exercise of contract? Do we see it as primarily an exercise of adjudication? There is a tension and a balance between these that plays out in different legal systems in different contexts, and in its resolution lays the answer to just about every interesting legal question in arbitration.

Now I think, in the United States as you might expect, the contractual model tends to be the dominant one. We see arbitration through the lenses of Contract, and answer questions in the same way. So, for example, we do not see arbitration in a way that pre-supposes a decision maker that decides on the basis of legal rules. We do not assume that an arbitrator is going to decide the way a judge decides. We think that if the parties have not reached an adequate level of agreement, then an arbitrator can nevertheless make a contract for them. (It is thus a familiar proposition that what might otherwise be a fatal "uncertainty" of terms can be cured simply by adding an arbitration

1 Burg Family Professor at the University of Texas at Austin School of Law.

clause.[2]) We do not expect that the arbitrator will follow the law necessarily. We do not expect that he will track the course of official jurisprudence, or write reasoned decisions explaining how he arrived at his conclusions.

Just Molière's M. Jourdain was astonished to find that he has been speaking prose all of his life, I think an American arbitrator would be astonished to find that he had been acting like an *amiable compositeur* all his life without actually hearing the word. American arbitrators do not write reasoned decisions; they do not write opinions the way judges do. In theory the European model, the jurisdictional model is very different for all of these reasons. European arbitrators are expected to write opinions, reasoned opinions, which is a matter of *ordre public*. It is unthinkable in Europe that an arbitrator can make a contract for the parties. European arbitrators are expected to adhere closely to legal principle. The UNCITRAL Model Law on International Commercial Arbitration – in this respect closely modelled on civil law arbitration principles – reminds us that the arbitrators are only permitted to act *ex aequo et bono*, only permitted to decide on equitable principles, if the parties have expressly authorized them to do so – but without expressed authorization they are not allowed to depart from what an official public judge would do.[3] No such need for such authorization exists under the American model.

---

2 See, e.g., *Lafayette Place Associates v Boston Redevelopment Authority*, 694 N.E.2d 820, 826–27 (Mass. 1998) (although the contract left undetermined "exactly what was to be included" in the parcel of land being sold as well as the price, it also specified that "appropriate details of the purchase and sale ... shall be resolved by arbitration", and thus "created a means for resolving disputes that might arise in the course of effectuating the ultimate sale"; "to borrow Justice Holmes's metaphor, the machinery was built and had merely to be set in motion"); Walker v Keith, 382 S.W.2d 198 (Ky. App. 1964) (lease provided that rental was to be fixed "as shall actually be agreed upon" by the parties and to be based on "comparative business conditions"; held, provision was too "indefinite and uncertain" to enforce; such provisions "have been the source of interminable litigation" and "courts sometimes must assert their right not to be imposed upon"; however, if the parties "had agreed upon a specific method of making the determination," such as the decision of an arbitrator, "they could be said to have agreed upon whatever rent figure emerged from utilization of the method").
See also Leslie v Leslie, 24 A. 319 (N.J. Ch. 1892). Disputes between the two owners of a close corporation "became so bitter and dangerous to its prosperity" that they wished to separate, with one of them retiring from all participation in the company's affairs. "But which should sell – who should go out – was the point of difficulty about which they could not agree." So they "were willing to leave the question as to which one should retire by the sale of his stock, and what the other should pay him for his stock, to be settled by arbitration". Id. at 321. (The court ultimately vacated the award, though, because it had purported to decide matters not submitted to the arbitrators, and because it was "uncertain and inconclusive").
Cf. Foley v Classique Coaches, Ltd., [1934] 2 K.B. 1, 11 (C.A. 1933) (requirements contract "at a price to be agreed by the parties in writing and from time to time"; held, an implication of a "reasonable price" is justified, and "if the parties cannot agree as to what is a reasonable price then arbitration must take place"). Note that since *Foley* was decided long before general acceptance of the notion of "separability", the Court of Appeal was required first to find that an "effective and enforceable" contract existed even without regard to the arbitration clause. In our day the enforceability of the contract should properly be left to the arbitrators themselves; once in place, they may – but of course need not – take it upon themselves to go still further, salvaging a defective contract by filling in the missing terms.

3 UNCITRAL Model Law, Art. 28(3).

Now, I might note parenthetically that one of the very strangest aspects of American arbitration law is that a number of American States in the United States, a number of the biggest American States, Texas, California, Florida, Illinois, have all enacted the UNCITRAL Model Law – and done so verbatim.[4] I do not know what they thought they were getting at – I cannot imagine what was going through their minds when they did that. They passed it verbatim. They used the words "*amiables compositeurs*" even though "*amiables compositeurs*" does not mean anything in English. Nobody in Texas or California knows what this word means. In some states like North Carolina they tried to translate it. They translated it "amicable compounder" which is even sillier and more foolish.[5] And that just shows, I think, the dangers of slavish and foolish adoption of foreign models when you really do not understand the model that you are following. But these statutes have pretty much been ignored, as they should be.

The difference between the European model and the American model still remains. Now, I think that difference can be overdrawn – it can be exaggerated because I think it is fair to say that in any legal system arbitrators do try their best to model their awards on what courts would do. That is what the empirical evidence suggests.[6] And that plausibly follows from what arbitrator incentives are likely to be. It is easier to follow what the public law is. It is probably congruent with the expectations of the parties, who probably do not really want justice from arbitrators, they want certainty. For "justice" means what the arbitrator will eventually find to be just, and that may seem a little too dangerous. The parties want the certainty of announced law.

Following the official public law gives the elite lawyer or the elite law professor, who is the typical member of an international arbitration tribunal, the chance to show off the usual skills by which they have come to define themselves. So, I think it is fair to say that members of international arbitration tribunals usually do try to follow the law, but they do feel able to depart from it when they think it is best to do so. In any event, the parties are aware of the fact that they are counting on the arbitrator's "take" on the law, the arbitrator's own reading of the law, the arbitrator's own working out of legal principles and that might not be the same as what a public and official court is likely to do. They are necessarily aware of this because, under any legal system, it is understood that the arbitrator's decision, no matter how legally flawed, is not going to be subject to overturning or annulment simply because it is legally flawed. The usual ground for

---

4 See, e.g., *Texas International Arbitration and Conciliation Act*, Tex. Civ. Prac. & Rem. Code § 172.102(d); Cal. Code Civ. Pro., Tit. 9.3, Arbitration and Conciliation of International Commercial Disputes, § 1297.284.

5 N.C.G.S.A. § 1-567.58.

6 Soia Mentschikoff, *Commercial Arbitration*, 61 Colum. L. Rev. 846, 861 (1961). This often-cited study of commercial arbitrators found that 80% of the respondents "thought that they ought to reach their decisions within the context of the principles of substantive rules of law, but almost 90% believed that they were free to ignore these rules whenever they thought that more just decisions would be reached by so doing". Note that the survey was conducted at a time long before it became commonplace to entrust arbitrators with questions of mandatory, regulatory law – although Mentschikoff still found the results "curiously parallel to the attitudes that seem to be implicit in our appellate courts".

annulment of awards in any modern system, gives no basis for annulment simply on the grounds of legal error. Judge Posner of the Seventh Circuit – being typically quotable – said that no matter how "wacky" an award may be, it may not be overturned on that basis.[7] And that I think is generally understood, whether one is an American arbitrator or a European arbitrator.

More fundamentally, this distinction between the so-called contractual and the jurisdictional model of arbitration falls away, to some extent, to the extent that we recognize that under either model arbitrators are operating under a mechanism of mercantile self-government. That is to say, they are operating under a role; they have a role as part of a mission that is given to them of changing and adapting the rules of law, more or less openly to suit the needs of the commercial community. I am referring, of course, to what is often called "Lex Mercatoria" (The Court of Arbitration for Sport in Lausanne is beginning to refer to something called the "Lex-Sportiva", but if we are going to use a Latin term, let's stick with "Lex Mercatoria" which is more common anyway). Whatever the term we use, at the very least this means that any interpretation of contracts has a place for trade usage – and in fact the Model Law directs the arbitral tribunal to take into account in its decision making to the usages of the trade applicable to the transaction.[8] This is the minimal interpretation of what "Lex Mercatoria" means. When I say it is the minimal interpretation, I mean it is the most banal, the most simplistic and the most trivial interpretation. But, it is a starting point. It never overrules or overcomes the choice of the parties. It simply recognizes that the decision of the arbitrators is intended to incorporate the understandings and practices of the parties as rules of decision. National state courts already give effect to the understanding and practices of the parties. These understandings and practices may already be so widely shared that the precise national source of the rule, whether it is in State A or State B, may not be crucial because they are so widely shared and that the arbitrators may indeed be better placed to understand and appreciate these rules.

The truism, that arbitrators are likely to be sensitive to custom and usage is a starting point. But the notion of "Lex Mercatoria" goes further and is more important. It goes further because arbitrators when they look to customs are able to work out more functional solutions as the harbingers of legal change. There are cases where the rule that would otherwise have a claim to be applied, that would otherwise have a vocation to be applied, should not be applied. It should not be applied because it may be obsolete. It should not be applied because it may be parochial. "Obsolete" and "parochial" are, of course, just pejorative terms, but what they mean is this: Certain rules may well have been suited for the particular need of a particular locality but they are no longer

7 *Wise v Wachovia Securities*, LLC, 450 F.3d 265, 269 (7th Cir. 2006).

8 See *UNCITRAL Model law on International Commercial Arbitration* art. 28(4); cf. Craig et al., International Chamber of Commerce Arbitration 626, 633–34 (3rd ed. 2000) ("The reader reflecting on his own national law will doubtless find support for the applicability of usages" – but this notion alone may be so mundane that "scoffers might reflect that if this is all there is to it, they have been mercatorists all along").

particularly well-suited for the needs of international trade. Therefore, if they are inconsistent with the needs of international trade, as an alternative to the usual conflict of law inquiry the arbitrators may choose a rule that is better suited to the needs of international trade. That is just an alternative to a conflict of law inquiry.

But there is a third point that I think is more important still and that is this: I think we ought to wonder whether courts really have a monopoly or should have a monopoly over the elaboration of the law. That is to say, are courts likely to be most responsive to the needs of participants in the general market? Is it not possible that arbitrators might be more responsive to the needs of participants in the international market? It rather seems naïve to take as a self-evident premise the unfailing and continuing ability of judges and juries to produce, over time, reliable results that remain responsive to the needs of participants in the market or of the general polity: In fact, it may be the peculiar contribution of arbitrators to test – "in terms of their inherent soundness"[9] – these rules of law, questioning, qualifying, and reshaping them, constructing brick by brick the "*Lex Mercatoria*" by realigning arbitral decisions with changing commercial practices.

Very often I am sure we all have seen cases where there are technical rules – let us say of the law of sales – clearly applicable to a given case, which are ignored by arbitrators because they seem out of date. Twenty or thirty or forty years later national codes and national courts catch up with arbitrators. Arbitrators were ahead of their time. And arbitrators ignored these rules of law because they saw that they were out of date and it is only later that the law, the positive law of the codes or courts, gradually caught up with them. Interpretation of courts are only correct in some positive sense and are only correct for the moment, but there is no reason to assume that decisions of courts or codes are really correct in the sense of being responsive to the needs of the users.

And then, one final general point. When we are talking about the law, we obviously have to distinguish between, on the one hand, mere rules of construction – what the common law calls "default rules" or "gap-filling" rules and I think the civil law calls suppletive rules – and on the other hand, mandatory rules or rules of immediate application. Most rules of commercial law are just gap-filling rules that apply where the parties have not expressly supplied one by themselves. These "general rules of law" "hold" only when there is no "common understanding" that is directly furnished by the parties themselves – or which can be found in the background, of usage and prior conduct, against which they have dealt with each other.[10]

But increasingly, as we know, commercial disputes are being swept up with statutes of regulatory concern and even state rules of mandatory and regulatory concern are

9 Soia Mentschikoff, *The Significance of Arbitration: A Preliminary Inquiry*, 17 LAW & CONTEMP. PROBS. 698, 703 (1952).

10 UCC § 1–303, cmt. 3.

applicable to a purely commercial dispute. In these cases conflict with state interest becomes palpable and we are increasingly seeing erosion of the illusion that public courts are the only sources for the generation of applicable norms. Now, even in matters involving mandatory law, there is room here for dialogue between arbitrators and courts because even here there is room for, on the part of arbitrators, creativity in adapting the law and pushing the law in particular directions. On the part of courts there is room for some deference towards arbitration in the sense of deference towards an appreciation by arbitrators of context and situation. Now, there are a number of cases I would like to bring to your attention and I do not really have time for all of them, I think, but let me mention one or two.

A very good example is a recent decision by the Court of Appeals of Ghent.[11] This involved a non-competition agreement. In Belgium, there is apparently a rule – a very common rule – that in employment cases, non-competition agreements are void unless for a limited reasonable period. If they are not stated to be limited to a reasonable period, they are void completely – that is to say, a court will not blue pencil them, a court will not reform them, a court will not re-write the provision, a court will not restrict it back to a reasonable time. They are completely struck out and void because otherwise people will not be deterred from overreaching. So they are completely eliminated. The case went to arbitration. There was such a clause which provided, in sweeping terms, for an unlimited unreasonable period. The arbitrator interpreted the clause and concluded that it was implicitly limited to a period of five years. Then he said, that is the intention of the parties, it was implicitly limited to five years. And then he enforced it – because now, it was limited to five years. And the court said, even though the clause itself was unlimited on its face, the arbitral award limited it, it was now limited. It was limited because the award limited it. It was therefore a limited award and therefore the court had to enforce it. The sovereign interpretation of the arbitrator saved the award, saved the clause from annulment. The solution therefore, as a matter of contractual construction, once it was phrased as a matter of contractual construction, contractual construction being within the sovereign appreciation of the arbitrator, the problem of mandatory law was eliminated.

Let me mention one more case involving a sort of dialogue on mandatory matters between courts and arbitrators. An English case involved the exportation of carpets from Iran in violation of the Iranian revenue laws.[12] The case went to arbitration, a Jewish arbitration tribunal in London. The arbitration tribunal said the agreement was illegal under Iranian law, but since Jewish law applied, this had no effect on the transaction and so it enforced the agreement. The Court of Appeals set aside the award on the grounds that the award said it was illegal and therefore it was not enforceable in any way – after all, the award said on its face that it was illegal.

---

11 Gent (7ème Chambre bis), 3 Dec. 2007, R.D.J.P. 2008, at 131.
12 Soleimany v Soleimany, [1999] Q.B. 785 (C.A. 1998).

Now, to me this is not about the illegality of awards or adherence to mandatory rules – rather, this is about the imprudence of the arbitrators in saying in their award that the award was illegal. If they had said something else, the award would have been enforced. The court would have deferred it to the arbitrators if the arbitrators had merely used other language indicating that the award was not in their view illegal.

I think once the importance of mandatory law is filtered through deference to the arbitration process, the importance of deference to the arbitration process becomes an important transnational policy that takes over. The "*Terra Armata* case", with which you are probably familiar, I think, is a good illustration of that.[13] Here the arbitrators, sitting in Switzerland, had rejected assertions that the underlying contract was invalid under EU and Italian antitrust law. The Swiss Federal Tribunal said, first, that it is absolutely mandatory that arbitrators consider European Union Competition Law: Even if the contract is governed by Swiss Law, they have to consider the validity of a contract under EU law if asked to do so – and a refusal to do so will lead to vacatur on the ground that the tribunal "erroneously held that it had no jurisdiction".

Nevertheless, – and paradoxically – the court went on to hold that the "provisions of competition law, whatever they are, are not part of the essential and widely-shared values that make up the foundation of any legal order". So a violation of those provisions is not "incompatible with public policy"; a court will therefore "refuse to re-examine [*refuse de revoir*] the way in which the arbitrators have applied the law". As long as they have applied the law, we are satisfied.

I told this story before, so if you have heard it I apologize – but it is a great story and so I am going to tell it anyway. At the University of Geneva law faculty, in the common areas of the law faculty there are, or at least there were until very recently, large signs that say "Thank you for not smoking in this area and if necessary – '*le cas écheant*' – for not throwing your cigarette butts on the ground". That to me is an injunction that does not lay claim to being taken with a great deal of seriousness, and the same thing is true of the cases I have just been discussing. Thank you.

13 Tensacciai v Terra Armata, [2006] Rev. de l'Arb. 763, 768–69 (Trib. Fed. Switz. 2006).

Arbitration Tribunals

BEN STEINBRÜCK[1]

A. Introduction

Thank you very much. I will continue with transnational law, as we have just heard something about transnational public policy.

It is well known that international commerce disputes typically arise between parties from different countries. Often these countries also belong to different legal cultures. In these cases, the parties and the arbitral tribunal have to find a common ground in order to successfully resolve the dispute. Parties often opt for arbitration in a neutral forum according to a neutral law. They simply choose the arbitral seat in a third state and choose the law of this or another neutral state as the applicable substantive law.

Sometimes, however, parties cannot or do not want to agree on such a third state. They would rather like to solve their disputes according to legal principles and rules that transcend the boundaries of national law. This means that they would like the arbitral tribunal to apply common or general legal principles or some kind of transnational law. This sounds like a good idea. But could it work in practice? Does there exist a transnational body of sufficiently developed law that arbitral tribunals could apply? And if so, how is this law created? Do arbitral tribunals create it themselves or do they refer to some pre-established sets of rules and norms?

In my presentation, I will outline the development of a process that is often called "the emergence of transnational arbitration law". I will first discuss a case in which the parties rather unsuccessfully tried to "transnationalize" their contractual relationship in order to bridge the cultural gap between them. In the second and third part, I will deal with more effective efforts to create transnational substantive and procedural law in the past decades. We will see that these efforts were successful largely due to a lively and fruitful dialogue between the members of the arbitration community.

---

1 Research Fellow at the Max Planck Institute for Comparative and International Private Law, Hamburg.

B. How to reconcile different legal cultures in International Arbitration

I. The Channel Tunnel project: the tronc commun doctrine in practice

A good example to illustrate the attempt to reconcile different legal cultures in arbitration is the famous Channel Tunnel case. This case was heard in the English courts almost 20 years ago, after one side had applied for interim relief in England.

The Channel Tunnel project was one of the major international construction contracts of the 20th century. The contract was concluded between the Anglo-French concessionaires – Eurotunnel – and a group of Anglo-French companies. The complex dispute resolution agreement specified Brussels as the seat of the arbitration. The choice of law agreement between the two entities did not refer to the national law of either party, nor indeed to any national system of law.

Instead it provided that the contract would:

> "*... in all respects be governed by and interpreted in accordance with the principles common to both English law and French law, and in the absence of such common principles by such general principles of international trade law as have been applied by national and international tribunals*".

The solution adopted by the parties is sometimes called the *tronc commun* doctrine: It is based on the idea that if the choice of a specific national law proves unacceptable, parties may want to apply the common parts of two (or more) different systems of law to the matters in dispute.

This doctrine has obvious charm: The parties try to find a common legal basis that is acceptable to both of them. Yet, in the Channel Tunnel case these advantages turned out to be rather illusory: For each of the many disputes that arose under the construction contract the English and French lawyers on each side had to determine what the answer was likely to be under the applicable principles of their own legal system. Then they had to work out to what extent, if at all, these principles were common to both systems of law. Very often the answers were unclear. How should a party know its rights and obligations under the contract when the content of the applicable law remains vague?

In the end, the choice of law agreement called for a proper comparative law analysis of English and French contract law. Let us, therefore, examine to what extent the comparative law method can promote the resolution of disputes in cases like this.

II. The role of comparative law

Before legal principles can be compared, we first have to establish what English and French lawyers have in mind when they refer to "general principles" in their own legal system. Here the problems already begin. For example: Do "principles" under English law and French "principes" have the same meaning and function in their legal systems? Are legal principles a legal source in English law that can be directly applied like in French law? And what about "rules"? Can we look for common rules as well? And can "legal rules" be translated by "règles de droit"?

There are no short answers. This is why there are libraries full of books on these issues. But do the arbitrators and counsel have to read all this material? Of course not, since comparative law teaches one important lesson in this respect: While different legal systems might operate in a very different manner, they often produce the same or very similar results. Thus, instead of comparing single legal rules and principles, comparative lawyers prefer to study legal problems and their solutions in the different legal systems. This approach is called the functional method of comparative law. In the Channel Tunnel case this method certainly helped to solve some of the disputes: Instead of looking for common principles, the tribunal and counsel merely searched for "common results" and ignored the dogmatic foundations.

However, whether such an approach is successful, depends on the particular legal question. Sometimes it might fail to provide the required answers, simply because legal principles are incomplete. They do not provide the set of common norms, which is necessary to cover all contractual disputes.

Let us consider the following example: One of the many issues the parties in the Channel Tunnel case argued about, concerned the question whether a particular claim was time-barred. We all know that contractual rights are subject to limitation periods. The crucial question is: When do limitation periods expire? After two years, three years or even 30 years? When does the relevant limitation period start to run? What does a party have to do to suspend or interrupt a limitation period? Different legal systems adopt different solutions in this respect.

Another example is the application of the principle of good faith: Continental lawyers will certainly agree to the proposition that contracts have to be interpreted and performed in accordance with good faith; "La bonne foi contractuelle", for instance, is firmly enshrined in the French Civil Code. English lawyers, however, disagree. Sir Roy Goode, a renowned English law professor, summarizes the English position on good faith as follows:

> *"We in England find it difficult to adopt a general concept of good faith. ... The predictability of the legal outcome of a case is more important than absolute justice. ... The last thing that we want to do is to drive business away by vague concepts of fair-*

> *ness which make judicial decisions unpredictable, and if that means that the outcome of disputes is sometimes hard on a party we regard that as an acceptable price to pay in the interest of the great majority of business litigants."*

This brief survey just gives an idea of the problems that an arbitral tribunal might encounter when it is asked to apply the common principles of two (or even more) legal systems. A thorough comparative law analysis of two national laws is obviously not what the parties of the Channel Tunnel had in mind when drafting their contract. It is simply too time-consuming and costly and might well produce more questions than answers.

Similar problems might arise in respect of the term "general principles of international trade law as applied by national and international tribunals". It is true that the application of general principles of law is attractive. The beauty of general legal principles lies in their omnipotence. Some even argue that contractual disputes could be solved solely with the complementary principles of pacta sunt servanda and good faith. As we have seen, this is rather a continental or civilian perspective.

But, even if we subscribe to this view, many questions may be asked: What is the relevant "trade law" for a cross-border construction project? Which tribunals have applied such a law in the past? Where do we find those decisions? Do these rulings add up to a comprehensive system of international trade law? Again, things are getting complicated once we start taking the wording of the agreement seriously.

So, what should an arbitral tribunal do when it is faced with a choice-of-law clause that calls for the application of common or general principles? Could it maybe decide the dispute "ex aequo et bono", which means that it issues a ruling on the basis of what is fair and reasonable in the circumstances of the case without being bound by any legal rules? Many academics and practitioners will argue that in those situations the tribunal should simply apply the "Lex Mercatoria" as a transnational legal standard.

This brings me to the second part of my presentation, which deals with transnational substantive law.

C. Transnational substantive law

I. Lex Mercatoria materialis

The term "Lex Mercatoria" is mostly used as a catch-all for alleged rules of international commerce that are not based on a specific national or supra-national legal system, including international treaties such as the UN Sales Convention. These rules are therefore considered by some jurists to constitute an autonomous legal order. They may be roughly split into two groups: trade usages, codified terms and custom on the one hand and general principles of law on the other.

II. Unidroit Principles of International Commercial Contracts, PECL

Parties may also choose the Unidroit Principles of International Commercial Contracts or the Principles of European Contract Law. These are sets of rules primarily written by academics steeped in the civil law tradition. Being based in comparative law and common sense, they are regarded as the "ratio scripta" of international contract law. Both preambles suggest that "they may apply when the parties have agreed that their contract be governed by general principles of law, the "Lex Mercatoria" or the like".

III. Dialogue within the arbitration Community: arbitral precedents

This leads us to the next point: Do arbitral tribunals apply the "Lex Mercatoria" or the Unidroit principles in practice? And if they do, do they refer to each other's decisions? In other words: Is there a dialogue between arbitral tribunals through a system of arbitral precedents?

The short answer to the first question is: Yes, tribunals apply the "Lex Mercatoria" or the Unidroit principles, but not very often. Empirical studies have shown that parties very rarely choose a non-national legal standard. Also, arbitrators consistently show restraint in cases where the parties have failed to choose the applicable law.

In line with these findings is the observation that there is no developed system of arbitral precedents. Of course, arbitrators are not bound by earlier decisions which have dealt with the same issues. But there is not even a practice of regular cross-references for authoritative purposes. A recent study by Professor Kaufmann-Kohler, for example, has shown that commercial arbitrators do not systematically quote earlier cases. If they do so, then usually just to illustrate the operation of national or institutional rules. Thus, contrary to investment and sports arbitration, where tribunals regularly refer to earlier decisions, there is no self-standing rule creation in commercial arbitration.

Why is this so? Because there is no need for norm creation in international commercial arbitration. The applicable national laws are well developed and sufficiently predictable, so that arbitrators may confine themselves to deal with their own disputes, which are usually fact-driven and contract-specific. Moreover, arbitrators have broad discretion in determining and applying the law governing the merits. Commercial arbitrators are inclined to transnationalize the applicable rules in order to remove the dispute from the ambit of a possibly inadequate national law. As a consequence, the applicable law is "a law newly minted by the arbitrator on each occasion, every contract the subject of its own individual proper law", as Lord Mustill once put it.

There is an additional phenomenon: Arbitration practitioners increasingly turn their attention away from the applicable law and focus on the procedure, which is often much more important. I will therefore turn to my third part: The development of transnational procedural standards in international arbitration.

D. Transnational procedural law

I. Transnational procedural standards – "best practices"

For some time already we have been witnessing the emergence of an international consensus on how to conduct international commercial and investment arbitration. This consensus is usually labelled "best practices" or sometimes more weightily "Lex Mercatoria arbitralis".

1. UNCITRAL Arbitration Rules, Institutional Arbitration Rules

At the heart of this development is the principle of party autonomy that modern arbitration laws are promoting. Arbitration proceedings allow for the use of customized rules or the choice of institutional arbitration rules that offer the desired procedural balance. Prime examples of such "private norms" are the UNCITRAL Arbitration Rules of 1976 and the numerous institutional arbitration regimes, such as the ICC Rules on Arbitration or the Rules of the London Court of Arbitration.

2. IBA-Rules on the Taking of Evidence in Int. Commercial Arbitration

There is also important "soft law" in the field of evidence taking: The IBA-Rules on the Taking of Evidence in Int. Commercial Arbitration of 1999. These rules strike a successful balance between the various legal traditions in this area. Starting from the premise that discovery is an important tool in private adjudication, they establish a general obligation to produce documents requested by the other party. Yet, the IBA-Rules preclude US-style fishing expeditions by imposing rather strict requirements for such requests. Furthermore, the tribunal exerts much more control over the discovery process than American courts do. Arbitrators and counsel often adopt the IBA-Rules in whole or draw on them selectively.

This system-neutral model of carefully calibrated and controlled access to evidence proved inspirational to the drafters of the Unidroit Principles of Transnational Civil Procedure.

3. Dialogue within the Arbitration Community

These "private norms" are the product of a fruitful dialogue within the arbitration community. The rules were largely drafted by international practitioners who operate in venues like London, Geneva, Stockholm and New York. Although their different legal backgrounds might here and there generate some distinct legal styles, they are less and less committed to a particular domestic legal order. Many of them are thus becoming cosmopolitan representatives of their profession, at least in the Western world. Besides this group of top-ranked arbitrators a number of other networks and associations are rapidly emerging, many of which are also specifically designed for the growing number of young arbitration practitioners.

E. Conclusion

In conclusion, I would like to emphasize the following points:

1. We have seen that national legal standards are becoming a distinct feature of international arbitration.

2. In practice, transnational procedural law plays a bigger role than transnational substantive law, although it is not always easy to differentiate between both areas. In essence, we observe that a transnational "method of adjudication", which combines procedural and substantive elements, is emerging. It is based on a growing consensus on how arbitrations are conducted, how decisions are reached, and what should be taken into account for such decisions.

3. The dialogue within the arbitration community as the basis of this process will certainly continue. If it is further extended to other parts of the world in the future, we may indeed have one day a truly globalized arbitration culture.

Thank you.

Dialogue Between Courts in Times of Globalization and Regionalization

PER RUNELAND[1]

A. Introduction

I wish to thank the organizers for giving us such an extremely fruitful topic to discuss. My job is to cover dialogue in arbitration as seen by an international arbitrator. My practice covers both the London arbitration market, where I have been active for 25 years, and the continent of Europe, generally in arbitrations where at least one party is from the former Soviet Union. Typically, my arbitrations have their seats in Stockholm, London, Zurich, Geneva, Paris, Vienna, Moscow or Kiev. I may add that, these days, many disputes that are really Russian appear in international surveys as disputes between companies domiciled in Switzerland, the United States, the British Virgin Islands or Cyprus.

B. Dialogue between the tribunal and (counsel for) the parties

In international arbitration, it is essential for the tribunal to be aware of any cultural differences and to attempt to move the proceedings forward efficiently, without surprises, and with visible attention to a reasonable balance between efficiency and fairness. It is unlikely that all parties will be satisfied all the time, but no openings should be left for later attacks on the validity or enforceability of an award based on lack of communication and failure to secure an environment of fairness. Some participants in international arbitration speak of fairness, others of due process, natural justice, or equal treatment of the parties, all of which terms are less than precise in their interpretation, especially in a cross-cultural environment. A tribunal that deals with these issues openly in the course of the arbitration does itself and the successful party a great favour by staying ahead of later opposition, post award. Where the co-arbitrators have experience of a legal environment that is different from that of the chairperson, they can make a significant contribution in this context.

---

1 Consultant with the International Arbitration Group of SJ Berwin, London.

C. Dialogue within the tribunal

One of the great benefits of the traditional three arbitrator panel is the opportunity it gives the arbitrators to discuss the case while it is being heard and while deliberating over the award. All arbitration rules require arbitrators to be independent of the parties and impartial, and the dialogue works best when this requirement is fulfilled. Parties should realize how they are best served by appointing arbitrators who are independent and are seen to be independent. Any bias reveals itself as soon as the arbitrators begin discussing the conclusions to be drawn. If the arbitrators realize that an arbitrator is not going to deal with the case on its real merits, then the dialogue within the tribunal suffers immediately. It becomes meaningless to discuss issues after an arbitrator has taken an entrenched position. Open and unprejudiced dialogue keeps the arbitrators, all of them, involved in the deliberations and influences the quality of the award positively. This also makes the tribunal's internal functioning professionally more satisfying and more enjoyable. If one arbitrator declares a firm view at an early stage, in terms that indicate that a dissenting opinion will be coming if the view is not accepted as the tribunal's view, then the effect is typically to exclude that arbitrator from the evolution of thought within the tribunal. I saw an interesting example of this in two recent parallel arbitrations regarding the breach of a lease agreement concerning a commercial building. The building was owned by two landlords who were related companies. When the tenant started an arbitration demanding damages for breach of contract, the landlords appeared to have decided to make the arbitration as difficult as possible. They appointed two separate arbitrators in the two arbitrations which had the same arbitrator appointed by the tenant, and the same chairman appointed by the arbitration institution. We prefer to speak of arbitrators appointed by a party rather than arbitrators belonging to that party, but in this case it seemed that the landlords had got their advocates inside the tribunal. The effect was that the awards were drafted with input from the chairman and the other arbitrator, with the third arbitrator limited to drafting and submitting dissenting opinions. Nevertheless, it was important to keep the third arbitrator fully involved in the deliberations. Otherwise the tribunal risked committing the kind of procedural defect that would render the award vulnerable to a challenge or lead to successful opposition at the enforcement stage.

The situation also frustrated the dialogue between counsel for the parties and the tribunal, on the one hand, and the witnesses, on the other. The hearings were separate, but much of the material was the same. However, the progress of the second case was not identical to that of the first, and the examination of witnesses resulted in slightly different facts being made available to the tribunal and the parties. Even the witnesses themselves became confused when appearing in the second hearing. Surrounded by the same counsel and arbitrators, except for the third arbitrator, they tended to refer to their statements in the first arbitration, forcing the chairman to put them back on track and underline that the tribunals were different even though the underlying contract and facts were the same.

D. Dialogue between the arbitral tribunals and the courts

The cases I just mentioned also gave rise to interesting arguments and deliberations concerning the relationship of arbitration and court proceedings. In separate earlier arbitrations between the same parties, the tribunals had decided that the landlord's failure to renew the lease was a breach of contract. Before the second arbitrations were started, in which the tenant claimed damages for breach of contract, the landlords had brought successful actions before the courts asking for the arbitration awards to be set aside due to a number of alleged defects, of which an argument based on public policy was the most important and successful. The theory was that rights, even leasehold, relating to real property require registration, and registration can only be effected by the competent government agency. Only ordinary courts, not arbitral tribunals, can require the registration of real property rights to take place. The courts found that the first tribunals had exceeded their powers when determining that certain conduct constituted breaches of the relevant leases. Such questions could only be determined by the courts. In the second arbitrations, the landlord argued forcefully that the tribunal had no right to order the payment of damages because the fact of breach of contract had been established in awards which had been set aside by the courts. The tribunals decided to turn a deaf ear to that argument. We have yet to see the end of this continuing dialogue between the tribunals and the courts.

E. The court/tribunal dialogue in setting-aside proceedings

I turn now, to a dialogue where the courts often have the last word, namely when arbitral awards are set aside, in this case, appropriately for our subject, due to a failure by the tribunal to hear the parties properly, a lack of adequate dialogue. I want to illustrate this point by two cases, one from Finland, where a challenged award was upheld, and one from Switzerland, where a questionable award was referred back to the panel of the Court of Arbitration for Sport.

F. Comesa GmbH v Polar Electro Europe BV

On 2 July 2008, the Supreme Court of Finland upheld an award given on 14 June 2004 by a unanimous tribunal in Helsinki. The arbitrators, three Finnish practicing lawyers, had to consider a claim by Comesa GmbH (the "Distributor") against Polar Electro Europe BV (the "Supplier"). The claim was for "distribution indemnity", claimed by analogy with the termination compensation available to agents, although the contract involved was a distribution agreement which contained a clause stipulating that, in the event of termination, the Distributor was not entitled to any compensation. The written and oral submissions of the parties focused on the Distributor's right to compensation based on the analogy with the rules applying to commercial agents. The contract was governed by the laws of Finland and "the internationally mandatory Austrian law".

The parties, and in particular the Distributor, presented a full history of their commercial relationship. It included a series of warranty claims and supply difficulties.

The tribunal held that, in this case, no agency rules could be applied by analogy. The clause whereby the Distributor had waived any right to compensation upon termination was binding in principle. However, the Distributor had accepted it in the expectation that a sufficient reward for its work could be earned during the term of the contract. The facts shown by the Distributor made it evident that the Supplier's manufacturing problems and the large number of warranty claims handled by the Distributor had reduced the Distributor's income in an unforeseen manner. Under those circumstances, the Distributor had not waived its right to indemnification. Hence, the Distributor was entitled to reasonable indemnification, putting it in the same position as if it had been able to conduct its business without the disruption caused by the Supplier.

Section 36 of the Finnish Contracts Act allows a contractual provision to be adjusted or disregarded if its application would lead to an unreasonable result. The tribunal held that, if it was not adjusted, the contract clause whereby the Distributor gave up any rights to compensation would lead to an unreasonable result due to changed circumstances (the disrupted supplies and the quality problems). The tribunal found legislative support for the position that whereas a court (or tribunal) cannot adjust unreasonable provisions ex officio, a party should be considered to have invoked the unreasonableness of a clause if it contested the other party's claim and presented views concerning unreasonableness. Further, a claim that a provision should be declared null and void or set aside due to a mandatory provision of law includes a secondary claim for adjustment of the contractual stipulation under Section 36 of the Finnish Contracts Act.

On the evidence presented, it was impossible to compute the revenue lost by the Distributor, but under the relevant rules of procedure, it was permissible to estimate it. The tribunal found that €1,200,000 was reasonable indemnification and awarded that sum. The costs of the arbitration were split so that the Distributor had to bear one third and the Supplier two thirds.

The award was challenged by the Supplier on the ground that the arbitrators had based their ruling on general contract law although neither party had specifically invoked it. The courts of first and second instance set the award aside, but the Supreme Court overruled their judgments. In doing that, the Supreme Court had to decide if the arbitral tribunal had exceeded its authority or deprived a party of a sufficient opportunity to present its case, to be heard. The Supreme Court first addressed a concept applied in Nordic laws of procedure, namely the party's "burden of allegation". It noted that the Distributor had invoked several circumstances as legal grounds for its claim. The Supplier had responded to those factual allegations. The Supreme Court stated that the reason why the award should not be set aside was that it had not been based on any facts not invoked by the claimant and on which the respondent had not been entitled to comment.

With respect to the principle of *iura novit curia*, the Supreme Court underlined that the tribunal was not bound by the legal reasoning presented by the parties. Further, a claim to declare a contract clause invalid could be deemed to include a secondary claim that the unreasonable clause be adjusted or set aside. Consequently, the Supreme Court held that the tribunal had not exceeded its authority and had not failed to give the Supplier a sufficient opportunity to present its case. In view of the facts of the case, the Supreme Court held that the tribunal's determination, not declaring the liability clause invalid, and not dismissing the claim in its entirety, could not have come as a surprise to the parties.

G. José Ignacio Urquijo Goitia v. Liedson da Silva Muñiz

The Swiss Federal Supreme Court published a decision on 4 March 2009 whereby it annulled a Court of Arbitration for Sport ("CAS") award due to the violation of the right to be heard. In this case, José Ignacio Urquijo Goitia ("the Agent"), a players' agent from Spain, entered into an agreement with Liedson da Silva Muñiz (the "Player"), a footballer from Brazil, giving the Agent the exclusive right to represent the Player in Europe. In 2003, the Player contracted with a Portuguese football club, without the Agent's involvement. However, the Agent demanded his commission and started proceedings at the FIFA Players' Status Committee. The Agent's claim was rejected and the dispute went to the CAS. The CAS Panel upheld the FIFA decision, noting that the contract was governed by FIFA rules and supplementary Swiss law.

The Agent underlined that having an exclusive agreement with the Player, he did not need to show that he had been instrumental in the making of the contract with the football club. The CAS Panel rejected this argument and referred to a mandatory provision in the Swiss Federal Law on the Employment Exchange and the Hiring-out of Personnel. It provides, in particular, that any stipulation is null and void if it prevents a person seeking employment, being contractually bound to one broker, from using the services of any other broker, in effect invalidating exclusive agreements in this area. The Agent then requested the Federal Supreme Court to set aside the CAS decision, arguing that he had not been given a chance to present his case because the application of the legal provision deemed relevant by the Panel was not at all addressed in the course of the CAS proceedings.

The Federal Supreme Court reviewed the interaction of the principle of *iura novit curia* and the right to be heard. The Court noted that the application of the Law on Employment Exchange etc., required certain connections with Switzerland, which were absent in this case. Hence, the Agent could not have foreseen that the CAS Panel would base its decision on it. The Court ruled that the CAS Panel should at least have permitted the parties to comment on the legal provision that decided the outcome of the case. By failing to provide this opportunity, the CAS Panel had violated the Agent's right to be heard and the dispute was referred back to the CAS Panel.

H. Procedure or substance?

These two cases are remarkably similar as to the principles involved. They reply to the question if arbitrators may rely on a statute that has not been mentioned in the course of the proceedings. Further, it appears that, in both cases, the respective Supreme Court helped obtain a result that was fair in the circumstances. The Distributor in the Finnish case certainly deserved some compensation, and the Agent in the Swiss case was entitled to his commission on the basis of his exclusivity under the existing contract. It is tempting to see the decisions as results of an undeclared review in substance rather than as the expression of any fundamental differences between the practice in Finland and Switzerland with respect to due process. However, there is a material difference between the two cases in that the Finnish case, where the award was upheld, concerns the application of a basic principle of civil law that was undoubtedly applicable in the case, whereas in the Swiss case, the arbitral tribunal applied a law that was in fact not applicable, and hence the parties could not possibly imagine that it would be applied. In the Finnish case, the arbitrators knew the law. In the Swiss case, as determined by the Swiss Supreme Court, the tribunal did not know the law and applied a legal provision in error and without discussing it with the parties. This was put right when the Court quashed the award.

I. Precedent in international arbitration

Within the time available, I have been unable to deal with the dialogue between tribunals that arises when previously decided cases are relied on by the parties or the tribunal when arguing and deciding the case. This interesting area, involving the role of arbitral precedent, will have to be left to another day, unless somebody wants to comment on it during the discussion session.

Discussion

PETER NOBEL

If we may now open the discussion. First the questions that have come up during the presentations.

MRS. PAIR

I have a question for Mr. Steinbrück. The quotations that were mentioned by you where arbitral tribunals quote each other, or the lack thereof, is that true for procedural questions as well? Say you have an international institution like the international Chamber of Commerce or the Stockholm Chamber or the Swiss Chamber, do arbitrations that fall under the same institutional rules quote each other on procedural questions because the procedural questions are always the same? They are not as fact-intensive as the material law questions.

BEN STEINBRÜCK

It is true that if tribunals refer to each other, they do so primarily with regard to procedural issues. On substantive law, in contrast, they hardly ever refer to other awards. This is at least my impression since there is not much material available. Most arbitral awards are confidential and it is very difficult to get the entire text of an award. Often, we only have a summary. But the empirical studies that were conducted in this field reveal that quotations often refer to procedural or choice-of-law questions. In particular, the determination of the applicable law is often not clear. Do tribunals have to apply national conflict of law rules, and if so, which ones, or can they directly apply the substantive law? In this respect national laws still differ from each other. That is why tribunals tend to look for guidance in other awards. But there appears to be no systematic cross-reference system in commercial arbitration. The situation is different in ICSID arbitrations and investment arbitrations in general and in sports arbitration. The reason for this is that these are areas where the law is not yet very well developed, so tribunals often have to create the law themselves. The Court of Sports Arbitration, for example, systematically refers to its earlier awards. This is necessary because especially in sport law cases you need predictability. When you have to rule on doping fines, for instance, you cannot do one thing in one case and then do something else in a comparable case. The basic principles have to be the same in both cases.

MRS. PAIR

Are they only for the same rules, like when Swiss Chambers or Swiss rules are only quoted by other Swiss arbitration cases, or when ICC rules are only quoted by other ICC cases, or is that inter-organizational?

BEN STEINBRÜCK

I do not know whether you can give general answers here. There might be tribunals that systematically refer to other ICC tribunals. If you are working in a big law firm, where you have access to a lot of awards, you might well quote your own or your colleagues' material, which might actually be unfair if your opponent does not have this material because it is not published. In such a case, the tribunal might only get one-sided information. And, of course, if you have an ICC tribunal, you may well look first for guidance in other ICC cases. But as I said, there does not seem to be a coherent system yet.

ALBERTO ALEMANNO

A very short note on this. We all agree that one of the preconditions for judicial dialogue is the public availability of judgments. Yet, as is well-known, in international arbitration these awards are by definition not available and just a few reach the general public, as you have rightly pointed out. As such, they represent the peak of an iceberg. So, I really wonder how can arbitral awards circulate freely and maybe be quoted as you said. More in general, I would say that arbitrators, unlike judges, have fewer incentives to quote and to make references. They do not really need to do so. Apparently, they do so only when, for procedural reasons, they do not want to appear inconsistent because they belong to a family like the ICC or other systems.

PETER NOBEL

Arbitral decisions are usually known only by accident, and this is one of the main reasons that it is very hard to develop consistent principles understandable, however, since one of the advantages of arbitration is the confidentiality. For lawyers it is an awkward situation. Please.

PIERRE TERCIER

Just a footnote to what has been said: In fact, we have to distinguish between the substantive and the procedural law. If we take a look at the procedural law: I am not sure that there is "typical" ICC case law. The rules are so general that procedural matters start to get interesting when going into detail.

But coming to the substantive law: It is true that there are not sufficient publications of awards. As we see more and more, especially counsels and arbitrators are very proud to promote the quality of their work and the perfection of their product in journals. But there is another point to it and this is, from a sociological point of view, very interesting: Arbitration constitutes a more or less closed community. The people dancing on this "arbitration parquet" are used to work together. This results in a spontaneous generation of law being created by people knowing each other and working together. Of course, there are not always the same people working together in one tribunal, but it is still a small community. I am not a sociologist, but I am sure that it would be an extremely interesting subject matter to see how this generation of law evolves. The last point, I want to mention in this context, is the control of arbitral awards by state courts, even if this control is used in a very reluctant way. It is true to say that there is no jurisprudence because we have no Supreme Court controlling what the tribunal is doing.

PETER NOBEL

Thank you. You know we talk a lot about the law. We always talk about the law, but we rarely talk about the facts. When I started at the Commercial Court in Zurich, as a young man, there was an experienced judge and he said, "Why are you always talking about the law? Establishing the facts makes a sentence unattackable by the federal court." You have got to present the facts in a way that the law becomes very clear. This is maybe also in arbitration, you know, it is a long process to establish the facts, but once they are on the table, very often things become clear. If you establish the facts, if you get the reality out of the past, if you realize when witnesses lie or when they have been prepared to much, if you look at the circumstances of the documents, then law, at least in my experience, becomes the easy part.

MARKUS MÜLLER-CHEN

Actually, it is not a question, but a remark that goes along the lines of what you have just said and we are talking about dialogue here, right? Dialogue means that we should understand one another. I often doubt that we truly understand one another, especially in an international arbitration setting where, as we have heard, decisions are formed under various sets of rules and people come from different legal and also cultural backgrounds. One thing, I am being really interested in, is, if we truly understand one another. For example, we saw that when quoting cases, we rarely talk about the procedural foundation of these cases. How did the substantive law that eventually is expressed in the decision, come to be? The same question relates to the fact-finding process and to the terminology used. We sometimes think we speak about the same things, but if you truly look at it, we kind of do not. I think it was you, Professor Rau, mentioned the good faith provision. That is a typical example of where we do not truly understand one another. So, in your experience, is that a problem and if it is, how can we take steps to better understand one another?

BEN STEINBRÜCK

This refers to my topic. What I tried to say is that there is a community of arbitrators, a growing community, that understands each other pretty well. They have often studied in different legal environments and know something about US law, about English law, about continental law. Over time they get the perception of different legal cultures and are able to merge them. This is what Pierre Tercier has just said, they understand each other when working together. This is what I meant with a common method of adjudication. It is true that it might be a rather small group of international arbitrators, and a national arbitrator who is working more on the national level might have problems in getting a grip of a foreign law when he has to deal with foreign arbitrators in an international setting. But the example of the IBA rules simply shows that there is an emerging trend of two different procedure cultures. Parties very often disagree, after an award has been rendered, on the question whether the proceedings were fair, whether the procedural balance was established. And the fact-finding parts are crucial elements here. There has been published a survey on arbitration awards applying the IBA rules, which shows that parties often try to challenge the application of the IBA rules in state courts. They attack the awards on the grounds that they were not heard properly, that they submitted something to the tribunal that was not taken into account or they asked for a certain document that they did not get. At the moment, these rules are still rather new and that is why their application is challenged before the courts. But, once a more, coherent general practice is emerging in this respect, it can be expected that less and less awards will be challenged in the future on these grounds.

ALAN RAU

I think I sort of agree with that answer. If people go about trying to do things, it usually works pretty well. I think where they get into trouble is when they try to find words for things and when they try to pin down legal concepts and that usually ends in disaster. That is why arbitration practice and procedure works very well across the traditional civil law/common law lines. However, attempts at theoretical classification in this area always leads to the kind of silly results that I was talking about.

LARS BAY LARSEN

I just could not help a comment to what Ben Steinbrück said both in his last comment and in his intervention, as I can easily understand the difficulties involved in deducting and identifying common positions in different national legal systems with a view acquiring step by step a commonly accepted basis for international arbitration. In fact it is not so far from the exercise that everybody involved in international jurisdictions are confronted with. However, we sometimes may seem to be doing it in the reverse order. When I am working as a reporting judge with a case concerning a possible infringement one way or another of community rules by say German Tax Law that treats daughter companies in Holland differently from domestic German daughter companies; then I must first analyze and understand the German system of company law and company tax law, eventually adding the Dutch company tax law system to it. And I may even have a fairly clear idea what the company law and the company tax regulations are in this area is in my own native Danish system. But still there are twenty-four other national jurisdictions. And I may get to the point where I believe that there is a real problem in the German system that my Court, the ECJ, will have to address in our judgment. But sometimes that could be phrased in three, five or ten different ways. And sometimes you speculate what difference it will make in say Portugal, if we choose model A, B or C, if Portugal for one or another reason has chosen not to submit any observations in the case? Maybe by taking one or the other or two for me equally good routes to the result I have to go to, I may overturn, accidentally, something in the Portuguese company tax system, which maybe was actually not causing any difficulties just because I do not know it sufficiently well. You may regard this as just another confession of personal incompetence, but reality is that nobody masters 27 national legal systems to perfection.

CHRISTOPH PAULUS

This is one request for clarification to you, Alan, and one question to you, Mr. Runeland. You mentioned that arbitrators sometimes have a solution for the interpretation of a law which is forty years ahead of the state judges. If this would be meant to be a plea for the excellence of arbitration law, I would add a little warning, because how often do you have dissenting opinions within the state courts (I think primarily of the Constitutional Courts) which are ground breaking, not for today, but for the future. Therefore, I would not say that this is something specific of the arbitration system. This is one thing.

And the question to Mr. Runeland: How is the second award which you have attributed this damage award. Is it enforceable?

PER RUNELAND

The answer is, we do not know because it is a very recent decision. We know that it will not be fulfilled voluntarily and this is part of, as I see it, an ongoing dispute about the competence of arbitration and the courts and this goes far beyond the poor parties in this case.

ALASTAIR MULLIS

I am struck by this idea of shared understandings. Can I ask the four of you to define "Lex Mercatoria"? I suspect we will get four different answers.

BEN STEINBRÜCK

That would have been my answer. You get four different answers. The situation is very unclear. When you look for a definition, which I did before this conference, you will find several ones. For some, for example, the "*Lex Mercatoria*" is part of transnational law, for others transnational law is just another term for "*Lex Mercatoria*". Professor Gaillard has said that "*Lex Mercatoria*" is rather a method than a law. As a method, it is what I have tried to describe as a transnational application of national law.

ALAN RAU

I think you will get four different answers from each one of us – and so you should, because I think there is no one answer, nor should there be. But the notion of Lex Mercatoria can intelligently be deployed in a whole range of situations – from the most banal (that is, the recognition that everybody contracts in the light of the surrounding custom and usage, a fact that makes everybody a "mercatorist") – all the way to the other extreme (that is, the recognition that arbitrators are often better placed than judges to take into account what is in the interest of commerce, which means that they can come up with solutions which are different from what a court would come up with but which better serves the interest of commercial law and which may, in fact, be what the "official" body of commercial law will be forty years from now) – and indeed, any position intermediate between these two.

The occasional suggestion that "one should merely consult what the books say", is presumably not intended to be taken seriously, but if it is, it is naively unreflective: It both begs the question for what reason can there be to assume that they know better than we do? That leads to infinite regress. (What if the "books" one day begin to refer to us?)

PER RUNELAND

It is not a definition, but it is a comment, because in my practice I do not apply it. If I see it, I will not apply it. The usefulness of "Lex Mercatoria", when you have a tribunal that is going to find an applicable law of some kind, is, in my view, here to support the arguments. When you have some reasonably applicable rule of law and it is not absolutely clear that it is applicable, then counsel will line up UNIDROIT principles and they will say, this all tells me this, and if the arbitrators are persuaded, they will take that with them and then they go back and find the solution in a positive rule. It is not wasted time, necessarily, even though you do not see a reference to "Lex Mercatoria" in the award.

PETER NOBEL

For me it is what I find in books about "Lex Mercatoria" but I have never used it in reality. At the end, it might be the result of a careful comparison of different solutions. But "Lex Mercatoria" as a body of law does not exist.

Maybe, Mr. Runeland, you could explain in a moment, why the Swiss were so stupid to set aside this second arbitral award.

PER RUNELAND

The Swiss are never stupid. You know more than I do, as always. That was a case where the tribunal applied a rule of internal Swiss law having to do with the labour exchange etc. to an international context. This had not been discussed with the parties at all and the parties were international, there was the Spanish agent, there was the Brazilian footballer and there was another international club. So, the only Swiss connection was, in fact, the Court of Arbitration. So, the Court of Arbitration found this undiscussed rule and based the decision on it. I think, I agree with the Supreme Court decision when they sent it back. I do not know what actually happened later, if it has been decided a second time. But they sent it back to the panel of the Court of Arbitration of Sport and said, you have to look at this again and presumably discuss this question with the parties. So, I think that the observation I would make from my outside point of view, is that it looks pretty reasonable that in this case the jura novit curia principle cannot really be applied because there are two weaknesses, if I put it like that. Number one, it seems to be the wrong law and, two, there was the wrong result. So, if you have the wrong law and the wrong result, I think you can look at it again.

PETER NOBEL

You know, for us, in many instances, it is enough that the arbitral court is in Switzerland. We do not care much that other pieces of the case are related to Switzerland. But there is a rule, you know, the right to be heard. In Switzerland it comprises also that you do not surprise the parties with your judgment. So, you must not tell what the decision will be, but the legal issues around the avenue of decision must have been commented by the parties. So, no legal surprise is part of the right to be heard. And the right to be heard is one of the few, very few grants to set aside.

ALAN RAU

Can I ask Per one question that we have not really talked about at all, but which I think is really basic? He was talking about the party-appointed arbitrator and he said, the arbitrator appointed by the party should play the game fairly, which, of course, I have no question with. The arbitrator who plays the game too openly and too blatantly, who is too obviously partisan, hurts the credibility of his own side and of the process, of course, that is right. But my question would be whether the whole institution of the party-appointed arbitrator is not somehow called into question by this, – because, what it does not take into account, what this structure does not take into account is the force of self-deception: That is to say, it is very obvious to everybody that the party who has appointed me once is more likely to appoint me again. I do not have to be dishonest to be influenced by the party who appointed me first. Now, it may well be that the institution of the party-appointed arbitrator is justified by the fact that this is true on both sides and so there is off-setting partiality and so it sort of cancels each other out. But we really cannot pretend that the arbitrator who has already been appointed by one party is really suspended in neutrality between the two litigants. We cannot pretend that unless we are just closing our eyes to the truth, can we?

PER RUNELAND

I have two comments. You know there can be dissenting opinions in arbitration. And in the long history of the world, there is not one dissenting opinion given by a party-appointed arbitrator against the party that appointed it. This tells us something about the function of the party-appointed arbitrator.

But the positive side is that the party-appointed arbitrator has a legitimate right and duty to make sure that the case, as pleaded by the party that appointed him, has been well understood within the tribunal. So, if the arbitrator does this and the arbitrator appointed by the other side does the same thing, you have a sort of neutral environment and there is a proper division of labour and there is no unfairness in it.

CARL BAUDENBACHER

I would like to point to a parallel between arbitration and adjudication by international courts. In arbitration you have party-appointed arbitrators and in international courts you have a judge from each Member State, in most cases. There is now one tribunal in the European Union which follows a different system; that is the EU Civil Service Tribunal, where there are only seven judges for 27 Member States. That means, they could not follow the one judge per country approach. But if you have one judge per country, then the question is how these judges are chosen. Right now, it is for the individual governments to pick them. It may then happen that a judge looks back to the capital where he comes from in a politically sensitive case. My experience is that such a judge loses credibility. He or she loses influence. You may play this card in a real vital case once every five years, but if you do it too obviously, you are out of the game. At least in this country, or in Germany, the situation of a party-appointed arbitrators is not much different. But there may be other traditions. Actually, I could just confirm that I agree a national judge plays the national card in one or another way. However, it is not the task for us to do so, that is the task for the agents of the government when they plead the case.

PETER NOBEL

To be frank, from party arbitrators, at least in my experience you can expect almost everything; from lawyer to very independent arbitrator. The worst case was probably an arbitration about a missing train. And when we found out why the train was missing, the party arbitrator was also missing, he disappeared.

ERICH SCHANZE

May I ask a question to the practitioners on the panel? Lon Fuller, who at least later in his life has been a fairly seasoned labour arbitrator, made the following point in his class at Harvard in the sixties: If you propose a settlement as an arbitrator, and the settlement is not accepted, you should quit. In practice, he would closely observe this rule. Notwithstanding my own observations, I would like to ask this panel: What is your attitude here? Do you quit, or do you stay on for making a binding decision?

ALAN RAU

Well, if you propose a settlement to the parties which is not accepted? That is a very difficult question. I should probably stop there. My first question would be, what are you doing proposing a settlement to the parties? What business is it of yours to be doing that? But my understanding would be that this is much more common in the labour situation than a commercial situation.

Well, what strikes me as interesting there is one foolish step after another in this scenario, isn't there? I think it is a foolish step to make that proposal – and on top of that, then it is a foolish mistake to quit after the proposal is turned down. But I am very much out of sympathy with this hypothetical, I am afraid. I would better turn over to my colleagues.

PETER NOBEL

In my opinion, the first step is not the foolish step in all instances. It might be a very wise step, but the time has come for our keynote speaker.

Keynote

Arbitrators and Judges – Opponents or Collaborators?

PIERRE TERCIER[1]

Introduction[2]

Ladies and gentlemen,

It is a great honour and a great pleasure to present to you the so-called keynote speech about the dialogue between arbitrators and judges with the fascinating subtitle: "opponents or collaborators". I would prefer the subtitle "competitors or co-operators".

Before my retirement as a professor, one of my goals has been to develop the dialogue between professors and judges; between "Rechtsprechung und Lehre". And after my retirement, especially in my last function as Chairman of the ICC Court of Arbitration, I strove to develop the dialogue between arbitrators and judges. Thus, the theme precisely fits my occupation.

A first remark: I will give a speech. It is neither a lesson, nor a formal lecture. And I will try to put some footnotes in order to address questions that have been discussed this afternoon.

Secondly, what is a keynote? A key can be used to open a door and to show people new and original premises and rooms. But a key can also be used to close doors, to confuse people and therefore to leave them alone and without orientation in the new rooms. I will do my best to not close, but to open doors.

I think that we shall first consider the reason and the scope of a possible dialogue between arbitrators and judges (A). We will then be able to address two sides of it: One is what I call the official or the formal relation between arbitrators and judges (B). On the other side I want to discuss the question of informal relations, of the informal dialogue (C).

---

1 Professor emeritus at the University of Fribourg, Honorary Chairman of the International Court of Arbitration of the ICC, Paris.

2 The following text is a revised and adapted version of the keynote speech given at the occasion of the 2nd St. Gallen International Dispute Resolution Conference, 15/16 October 2009, St. Gallen, Switzerland. It keeps its oral character without scientific references. The text has been revised by BLaw Eva Molinari.

A. A dialogue

What is a dialogue? A moment ago, Professor Peter Nobel made good demonstration of his culture: The Greek word "dialogos" refers to a speech, to an exchange of views and ideas among people. Those people firstly have to have something in common. Otherwise they discuss in parallel tracks without meeting each other, which would emerge into a totally useless encounter. On the other side, they also have to have some differences. Otherwise their discussion is boring, since they will all say the same thing. So what is different? What is common?

I will start with what is common (I) and then continue with what is different between judges and arbitrators (II). And using Professor Carl Baudenbacher's field of specialization, I will also consider this from a market perspective.

I. What is common between judges and arbitrators?

Common is clearly the role that judges and arbitrators play in the functioning of society. We want justice. In case of a dispute between two or more persons or entities, judges as well as arbitrators have the power to decide who is right and who is wrong. This is indeed an extraordinary power and in my view one of the most presumptuous tasks in society. Judges and arbitrators decide on the basis of general principles. Besides the "lex mercatoria" we use norms, abstract concepts applicable to everybody.

A further common point is that arbitration may be used in exactly the same way and also in the same fields as litigation before state courts. Of course there is a certain number of fields that are closed markets and thus monopolies of state judges; namely the fields of criminal law, family law and administrative law. However, it is worth mentioning that those closed markets are more and more contested and penetrated by arbitration. This development can very clearly be detected in administrative law, partly in family law and in some countries even in criminal law. But leaving this question aside and addressing mainly the field of private law and especially of contract law, it is evident that judges and arbitrators work on the same grounds.

Furthermore, judgments rendered by Swiss state courts are enforceable in Switzerland, but also in foreign countries as far as there exist multilateral or bilateral treaties. The same applies to arbitration, i.e. to decisions rendered by private persons outside the classical legal framework of a state. An arbitral award has the same value as a judgment rendered by a state court and may – with the help of state organs – be enforced in Switzerland but also abroad. The enforcement of arbitral awards in foreign countries works even better than the enforcement of a judgment thanks to the extraordinary extension of the New York Convention. The New York Convention, and before it the Geneva Conventions 1923–27, are extraordinary tools. They were the start of the globalization of international dispute resolution. And today 144 States accept to enforce a decision rendered by private persons and to do it much better and much easier than they would enforce a state judgment.

Judges and arbitrators are indeed on the same market and satisfy the same needs.

Here I would like to put my first footnote concerning the role of the arbitrators in settlement: I fully agree with what has been said by Professor Peter Nobel. It is also the role of the arbitrator to help the parties in participating in the dispute resolution process and in finding a settlement. But there is a risk: Depending on the procedural framework, and especially in the common law tradition, it is forbidden to mix alternative dispute resolution methods (ADR) and arbitration. Namely, the mediator has not the right to act afterwards as an arbitrator. The merger of ADR and arbitration in one and the same procedure is probably more developed in civil law countries and is extremely well developed in Zurich. But there, another risk emerges, and it is an important one:

As we have heard before, a criticism against arbitration is that arbitrators are still splitting the baby, meaning there is a tendency of arbitrators to not grant everything required by the parties, but only a part of it. In other words, there is a tendency to go for compromises. The problem arising in connection with those solutions based on a compromise is that they are sometimes very unpractical: Especially in the banking and finance sector, the goal of the parties is to get 100% of what they have required. When arbitration is linked to the idea of ADR, they will not go for arbitration, fearing that the arbitrator could grant them less. There, the parties are better advised to go before a state judge where it is more likely to get the full amount asked for.

II. What is different between judges and arbitrators?

The main difference is the basis for the activity of judges and arbitrators: Judges are appointed and paid by the state to render justice between private persons and to decide on all cases that are submitted to them. On the other hand, the arbitrators' activity relies on a very different basis. It relies on the contract accepted by the parties. What exactly do the parties accept? They accept to waive their fundamental rights to go before a state judge and therewith they waive all advantages linked to state justice: control, clear procedural rules, and assistance in case of difficulties. They abandon those rights and advantages because they consider them to be replaced by an institution of the same value and because people of their choice replace the judges. The parties place their confidence in the arbitrators who they chose for the particular case and due to their specific skills and experience.

As a result: Choosing arbitration means choosing a totally different way and arbitral proceedings will therefore also be used and applied in a different way than court proceedings.

Judges and arbitrators are in the same market and supply the same needs but with clearly different services.

To present the issue this way is simple and therefore it is – like all simple descriptions – wrong. In line with the classical distinction of competition law we should differentiate between several markets: Investment arbitration and commercial arbitration, sports arbitration and other arbitration. We could really identify a lot of markets.

But I will in the following concentrate on one specific market, a market whereon we will find arbitrators and judges: I will take the example of an international case with seat in Switzerland.

B. The formal dialogue

There must be some sort of formal dialogue between judges and arbitrators. Indeed, since arbitrators never interfere in the field reserved for judges, judges may be invited to intervene in the arbitration proceedings. This intervention may occur at three different levels:

The first level is at the beginning of or during the arbitration in order to facilitate or to control the functioning of the proceedings (I).

Secondly, once the award has been rendered, the judge may intervene based on recourse for annulment in order to control the award (II).

The third possibility for intervention is when the judge is asked to provide for help for the enforcement of an award (III).

This already manifests that arbitration is still embedded in a legal frame, normally being the frame of the seat of arbitration or the place where enforcement is required. It is worth noticing that there is an extremely interesting and strong trend, especially in French Law, to disentangle the arbitration from any control of the judges at the seat of arbitration. This trend results from the conception that the arbitral award is an international decision solely based on the consent of the parties and free from any limitation by the procedural law of the seat of arbitration. However, this delocalization of arbitral awards has not been accepted in Swiss Law and I bet that it will not be adopted in the close future! I will therefore take the approach of what Emmanuel Gaillard said to be the old "Westphalian style", considering that the judge has still something to say in the field of arbitration.

But let us turn back to the three procedural stages where an intervention of the state judge is possible:

I. The arbitral proceedings

The first level consists of the judge (juge d'appui) assisting in the arbitration proceedings. This is a non-exclusive power since the judges are merely invited to intervene and to help the parties and the arbitrators. Therefore, these competences may be attributed to a third party, namely to private institutions especially devoted to arbitration. Examples for such institutions are the ICC, the LCIA, the Swiss Arbitration Association, the Stockholm Chamber of Commerce and others. Without any mistrust towards the judges, this delegation seems to me to be opportune since the decisions that are envisaged must be taken in view of the specificities of arbitration. The questions that may arise during the arbitration proceedings are not of a nature requiring the wise intervention of the judge, they are specific to arbitration. It is not easy for a judge, and it should be noted that they are normally local judges, to find the person appropriate to act as an arbitrator or to fill gaps left open by the arbitration clause. This is not for the reason that judges would not be competent, but they are probably generally less acquainted with a system based on consent and international practice.

I would like to point out that the reason why arbitrators say that they do not need the judges is partly because there are private institutions intervening at their place. Arbitration is a privatization of justice and it is really interesting to see the growing role of arbitration institutions in the functioning of arbitral proceedings. There should thus also be a dialogue with the institutions in order to avoid misunderstandings. There is still a lot to be done.

II. The control of arbitral awards

The control of arbitral awards falls into the exclusive competence of the judges; in Switzerland of the Swiss Federal Supreme Court. It is worth noting that under special conditions of law, as we know them for example in Art. 192 of the Swiss PILA, the parties in international arbitration may waive any possibility of recourse to the state courts. Furthermore, under the UNCITRAL Model Law or under Swiss law for example, the control of arbitral awards is limited to the constitution and the competence of the arbitral tribunal, the respect of a few fundamental procedural rights and the – in theory possible – control of the content of the award. These limitations are perfectly in line with the essence of arbitration. If the parties decide to privilege a private dispute resolution mechanism, they also have to assume the consequences of their choice, including the risks that are linked to it. To quote Emmanuel Gaillard again: "It was your wish, you have it". Therefore it is difficult for the parties to come back and to ask for the protection of the state court once they consider that their choice to go to arbitration has been the wrong one. The philosophy of the Swiss legislation and of the Swiss Federal Supreme Court fully concurs with this conception: There is only one instance for recourse and not two or three like in other countries. And the conditions for annulment are expressly limited and interpreted in an extremely restrictive manner by the Swiss Federal Supreme Court.

The Federal Supreme Court judges deal with cases in an average of four months. According to a survey conducted by Professor Felix Dasser, only seven percent of all recourses have been accepted and none of them on the ground of a discussion on the merits. This is of course exceptional and contributes strongly to the reputation of Switzerland as an arbitration friendly country.

However, judges are not called to make politics. They are not called to contribute to the promotion of Switzerland as the ideal place for arbitration. They are invited to control the application of the law in the field of arbitration and to control whether the arbitrators have followed the minimal standards required in order to justify the parties' waiver of the normal state procedure. The parties agree to be submitted to the final decision of the arbitrator of their choice. Nevertheless, they have not agreed to be submitted to anything. There is a limit to the freedom in arbitral proceedings and this limit must be drawn clearly and firmly. At the end of the day it is a judge that, in an exceptional case, has the last word in this formal dialogue.

III. The enforcement of arbitral awards

The third level is the level of enforcement. The judges, and here again we speak of local judges, are invited to control foreign awards. They will accomplish this task according to the criteria set up by the New York Convention. Those standards are practically the same as in most national legislations, but they have to be applied in an open way. The standards applicable to arbitration are less and less domestic; they become really international.

C. The informal dialogue

If the judge has to apply international standards, it is absolutely necessary that there is a dialogue between judges and arbitrators. The judges are the guardians of the minimal legal standards, but it is the arbitrators that are familiar with the principles commonly applied in the world of international arbitration. It is the arbitrators that know or should know what is practiced in international arbitration and what are the expectations of the parties. International arbitration is certainly linked to the standards applicable at the seat of arbitration, but arbitration is equally, by essence, a system fully integrated and developed in an international environment.

D. Perspectives and conclusion

Looking at the future, I think we should avoid two errors. The first one is the arbitrators' error to discuss questions and problems only within the community of arbitrators without any relation to the state judges. During the time I was at the ICC Court of Arbitration, I very much promoted this relation to the judges. The arbitrators have to explain the specificity of their task, the necessity to find predictable and acceptable solutions for parties of different origins and with different backgrounds. Arbitrators have to be tolerant, open and flexible. And they do not only have to explain these specificities, they also have to learn from the judges, who are the guardians of values that have to be respected in the arbitral proceedings. This has not sufficiently been considered and must be promoted in the future.

A second error is the error of the judges to neglect their possible integration into the arbitration process. It is true to say that this error has in Switzerland been committed by the Parliament, which decided that judges, especially our Federal Supreme Court judges, are practically no more allowed to act as arbitrators. There could certainly have been some abuse of this "double function", but arbitration is not the monopoly of a group of people. It must be open to all groups of people working in the field of procedural law, be it professors or be it judges.

I am sure that judges would benefit of the contact with the arbitration world. They could not only offer their experience, but could also learn to work in a way that differs from the one they are used to. During and through arbitration I have personally learnt a lot in respect of developing qualities and efficiencies in the procedure and it is in my view time that arbitration makes also a good contribution to the development of our domestic procedure.

Concluding, I consider that the dialogue between judges and arbitrators must be promoted. There is mistrust. It is true that on one side, judges often consider arbitrators as rivals; rivals that are indeed doing the same job, but in beautiful hotels and with much better remunerations. But that is too easy a way, too easy an excuse to avoid discussions.

On the other side, the arbitrators really have to avoid becoming a cartel, if I may use the words of competition law again. It is for the benefit of everybody to open the circle of arbitrators, not only for a practical reason, but also for very essential reasons:

Firstly, I am sure that we are now at the key point of the development of dispute resolution systems on one side, and the development of international commercial law on the other side. It is rare to see new contracts in which the parties do not go for arbitration and there is often not even a choice anymore whether to accept an arbitration clause in a specific contract or not. Arbitration is a system with advantages, but this development also bears its risks, especially because arbitration is a business as well as the exercise of an official activity and there is always the danger to mix those two things up.

Secondly, the law is changing through arbitration. It is changing because of the way the arbitrators are generating new rules. I think it is essential that arbitrators are open to other people when preparing those new rules; especially to judges.

To sum up: The key point is that we are experiencing the privatization of justice, the privatization of rule setting. It is absolutely necessary that this privatization is developing in line with a certain order and certain rules. The only way to achieve this is that arbitrators and judges search for a dialogue. What is a dialogue and what is needed for a constructive outcome? It is the opportunity to speak, but most important is the ability to listen. And the essence of arbitration is the ability and the art of listening.

Thank you very much.

Discussion

CARL BAUDENBACHER
Thank you, Professor Tercier, for your excellent final speech of the first day. I fully agree with his market-oriented approach. This is a market and you have defined the relevant market at the beginning. Switzerland is in a good position, but others are also trying to get a piece of the cake now. I am sure there are questions.

ALAN RAU
You referred to the Swiss legislation. About a decade ago Belgian legislation, as you know, provided a special regime for arbitration among foreigners and made a local annulment in Belgium impossible. That legislation was a fiasco as I understand it. It made people flee Belgium as a source, as a place for arbitration and the legislation was repealed. Now, the Swiss legislation makes it optional for foreigners as to whether or not they want to eliminate any possibility of a Swiss annulment. Do you have any sense of whether, how extensively people are taking advantage of this possibility of eliminating Swiss annulment? Is the Belgian experience being replicated in Switzerland in terms of people's reluctance to agree to eliminate any possibility of local annulment?

PIERRE TERCIER
I currently do not know, because we have no statistics on the issue. But what we see is that there are cases before the Swiss Federal Supreme Court and I would suggest two points if I may. I had a case where the tribunal considered that the party had waived its right to seek court review. Once the parties have agreed on a waiver, it will be applied. It is really very strong.

The second point is interesting, because the question arose in cases before the TAS, the Tribunal Arbitral du Sport. A certain number of statutes of sport organizations contained a waiver of the right to seek state control. The Swiss Federal Supreme Court decided that these waivers were not valid since the parties had no choice concerning the issue. As a result, if a party wants to waive its right to recourse, it must have sufficient freedom to decide on the issue. In the case of someone wanting to play handball, this person is probably not interested in what is contained in the statutes, and a real and free decision on the question of waiving the right to recourse is thus missing. It is, furthermore, interesting to see the reaction to this jurisprudence and that those waiver rules seem to be on the way again. However, there must be a control somewhere. But Professor Peter Nobel, it is probably you having the experience concerning this question.

PETER NOBEL

I would subscribe to this. The appeal, nowadays, is so much more limited, that people are reluctant to give it up, because not knowing what will come up, what the outcome will be, they prefer to have an ultimate, even so very limited control. This is my experience. The bad experience is, I have seen three federal judges without an appeal behind, and they became very, very free in the application of the law and even of the proceedings. So, in my opinion, an ultimate control, limited practically on constitutional grounds, in Switzerland is preferable to no recourse at all.

PIERRE TERCIER

Are you not shocked by the arbitration regarding Article 6?

CARL BAUDENBACHER

No, but one obvious question poses itself, although I may have raised it last year at this conference. But since we have the Danish judge from the European Court of Justice here, I may do it again. I mean one dialogue is obviously missing; that is the one between private arbitration tribunals and the European Court of Justice, because according to consistent case law, you do not accept references from such tribunals. I have never heard a really convincing argument for this, but probably you have one.

LARS BAY LARSEN

I am not ready to give a better argument probably than what you have heard already, which I think without refreshing my memory that it stems from the position of arbitration in the total legal order. Sometimes it is a tricky situation with the jurisprudence we have, even vis-à-vis other institutions which have a sort of semi-court nature. On the one hand they do not qualify the criteria in EU-law as interpreted by the ECJ to make a preliminary reference, but on the other hand we are left with the uneasy feeling that nevertheless they will have to apply European law. And maybe not just as an arbitration tribunal in a specific case, but consistently and repeatedly over time, and it would thus be very useful for them to make a preliminary reference. I can understand why you might wonder if we are a sometimes victims of our own jurisprudence in this area.

MR.VIGUIER

Thank you very much, Mr. Tercier, for this presentation. I have a question for you. I would like to know what is your opinion on the French conception of the award which is "Decision de Justice International" especially regarding its consequences in the development of the international commercial arbitration.

PIERRE TERCIER

Very shortly, because we could have a long discussion on this issue: On one side, I find it an extremely fascinating position. It is a position where you consider that there is a third level; that in fact, an award is an international award and as such not necessarily embedded in the legal order of the seat of arbitration. But to accept this position, you have to act on the assumption that arbitrators are "holy people", that they are perfect. And for the time being, I am a bit afraid of leaving arbitrators, and especially the parties, alone without any possibility of control. It would be a free card given to the arbitrators. I have thus a sort of realistic view, especially since I have seen quite a lot of arbitrators and arbitral awards when I was at the ICC Court of Arbitration. It is not that they are bad, but there must be a possibility of control since arbitration is a beautiful, but also an extremely risky system: Given that there are party-appointed arbitrators, it is possible that he/she is – in the worst case – partial. Furthermore, we have to consider that what is at stake is incredible. It is three people deciding on huge amounts of money and even if they are excellent arbitrators, I am sure that a control by state judges attenuates the risks linked to such decisions.

PETER NOBEL

I have a question, if you do not mind. You predicted a great future of arbitration. I believe it to some extent, but I listened to a conference of the General Council of Nestle and he says it is not arbitration, it is mediation. According to him, arbitration is too expensive, it lasts too long and it is disruptive. We go for mediation. This is the future. What do you think about this?

PIERRE TERCIER

First, I very much encourage the development of ADR or other methods of dispute resolution, like Dispute Boards, for instance. Dispute Boards work very well, as I have seen at the occasion of the Lötschberg project, where this system was inserted in all the contracts. However, such methods of dispute resolution are only a good way if both parties agree to play the game. At the end of the day, you have to keep arbitration for the case that the parties are not willing to cooperate in the way required by ADR or by the dispute board system. Thus, I think, the best way is a multi-tier system, in which you start with mediation and in case it does not work you go to arbitration.

Secondly, I am sure that it is possible to do better in arbitration and to avoid the criticism of arbitration being expensive, long and bad. It is possible – and we have good examples – to get decisions on very important cases within one year; something you would never achieve before state courts. Nevertheless, it is true that arbitration can be expensive.

Thirdly, there must be a certain control of the quality of arbitral awards. In that regard, I consider the role of the ICC Court of Arbitration in the scrutinizing process to be a very good system.

Arbitration is possible, but it is also possible to develop it. However, you are right, if possible, it is always better to mediate than to go to arbitration.

BEN STEINBRÜCK

Just a short comment on the delocalization theory in France. It is not only dangerous, but it is also unprincipled from an international private law perspective, because what French law is actually doing is that it always applies its own law. It is a simple "lex fori" approach. They pretend that this is an international or transnational legal order but, after all, French awards can be challenged in the French courts and they, of course, apply in the end French law. They call it differently, but it is always the very liberal French arbitration law. This is why it is an acceptable solution, but it ignores the choices made by the parties when they opt for certain legal systems. When parties choose their arbitral seat, for example, in Switzerland, then they expect to have the award controlled by the Swiss courts. But a French court, when they are asked to enforce an award or to recognise an award, they do not take into account whether the Swiss court annulled this award. That might be acceptable from their own perspective, but it ignores the choices made by the parties who went to Switzerland and not to France. So, in the end it is not really a delocalized theory, but it is a multi-localized theory because you always have to take into account very different legal orders and that is very difficult to handle.

ERICH SCHANZE

Only shortly on the matter of career judges as arbitrators. As usual, the clear Swiss air has produced good results by being conservative at this point. Many observers have doubts about the healthiness of the situation in Germany, where judges in high judicial functions are almost routinely appointed as arbitrators, particularly in matters of company law. There is a thin line between judicial independence and capture which may be also sometimes crossed by commissioning highly paid speeches of judges about recent decisions or salient problems of a specialized court.

CARL BAUDENBACHER

Just off the record. If you compare the salary of a German Supreme Court judge with a Swiss Supreme Court judge, that may also be one of the reasons.

MR. BURKE

Just from a commercial point of view. I am a commercial lawyer working for a multinational law firm. There a very clear point was made. If you do not have your facts right, you are never going to be able to resolve a dispute. It does not matter how you do that; if it is in front of a national court, if it is by way of mediation or if it is by way of arbitration. But to pick up the thread of mediation being the future, of course it will always be your first port of call because it must be, because it is a commercial reality. I think that when you look at how dispute resolution works, if you theorize it completely, you take away the aspect of the business drivers that force you as either an in-house lawyer or as external counsel for a company, what a business wants. And what a business always wants is they want the problem to go away. They want it to go away now. They do not want it to go away in a week or six months. The other thing is when you work on large infrastructural projects that have an international aspect to them, this is often factored in. Now, if they have not factored it in, in the cost of the project, they have just been stupid in their budgeting, but most large multinationals will have anticipated that there will be a problem, there will be a hiccup, so they will build this mediation step in, but they will always want a final, definitive and enforceable solution.

JAY WESTBROOK

Just briefly, you have said quite correctly that the effect of the growing trends in transnational arbitration is to create a privatization of international commercial law. And it is a quiet privatization; it is sort of not obvious that it is going on. The events of the last couple of years have made privatization of everything and the assumption that there is no public interest in commercial activity subject to considerable scepticism, even on our side of the Atlantic. So, I wonder if you think at some point that there might be a legislative reaction or a backlash against arbitration, which would be unfortunate in the context of this concern that we really do have public interest in commercial transactions and that someone has to vindicate them. As Alan pointed out, mandatory rules really are not effectively enforceable ordinarily in an arbitration.

PIERRE TERCIER

Two small points: The first point is to see the "retour du juge". There is now a large number of cases in which judges are coming back into the arbitration proceedings, especially and more and more concerning anti-arbitration suits, anti-arbitration injunctions and also claims for liabilities.

Secondly, there is an interesting debate on the mandatory rules. Where are they? Taking competition law as an example: Do arbitrators have to apply competition law? Yes? No? When? And so forth.

CARL BAUDENBACHER

Actually, that is a beautiful final statement. Thank you very much once more Professor Tercier.

Keynote

Judicial Dialogue – Challenges for Counsels

MARCO BRONCKERS[1]

It is, of course, good form to start a presentation by thanking the organizer and the chairman of the day for his kind words, but in my case today I have to add to that. Carl Baudenbacher actually sparked my interest in the phenomenon of judicial dialogue a number of years ago. I have followed his writings quite closely, as well as his activities as a judge. Those who know him a bit more personally will realize that judicial dialogue in Carl's case means something very concrete. Those who have seen him operate in Luxembourg can appreciate that even more.

What I propose to do today, is to take the perspective of a private practitioner in looking at judicial dialogue and see what challenges it brings. I propose to do that in two steps. First of all, what is judicial dialogue and in particular, how does the European Court of Justice engage in judicial dialogue? Secondly, what are we as private counsel, but obviously also as constituents, supposed to do with this phenomenon? What are the lessons we are supposed to draw from judicial dialogue?

In an academic setting as today we should start with giving a definition of judicial dialogue. I have found useful the writings of a judge on the German Supreme Court, Mr. Bornkamm.[2] He has distinguished five different levels of judicial dialogue, that go from taking account of what another court says, to feeling compelled to follow the ruling of another court. Yesterday, at the dinner table, I was told by my neighbour, Professor Paulus, that, in fact, there may be yet another level and that is that judges simply pick up the phone and start speaking to each other about their cases. My interest as a practitioner is to look at the 'upper' levels of judicial dialogue: At those instances where you feel that if you are able to cite the ruling of another court, the European Court of Justice will perhaps feel bound to follow it, or will at least be impressed enough to take this ruling very seriously into account.

---

1 Professor at the University of Leiden, Partner at Vermulst Verhaeghe Graafsma & Bronckers, Brussels.

2 I invite the reader of this transcript to consult some of my recent publications which give the full references to the scholarship and case law I refer to here. See From "Direct effect" to "Muted dialogue": Recent developments in the European Courts' case law on the WTO and beyond, in Views of European Law from the Mountain: Liber Amicorum Piet Jan Slot 403–416 (Bulterman et al. eds., Kluwer, 2009); Private Appeals to WTO Law: An Update, 42 Journal of World Trade 245–260 (No. 2, 2008); The Relationship of the EC Courts with other International Tribunals: Non-committal, Respectful or Submissive?, in Economic Law and Justice in Times of Globalisation: Festschrift for Carl Baudenbacher 51–74 (Monti et al., eds., Nomos, 2007).

If you review the case law, you will observe that the European Court has a habit of referring to other courts, particularly to courts from the European region: the European Court of Human Rights, and also the Court of Carl Baudenbacher, the EFTA Court. Alberto Alemanno in his speech of yesterday already gave you a good example of how the European Court of Justice took on board what the EFTA Court said on the precautionary principle. There are fewer instances where the European Court has referred to the International Court of Justice. That may not be so surprising as one would normally not have thought that what the European Union does falls within the scope of activity of the United Nations, although after Kadi that assumption is obviously up for reconsideration. Then there are a few instances where the European Courts have referred to WTO rulings and rulings of other tribunals.

Now, the interesting thing is that in the early 1990s the European Court of Justice actually went so far as to say that it might be bound by the ruling of an international tribunal. The mention of this possibility was pretty exciting for private practitioners, and European lawyers generally. Yet, whether the Court was truly conceding that it might be so bound by another international tribunal remains to be seen. To date the ECJ has never accepted that it is, in fact, bound by the rulings of another court. Perhaps the Court's early pronouncement was more of an olive branch that extended at the time before crashing down on the first emanation of the court that Carl Baudenbacher currently presides over, the EFTA Court. What you might observe is, certainly where tribunals are concerned which are situated outside of the European region (and I am referring again to these WTO rulings), that the Court seems to distance itself more from what is happening there.

Perhaps the ECJ shows more reluctance when the international tribunal does not look like a court. In the case of the WTO tribunals we are, of course, not speaking formally of a court, but of a "panel" or something quaint like an appellate "body". If that would indeed explain the ECJ's reluctance, we may not expect to see much judicial dialogue in the economic context, as we are unlikely to see courts in any formal sense appearing here anytime soon. We have been seeing a proliferation of international courts, of course, but not in the area of economic regulation. There we are stuck with panels, arbitrators, tribunals and so forth. For instance, in the International Herald Tribune of this morning, we saw a reference to the signature of the FTA Agreement between the EU and Korea, which has been in the works for quite some time. If you look at that agreement, you will see that again the parties have established an ad hoc tribunal to settle disputes between them. Furthermore, the EU a few weeks ago launched new negotiations with Canada on an FTA plus agreement. I am pretty sure that whatever dispute settlement mechanism the parties will ultimately agree on will not include the establishment of a court, but rather another ad hoc panel or tribunal.

What is going to happen with the rulings that will issue from these tribunals, which interestingly enough are all modelled on the WTO dispute settlement system? Will they be ignored by the European Court of Justice?

Since I am not sure that all of you have at their fingertips what WTO dispute settlement looks like, let me briefly recall how this system operates. It is pretty unusual, I would say, compared to the dispute settlement mechanisms found in many other international treaty regimes. For one thing, the parties to the WTO have accepted compulsory jurisdiction. There is really no possibility for a defendant country to say, "Oh, very interesting, you want to litigate against me but, well, where is my consent?" WTO litigation is also fast. The proceedings could last no more than two years, and that is counting two instances. In fact, the appellate instance, which is another unusual feature of the WTO, only takes two to three months to reach a ruling. This is exceedingly short. Painfully short, some people would say who actually prepare or read the briefs. Then, there are the detailed rules on countermeasures (retaliation) that the winning party can take in case the losing party fails to implement a ruling so as to induce compliance on the loser.

After the 15 years that this system has now been in place, it has produced a considerable body of case law that goes beyond WTO principles as such. I saw an announcement recently for a new book on the Vienna Convention of the Law of Treaties, and I am curious to see how the book will deal with all of the rulings of the WTO tribunals on the Vienna Convention.

But what has the European Court of Justice said about this system? It has said that it is diplomatic in nature. Now, that characterization I find difficult to square with the system that I have just described; and even more so, if I compare the WTO's mechanism to the dispute settlement systems of other international agreements. I do not fully understand how something that is perceived to be quite aggressive by many could be viewed as diplomatic by the judges in Luxembourg.

It may be that the Court is reading the possibility of a "buy out" into the WTO system. There is this notion that if a country does not want to follow a ruling of a WTO tribunal, it can simply submit to retaliation. In other words, some people argue that the losing country could simply submit to countermeasures of the other party, and that this would be an excuse for not complying with a WTO ruling. Frankly, I believe that that is a mischaracterization of the WTO system. It clearly does create international responsibility when you are being told by a WTO tribunal that you have not complied with your treaty obligations. That the WTO has introduced some kind of a self-help remedy, for as long as this impermissible situation continues, does not detract from the normative force of the WTO rulings. I do believe that the self-help remedy in the WTO is problematic. I believe that this remedy is too blunt, too medieval; in many cases it cannot achieve what it is supposed to.[3] But the fact that this remedy is medieval does not mean that it is diplomatic.

3 See Bronckers & van den Broek, *Financial Compensation in the WTO: Improving Remedies in WTO Dispute Settlement*, 8 Journal of International Economic Law 101-126 (No. 1, 2005).

Now, I have to add a word of precision here. The European Court has not said that it is not prepared to listen to the rulings of these WTO tribunals because they are diplomatic in nature. The argument the European Court made was that because there was a diplomatic element in the WTO dispute settlement system, it did not need to give direct effect to the WTO rules, which is a related but different issue.

Rather than dissecting in more detail whether the Court's reasons for denying direct effect to WTO rules are convincing, I believe it is more interesting to see what happened next. After having laid down the law that it did not want to give direct effect to the WTO (and its predecessor the GATT), the European Court created a number of exceptions to this rigid principle.

First of all, on the issue of direct effect the Court has said that if somehow the EU legislature (the Council of Ministers, the European Parliament) in a particular piece of legislation has made reference to an international agreement (and in particular the WTO), it will have no hesitation to give direct effect to this agreement in testing the validity or interpretation of that piece of legislation. So, the lack of direct effect seems to be more of a division of powers issue between the judiciary on the one hand and the legislature on the other hand, than a problem of whether or not the dispute settlement mechanism in the treaty is diplomatic or not that is guiding the Court here.

Furthermore, the European Court of Justice is firmly attached to the principle of Treaty-consistent interpretation: whenever a norm of EU law is relatively open and allows for more than one interpretation, the Court feels compelled to choose the interpretation that flows from and is consistent with the relevant international treaty to which the EU is a party. This principle does not permit the invalidation of an EU law measure on the basis of international law. But it is a very useful means to guide the interpretation of EU law.

Another interesting development in the case law occurred more recently. In some cases, the Court recalls in its jurisprudence that the WTO does not have direct effect in the factual section of the judgment. Then, the Court starts to interpret European law and it comes up with an interpretation that is pretty startling. In a few sentences the Court concludes that the EU institutions have committed manifest errors of assessment of the law. The Court is never prolific in its explanations, but these statements are really very summary. But if you go back to the factual section of the judgment, you will find that the WTO Appellate Body has already ruled that the EU measure is incompatible with WTO law. I submit to you that these are instances where the European Court is engaged in a dialogue with WTO tribunals. This dialogue may be muted. It may not be very obvious. But it is there.

This approach of the European Court makes sense. These international tribunals have the expertise to interpret the international agreement that is at issue. They have also received a mandate from the treaty partners, including the European Union, to interpret this international agreement. The fact that the European Court is listening to these international tribunals is also good in a practical sense, because it limits the potential liability of the EU for violating an international agreement.

I also think it is positive that the European Court is effectively applying a sort of "Solange" reservation to international law and international rulings: Rather than giving direct effect to an international rule or accepting that it is bound by an international ruling, the Court is using international law in order to interpret European law where it is the final arbiter. In other words, the Court reserves the possibility to deviate from the international ruling, presumably in exceptional cases. There may be new facts that have arisen after the international court or tribunal has rendered its judgment. It also depends, I would think, on what it is that the private claimant is asking. Is the private claimant asking the invalidation of an EU norm? Or is the private claimant asking damages? Is the international norm similar to an EU norm of which the Court has already given a different interpretation? Does the international ruling raise an issue of fundamental policy concern to the EU (a variation of what we saw in Kadi)?

In sum, these recent judgments suggest that the European Courts are willing to pay respect to international rulings. They seek consistency wherever they can, but they reserve a margin of discretion, a narrow escape route if you will, to reach a different conclusion in particular, exceptional circumstances. Now, what do you do with this burgeoning judicial dialogue as private counsel? I would submit to you that there are three things that a private practitioner appearing before the European Courts can and should do with this development.

A. Bring a bigger toolbox.

It is not good enough anymore to appear before the European Courts and know your EU law precedents. If you really want to make the best possible case for your client, you have to ask yourself whether there is not also an international issue or regime that could constrain the European measure that you are challenging, as this could help steer the debate before the European Courts. Now, this is easy to do in obvious cases. If you happen to represent somebody in an anti-dumping case before the European Courts, I am sure that you will be thinking of the WTO Anti-Dumping Agreement. But obviously the relevance of international law is not limited to instances where EU law is directly or explicitly connected to the international rule.

For example, we are now engaged in a debate in the European Union on climate change. I would submit to you that the WTO and other international agreements can become quite relevant to multiple elements in that debate. Furthermore, if you have a competition law case before the European Courts, international agreements may also be relevant. Think about the Microsoft case where Microsoft at some point started to invoke the WTO's TRIPS agreement on intellectual property right protection as a benchmark against which to test the Commission's decision. Consider, as well, the implications of human rights law to evaluate the process before the European Commission as a prosecutor and a judge when inflicting very high fines.

Accordingly, if the European Courts are reluctant to grant direct effect to international rules, there may still be something useful that a private practitioner can get out of the international sphere.

B. Do not overstate your case.

I believe that courts easily have a human reaction to the pleas they hear. Thus, if you say to a court that is going to cite something which the judges are bound to follow, I suspect the first reaction will be one of resistance. People prefer to think for themselves. This seems trivial, but if I look at a recent case, the FIAMM case of the European Court of Justice, I wonder whether the disappointing and in my view erroneous result was not in fact provoked, at least in part, by overstatement. FIAMM is a case where a few smaller companies in Europe, companies that produce spectacle cases, batteries and so forth, suddenly found that they could no longer export their products to the United States because of a prohibitive increase in US customs tariffs on their products. When they inquired why this had happened, they discovered the reason was that the United States had retaliated against the EU because the EU was not complying with a WTO ruling involving bananas. You can imagine their reaction: Involving what? These producers of spectacle cases etc. had absolutely nothing to do with the treatment the EU afforded to imported bananas. The WTO had been saying for years, in a series of rulings, that the EU preferences for its former colonies were not consistent with WTO law.

Now, it may be that the EU had an overriding public policy interest not to abandon these preferences immediately, thereby provoking retaliatory measures. But why should only a few Europeans have to pay the price for a general public policy choice? That seems to me to be a strong case to put before the European Courts, which you could plead in different ways and build on basic fairness. It seems that the lawyers of the claimants went in with guns blazing and argued that in the circumstances of this particular case the Court had to give direct effect to the relevant WTO rules. But the European Courts did not accept this plea and rejected the damages claim. I cannot help speculating that the outcome might have been different if the claimants had tried a somewhat different, understated type of argument. This might have run along the lines of: "You are not bound to follow WTO law, but in this particular case, which is not concerned with invalidity but with damages, there are good reasons to pay respect to what the WTO has said etc. etc."

C. Think strategically

There are instances where you can expect that it is difficult for the European Court of Justice to overrule a political decision of the EU legislature. An appeal to international law may then be helpful to the Court to justify its decision. Think for a moment about a company that has to fire a lot of people. What do companies do in situations when they have to take an unpopular decision? They like to call in an outsider, a management consultant for example, to tell them that this is really necessary. This helps management to sell the decision to the unions and other stakeholders.

Now, consider a case where the European Court is faced with a challenge of a highly emotional policy choice of the legislature, for instance in the area of food safety, bio technology, GMOs. Some of these choices appear pretty extreme, such as the so-called zero tolerance policy regarding GMOs. As a claimant you might appeal to a general European law principle, such as proportionality, to say that certain measures are really unsuited to achieve the policy aim that they are supposed to contribute to and therefore should be struck down by the European Court. That could be an interesting argument. It may even be a good argument. But is it an argument that will persuade the European Court to invalidate such a measure? These are not easy cases for the Court.

Do you remember the Hormones case, the first one of the 1980s? The European Court thought that the ban on hormone treated beef instituted by the EU was fine. Then, soon after the WTO was established in 1994, including the new SPS Agreement, the same measure was challenged before the WTO. The WTO Appellate Body condemned the EU ban for lack of scientific evidence that these hormones created a health concern. Now, I do not want to go into who was right or wrong here. I am just saying that to have an outsider take a second look at what you feel that the EU might or might not be able to do can sometimes be helpful.

Accordingly, if you think strategically, what you would want to ensure is that the European measure you want to challenge is first tested in the WTO. You will recall that WTO litigation goes pretty fast. Chances are, if you play your cards well, that you will get a ruling out of the WTO before the European Court is considering its judgment. Judicial dialogue might help to give extra comfort to the European Court to take an unpopular decision, even if the Court would ultimately base this ruling on an interpretation of EU law to keep its hands free for the future. In other words think strategically. Think about how a test case before different courts or tribunals might help your position before your own court, the European Court.

To conclude: Judicial dialogue, I believe, is an important phenomenon. Academically, one likes to point out that judicial dialogue helps to connect different legal systems. It helps to ensure that international tribunals, proliferating in number, are actually conscious of each other's work. And from a private practitioner's point of view, what judicial dialogue does, in very plain terms, is that it can help reinforce your client's position in litigation.

Perhaps you are thinking that it actually is only about grubby self interest that I applaud judicial dialogue from a private practitioner's perspective? But I remind you that the European experience has shown us that if private entities take their interests seriously, and invest in bringing their cases to litigation, they help tremendously to reinforce and deepen European integration. So, I submit to you that encouraging private counsel to use the phenomenon of judicial dialogue can also help to deepen and reinforce the salutary development of interconnecting different legal systems.

Discussion

CARL BAUDENBACHER

Thank you very much, Marco, for this marvellous speech. You gave a whole picture in half an hour of theoretical considerations and then also of very practical advice. I have a number of questions, but we have students here and lots of other participants.

MR. SANTOS

Professor Baudenbacher, I was just wondering, you were mentioning the Bananas case, earlier in your speech, and you were referring the judicial dialogue that actually emerged with the recommendations that the panel gave in the complaint. My question is directed towards this strategic thinking you mentioned and the political costs implied in complying or not complying with the measure. Why not just sign a free trade agreement with the ACP countries to get rid of the whole problem?

MARCO BRONCKERS

Well, I believe that is exactly what the EU has been trying to do. They call it now EPAs, Economic Partnership Agreements, with the former ACP countries. The problem for the ACP countries is the requirement that the EU is imposing on these EPAs: A reciprocal exchange of concessions and a mutual liberalization of the markets. For the ACP countries this requirement runs counter to their development policy. But the EU is saying that a reciprocal free trade agreement, which reduces and eliminates barriers to trade on both sides, is the only remedy left to try and square the ACP countries' wish to give their products preferential access to the EU market with the conditions set forth in Article XXIV GATT. That is where we are now. In other words, your thought is an absolutely sensible one, but it does provoke considerable reluctance on the part of the developing countries that can no longer claim unilateral preferences from the EU.

ALBERTO ALEMANNO

Thank you. Professor Bronckers, I am very sympathetic to your argument that allowing private economic operators to rely on WTO rulings would somehow strengthen the European integration process by judicializing the whole process, thus promoting legal certainty. This would finally provide justice for companies like FIAMM who – under the current circumstances – have no chance to obtain any kind of remedy. But what was lacking in your speech is the main argument which has historically been used by the European Court of Justice and also by the CFI, the idea that we cannot follow this path because this would go against reciprocity. In other words, why should the European Union be the first to allow people to rely on WTO rules when other partners like the US do not do it? And I know, there is an important difference between relying on the WTO rule or relying on a WTO ruling. I think there is a huge conceptual difference between the two, but, apparently, in FIAMM the ECJ did not want to follow the subtle line as they did in van Parys. So, I would like to know, how would you address this issue which is still on the table? Should you claim a case in this way?

MARCO BRONCKERS

Well, I would not like to depend on the mistakes of others in order to decide what is right for the EU; reciprocity is, therefore, not a consideration I would follow blindly. When we are talking about the FIAMM case (i.e., a private damages claim) and not about direct effect, I am not worried about the EU steering its own course rather than following whatever other WTO Members have decided. The point about FIAMM is this: If I see that a few of my citizens in the EU have to pay a price for a general public policy choice, I am sensitized by principles that we have recognized in our national European traditions, about the Sonderopfer theory, about *égalité devant les charges publics* and so forth, and I strongly believe that these citizens have a powerful claim to be compensated. I do not particularly care how other countries treat their citizens. I would like our EU to treat its citizens correctly.

CARL BAUDENBACHER

If I may just add a comment: The reciprocity argument is a fatal argument, because nobody will move. So, this is going to last forever. It is finger pointing and as long as you do not move, we will not move. It is the same in the area of international exhaustion of trademark rights where the ECJ has closed down the outer borders of the Community and is finger-pointing at the Americans, essentially. And well, unfortunately, my Court has given, in too last year. I did not sit in the case, that is why I can say "unfortunately".

ALAN RAU

I was very interested in what you were saying about how to argue strategically to courts. As a common law lawyer, I am very interested in the rhetoric of arguments that one makes before courts. It is also a question of psychology. I would think it would be very reassuring for a court to believe that the decision that it is being asked to make is in fact constrained by past decisions, because choice can be very threatening and I do not have to worry too much about whether the decision I am making is the right one; if in fact it falls very comfortably within the pattern of past decisions. So, I would think that what the advocate would be trying to do, would be to create the impression of inevitability. Not threatening, but to create the impression that what he is asking the court to do is, in fact, constrained by past decision patterns. Now, apparently, this does not seem to have a great deal of resonance in the European context and I was wondering why.

MARCO BRONCKERS

Your common law approach makes a lot of sense and is applied on a day-to-day basis by counsel pleading before the European Courts when referring to precedents of those same courts. In other words, if we are able to go before the European Courts and say this case is easy, because it really follows what you decided before, we do so without hesitation. I do not believe that there is much of a difference between what I understand to be the common law tradition and what we would call the civil law tradition when pleading our cases before the European Courts. Yet, I would caution against using terms like 'inevitability' when you go before the European Courts and start citing precedents of other courts, to which they are not bound and with which they are not necessarily familiar. That is where the subtlety comes in, in the pleading of those cases.

ULRICH HALTERN

Our subject is judicial dialogue, and unsurprisingly, the European Court of Justice features prominently in our discussions. Up to now, we have seen the ECJ as a major player in the judicial dialogue game – talkative, voluble, almost loquatious. The need to secure voluntary co-operation by national courts has made the European Court sensitive towards national courts' legal and political sensibilities. The ECJ appears always open to communication and discussion (which, of course, doesn't mean it is always willing to compromise). Now, however, we are running into WTO law. As we all know, the European Court is less open to communication with panels and the Appellate Body. It drives a pretty hard bargain; to remain within our dialogue metaphor, I can picture the Court telling the WTO panels and the Appellate Body, "I do not want to hear it, I do not care, go away." Of course, we could call this type of communication part of a "dialogue", but you will agree that this is a peculiar sort of dialogue. It is not the only peculiar dialogue the ECJ leads. In its MOX Plant decision, the European Court basically stripped the UNCLOS tribunal of its say in the matter, placing itself at the center of things and, even further, at the top of international court hierarchy. While in MOX Plant, this may have been hermeneutically defensible because of Article 292 UNCLOS, the European Court's decision and, above all, its tone (it is not what you say, it is how you say it) make for interesting and, to be honest, a little off-putting precedent.

What binds these cases (the WTO jurisprudence and cases like MOX Plant) together is the fact that when it comes to communication with international tribunals rather than national courts, the European Court seems slightly deaf and taciturn. Here is, for whatever it is worth, an intuition about why that is. The legal arguments the Court uses in these cases, the direction the decisions take, and the whole tone thing reminds me strongly of what EU Member State courts used to do in order to try and fight back ECJ judicative competence. We see this line of argument still when we listen to the German, the Polish, and other constitutional courts. National sovereignty figures strongly in such discourses. And here is the ECJ, engaging in precisely the same endeavour vis-à-vis international tribunals. Is it possible that the ECJ is actually about to construct something like post-national sovereignty of the European Union by pushing back outside jurisdictional intervention? If there was any truth to this intuition, judicial dialogue would be a window on the reconstruction of the legal and political imagination of the polity, in this case the European Union. Do you share any of these intuitions?

MARCO BRONCKERS

It is an interesting question. To what extent could you compare the relationship between the European Court and the national courts on the one hand and between the European Court and other courts on the other hand? I must say that, fundamentally, I feel at ease with the position of the European Court of Justice. Not if you look at it the way you described it, as an exercise in "I want to be boss in my own court and I do not want to follow other courts". But I feel at ease if I think about the European Court of Justice as the court to which I ultimately would entrust the decision whether a particular international ruling is right for my environment, for my culture etc. Francis Snyder once coined the term that the European Court of Justice is the gatekeeper of the European legal order. I am at ease with that. Do not get me wrong though. I would want the European Court to pay respect to the rulings of other international tribunals. I would not want the European Court to easily dismiss these other rulings. Maybe, some of the rhetoric in the judgments so far might suggest that the Court takes these rulings of some international tribunals too lightly. But I believe that the signals are really the other way. However that may be though, ultimately, I would let the European Court decide whether there are specific circumstances where we in Europe would say, this non-European ruling is not right, is not consistent with our traditions, policy choices and so forth. Of course, that is a legal policy choice, and it is a choice that I am entirely comfortable with.

Specifically, with respect to the WTO, I would say, you pay respect to the WTO as a rule, but there may exceptionally be cases where you would not want to follow a WTO tribunal. By reinterpreting WTO rulings as expressions of general European law principles, the European Court of Justice remains the ultimate arbiter, but is quite capable of paying respect to WTO rulings when it believes it can do so. I think if you look at recent ECJ cases, that is exactly what is happening.

LARS BAY LARSEN

Thank you very much. I thought it was an extremely interesting presentation. I will say a couple of things also as a response to the last remarks, because we at the ECJ are so often accused of being too activist, taking over the work of the community-legislator in Brussels and now at the same time we are perceived as and blamed for being too timid. But for us as EU judges there is a clear distinction, since we work on allocated powers and we try to be pretty careful not to go beyond those powers. Of course there is a specific problem vis-à-vis the big body of truly traditional international law and its various aspects. One can easily understand the political point: why should some small companies pay the full price for another conflict which the EU is having with its international partners. But one can also ask: is this necessarily a judicial decision to be taken, or is it not a political decision to be taken, not in Luxembourg but rather in Brussels, if there is a need to compensate. I will not make any comments on the specific case, which I was not involved in. Nevertheless, I would like to remind you that we do pass judgments in infringement cases where big member states have failed to comply with for instance the GMO regime to which we are internationally bound. And if a member state hypothetically would build its defence essentially on the fact that compliance with the international norms, which the EU has agreed to, would be very unpopular in national politics and lead to farmers blocking motorways, such a member state is not likely to succeed. So, it is not completely unfamiliar for us to operate in these areas even if they may be politically very sensitive. But we only do so, when we have been given the competence to do so by the EU treaties.

There is perhaps another element which may occasionally tend to support the perception of judges as a little timid in some of these areas, namely the very complex and highly technical character of some of these cases. It is often argued that the highly technical nature of a case may lead any court – national or international – composed of generalists to be a little less intensive in its judicial scrutiny of the legal instruments drawn up and negotiated with sophisticated technical expertise at hand. This may merit further reflection for judges, who are generalists and not biochemists, whether we act in a national or an international context.

MR. BURKE

Just when you look at this entire debate and all of this interaction that you speak of, it is predominantly economically driven, socio-economically driven and socio-politically driven. In many of these agreements we have carved out a little jurisdiction for various entities. I think quite a lot of people forget that because of the complicated interrelationship of these trade agreements and methods of dispute resolution that we have created for specific areas, knitting all of that together into a judicially coherent whole is a very, very difficult thing to do. Business groups can receive the short end of the stick simply because there are other factors at play beyond their sphere of operation. They end up paying penalties for living in a globalized economy. What I would like to know is, do you believe that we are moving slowly towards a degree of judicial certainty for those people who participate in the economic field, who are the ones who will ultimately bear the brunt of governmental decisions? Is there a thread of clarity that is emerging from judicial dialogue? Is there a degree of certainty that if you go to court, you can obtain a legal remedy?

MARCO BRONCKERS

Well, that is I believe the million dollar question. Why do we engage in treaty negotiations on economic issues? I believe the ultimate reason is predictability, making sure that traders know from day one when they start making investments whether their choices will ultimately be protected, whether they can rely on these international agreements. This is the paradigm that John Jackson, already in the 1970s, described as the move from power diplomacy where the private trader has no certainty whatsoever, to rule-based diplomacy where traders are offered more predictability. Maybe we are going even beyond rule-based diplomacy now, and are approaching rule-based enforcement. Nevertheless, while these questions are dear to lawyers, we have to recognize that they may not immediately resonate with business people. After all, how many business people realize that the investment decisions they make are protected by for them probably pretty arcane agreements like FTA's or the WTO? Still, let us hope that their legal counsels are aware of these developments and can give an informed advice to business people who are concerned about the protection of their investments in international commerce. Ultimately, I do believe that increased judicial dialogue actually helps to reinforce whatever predictability, legal certainty private business can derive from international agreements.

CARL BAUDENBACHER

Can I ask a very practical question Marco? You spoke about the reluctance of the ECJ to give effect to WTO rules or rulings of the WTO dispute settlement organs, but you alleged that it is not so that there is no effect at all. There may be some hidden effect. That may be assumed, but it may also be a little bit of second guessing, I do not know this. But, that is not my point. My point is that we have an old judgment from 1982 in the case Kupferberg, where it seemed that the European Court of Justice was prepared to open up the courts in the member states and its own court room for plaintiffs relying on such an international agreement. (In Kupferberg the ECJ granted direct effect to a provision of a bilateral free trade agreement.) Admittedly, that was done based on a hidden dialogue with the Swiss Supreme Court because the Swiss Supreme Court had been very parochial a couple of years earlier and closed down the courts in this country for claims based on free trade agreements. Now with Kupferberg we saw a development in the opposite direction as you know. Everybody speaks about the WTO not producing direct effect in the Community and yet Kupferberg is still there. If the EU-Korea Free Trade Agreement, for instance, has no direct effect in the Community, what does it have? Is Kupferberg still good law, or will Kupferberg fall? I know there are those who say, it is about time now, given that the European Union has become a world power, to take back Kupferberg and make everything dependent on reciprocity.

MARCO BRONCKERS

This is indeed the fundamental debate. What is the position of the European Court towards international agreements? The WTO (and previously the GATT) case law was always considered the odd man out because there the Court did not do what it was "supposed" to do if one were to follow Kupferberg. Then we have the recent Intertanko judgment where the Court has ruled that the Unclos (Law of the Sea Convention) follows the same fate as the WTO: none of the Unclos provisions is capable of producing direct effects according to the ECJ. This could be seen as another blow to Kupferberg.

Some observers have the following explanation. Because, the EU normally has a lot of negotiating power in the case of bilateral agreements, the ECJ may be more willing to give direct effect to these agreements. Whereas if we look at agreements in a multilateral context such as the WTO and Unclos, we are not sure that the EU will be able to get its way and so the ECJ denies them direct effect.

This is an interesting analysis, but I do not find it particularly agreeable from a legal policy perspective. There is an incompatibility here between law and power politics. I would prefer the European Court to give direct effect to international agreements, whether they are multilateral or bilateral, only in rare circumstances – as long as the Court continues to combine direct effect with supremacy. In other words, given supremacy, the only way to correct a court interpretation of a directly effective treaty provision would be a renegotiation of the international agreement (or withdrawing from that agreement). Unlike other jurisdictions such as the US, the EU legislator could not override an ECJ interpretation of a directly effective treaty provision as long as direct effect goes hand in hand with supremacy. Considering the concerns international (and also European law) creates about a democratic deficit, I find supremacy of international law a pretty hard thing to stomach.

In sum, I am in favour of limiting the Kupferberg doctrine to special cases, as long as the ECJ links supremacy to direct effect. I am in favour of the European Court giving respect wherever possible to international rulings and maybe doing it a bit more openly than the sort of muted way it has been using in respect of the WTO. I am also in favour of the European Court being the ultimate gatekeeper of the EU legal order and keeping the freedom to deviate in exceptional circumstances from what another international court has said.

CARL BAUDENBACHER
That was a clear statement. One last question please.

BEN STEINBRÜCK
I would like to know whether the different courts acting here are aware that from an international law point of view they are part of the phenomenon called 'fragmentation of international law'. The question is how do all these norms, you talk about, relate to each other? Is there a hierarchy of norms? Ultimately, every legal system is self-referential. The German Constitutional Court, for example, thinks it is the final arbitrator on German law, the ECJ thinks that as regards EC Law it is the final arbitrator. The WTO panels are the final arbitrators in relation to their law, and from a meta-perspective we see a fragmentation of international agreement or international law. There is this huge debate in international law on how these courts relate to each other and whether there exists a hierarchy of norms. I am wondering whether all of these actors in this process are actually aware and to what extent they are aware that all these different subsystems might not form a coherent picture. Judicial dialogue is certainly a way to form a more coherent system, but I would like to know from your experience whether these different courts are aware that they all try to take the top position, which, of course, cannot work.

MARCO BRONCKERS

You have used a word that I have difficulty with and that is hierarchy of norms. I have even more difficulty with the idea of a hierarchy between courts. If we get into that debate, I fear we will be provoking the worst instincts in the judges. So, I would not like to characterize the debate like that. That is number one.

Number two: I believe the relationship between the European Court and a national court is fundamentally a different one from the relationship between the European Court and international courts. The relationship between the European Court and national courts is almost like cuisine interne. Although one could discern some notion of a hierarchy where the interpretation of EU law is concerned, the European Court is studiously avoiding putting the cooperation it likes to maintain with the national courts in that way. More fundamentally, who is the ultimate gatekeeper within Europe of European values? Is it the European Court in Luxembourg or is it the national constitutional court? That is a delicate question, where I see a role for both the ECJ and the highest national courts. On the other hand, I have no hesitation to assign the gatekeeper role to the ECJ to define and protect European values in relation to other international courts or tribunals.

CARL BAUDENBACHER

Ok, thank you very much once more Marco. We break here.

Focus:
The Application of Uniform Law

Introduction

FRANZ WERRO[1]

I would like first to thank you both for organizing this conference and for inviting me. I am delighted to see that our panel will be dealing with a fundamental problem. Indeed, we have been asked to discuss in essence the following question: Can one legal international text, such as the CISG, trigger uniform law in different countries, with different legal systems in the absence of a common court? Obviously, this question is interesting because it relates to the more general question of the relation between the text of the law and the impact that such a text can have on the reality of the law.

We, especially the civilians, who grew up in the shadow of statutes, tend to believe that texts have the power to define the law. However, in that approach, we fail to recognize the importance of the social and cultural glue that gives a text its legitimacy and consequently its proper meaning. The point, of course, is of major importance. If it is true that, as I see it, texts only acquire their meaning in the light of the cultural assumptions, it is quite clear that, unless such assumptions are shared, one text of law will not trigger a common law in places of different cultures.

This is true at a national level where various cultures may coexist. Naturally, this is even more true on an international or transnational level. Naturally, and despite the much proclaimed "technical" character of contract law, the CISG is very much confronted with this problem, as it turns out that many questions in the life of a contract find a cultural answer. Before I give the floor to my distinguished colleagues, I would like to point out that this question is the very one that Europeans face today with respect to a possible European Civil Code or what is now referred to, more timidly, as the Draft Common Frame of Reference. As much as the idea of a common code might appear appealing, as a noble, exciting and almost revolutionary expression of what the Europeans can do together, I fear that, in the absence of a common cultural (pre) understanding, a common text will not trigger a common law, all the less so, if there is no supreme court in charge of applying that law and giving it its meaning.

Be that as it may, the difficulty of achieving uniformity does not preclude courts to engage in a dialogue and maybe to get to the definition of common principles. Article 7 of the CISG invites explicitly the courts to do so. Whether this provision does achieve this result without the existence of a pre-existing common understanding is again what we need to ask. Looking at what courts have done, it looks like more often than not they use foreign law, but only in very peripheral way, to back up a solution to which

1 Professor at the University of Fribourg and Georgetown University.

they have already come on the basis of their own law. Maybe the truth is that common texts cannot trigger a dialogue between courts unless there are forces that lead them to do so anyway.

These questions and others will now be addressed more fully of course by the members of the panel, whom I have the pleasure of introducing to you briefly. Let me begin first with Judge Achim Bender, who is the presiding Judge of the German Federal Patent Court in Munich and a lecturer at the Universities of Düsseldorf, Dresden and St. Gallen. Judge Bender will, among others, tackle the question of difference and understanding. Judge Bender will do so in the light of his rich experience in trade mark cases. Professor Alastair Mullis, who teaches at the University of East Anglia, will then take a closer look at the CISG and analyze the way in which courts do use foreign law and give an explanation as to why they do it so rarely and so timidly. Finally, Professor Erich Schanze, will revisit the biography of the CISG and try to give us an account of its success as an academic enterprise and its failure in practice. He will back it up by showing why in his view substantive law plays a very limited role in the settling of contract disputes.

The Application of Uniform Law

ACHIM BENDER[1]

Thank you very much for the invitation and especially for this preface with Professor Werro. Unfortunately, I am not a professor, I am only a poor judge and practitioner and so I come a little bit down from the high university level to the simple reality, to create in Europe an uniform law system. I will tell you a little bit what my experience was acting for ten years in Alicante in the OHIM office as a member of the Boards of Appeal and show you what the real problems are to create a harmonized and common law. However, the application of an international law system is a very, very difficult thing.

I go a little bit back: We have in Europe a common trade mark system. This is a good example for showing, how does function or how can or should function a uniform law. We have in the trade mark system in Europe two columns. We have on the one hand the national systems, which are harmonized by a directive from the Council. Therefore, all the European member states, 27 at the moment, should apply more or less the same law in substantial matters. This is the target that was inclined in this directive. On the other hand, we have in Alicante, the OHIM as an European institution. There, you can register trademarks and design rights and the substantial law follows a harmonized, a common rule which is in the same line as the directive has defined for the national systems. And therefore, it is very interesting, after having had for a long, long time a different substantive law in trade mark issues in the different national states, to come now in Europe to a common way. For my person, it was also an experience to come from the German Federal Patent Court, where I have acted before four years in the German trade mark issues and afterwards two years as legal assistant by the German Supreme Court, then to go to Alicante. It was a nice idea now to meet other colleagues from other countries and to create a new system.

And at the starting point 1997, we had no books. We had no judgment. We had only the legislation translated into the languages of all the member states. The first problem was: How to organize our system, how to come together with different nationalities and with different professional experiences. My experience was acting before as a judge in national issues, but I had no knowledge of the European or the international system. Then we had other colleagues who arrived from the Court of Justice in Luxembourg acting before as legal assistants together with European judges. These colleagues had a broad knowledge of European Law but no experience with the trade mark system. Furthermore, we had some lawyers who acted before in arbitration law, in franchising

---

1 Presiding Judge at the German Federal Patent Court, Munich, Lecturer at the Universities of Düsseldorf, Dresden and St. Gallen.

law without any relationship to trade mark law. Other colleagues arrived from the national offices. They were involved before in national administrative activities. In consequence, we had a broad spectrum of colleagues with very different experiences. Now we have tried to harmonize our experience and to come to a common approach. This is, you can understand from the experiences and from the languages, not so very easy. As I have started I have brought from Germany my books, my commentaries. A commentary is a word which does not really exist in English. I have found a translation: It is an article by article guide. I think it is a specific German word. Normally, in other countries there exist handbooks, to give indications how to apply the law, but this article by article guide is a very German attitude. Now, as I started, I have in my office, collocated my books, four or five commentaries and then my Greek colleague has come in. He was astonished, five books about the German trade mark law. I would be happy to find only the Greek law printed out. You can see that, therefore, the experience was a very different thing and the professional preparation for doing our work was also a very heavy issue.

Then the language problem. You know or you do not know that OHIM works in five languages. It was a compromise. In reality the most important language is English with 65% and I was astonished that German, with 20% of the cases, is the second important language. It depends on the numbers of applications. The language is not chosen by the office, it is chosen by the applicant. So, we have to follow what the applicant wants, and therefore because Germany is the leading nation in the application of trademarks, in the application of design rights, for three years it overrules the United States of America, and Swiss and Austrian applicants chose also the German language. Therefore, the German language is the second most important language. Then, follows French and Spanish with 6% and Italian with 2% and 1% are other languages. In absolute cases the applicant can choose all the 23 European languages. So, you can imagine we have to work in different languages and we have first to learn to understand each other. In discussions, we have found to the common language in English, but you can imagine that my poor Bavarian English was a little bit different from the English of my President, an Italian, who spoke his own English with some Italian words like "Gazzetta ufficiale" for "Official Journal", but we could understand each other. The best solution to find a clear line was to quote Latin terms. It was surprising that Latin terms have been present by all the lawyers. If you chose a word like, "res juricata", everybody could understand it. This was a clear term without any doubts. We spoke all the same English language. We used the same words but we do not understand each other. Why? Because everybody had in his mind his national system. His national system was very different from the national system of the other country. So, we must stop the discussion and say: Please, can you explain to me me how does your system in Italy function, how does your system in Greece function or how does your system in the United Kingdom function? After this excursion we needed to make, it was easier to understand the arguments of the colleagues and to come to a conclusion, which seems to go in the direction to a common solution.

The characteristic background is also very different. You must imagine such a situation: We have very different persons. I remember once in the morning, I heard a person crying in the hall: "I will bring you to a criminal court!" I was astonished. My Greek colleague runs to the hallway and says "Oh, it's only Stefano". It was my Italian colleague. He had a strong discussion with the Irish colleague. But nevertheless, in the afternoon they were sitting and taking coffee and without any problem. But you must acclimatize in this kind of discussion.

Then we had, this was the next heavy problem, no procedural rules. We had only to apply the textural rules, the right to be heard, that any decision must be grounded but nothing more. I prepared to you some examples in the hand-out, which will show you the problems. Nevertheless, as central rule we should apply principles of procedural law generally recognized in the member states. A very, very precise formulation. Additionally, it was wrongly translated in German. The correct translation should be "allgemein anerkannte Grundsätze" not "im allgemeinen anerkannte Grundsätze". There is a great difference, understandable only for German speaking people. In the other languages you have the same wording. What are these "allgemein anerkannte Grundsätze"? What are these principles of procedural law generally recognized? It is absolutely clear. My Greek colleague says, the basis of Europe is Greece culture. The Greek philosophy and the Greek law is the basis of the European law. You have to follow the Greek law. No, my Italian colleague is answering, the Greeks have nothing to do with law. They created many architectural events, but not law. Law is a Roman speciality and I represent as an Italian Roman law and the Roman law is the basis of Europe. You can understand that I tried a little bit to convince the colleagues, that we have in Germany also a certain tradition of law and it should be also reflected in Europe. You can imagine, that it was always a strong struggle what line we should follow. In substantial issues, whether a trade mark should be protected or not, or whether a likelihood of confusion exists, it was not so problematic. We can follow the one or the other line. If you are outvoted, you will not be convinced, but you can accept the result. However, in procedural issues it was sometimes impossible to find a compromise. We made in some cases a moratorium, saying: Now, the discussion is closed and we will reopen it two months later. Let us see if we will find additional arguments to come to a common result. It was sometimes very, very difficult to come to a common conclusion but, at the end, we must solve the cases. We could not wait. Therefore, we tried to develop some things.

I have mentioned one example in the hand-out. It was the question of notification by fax. We had in the OHIM a very new system. We had a paperless office. This was the name, but I have never seen so much paper in any office. Everybody has copied everything that was accessible, so the copier was always going around. But, nevertheless, we transmitted all our decisions by fax to the parties. There raises the question: What is a relevant date of receipt by decisions by the parties. We had only the rule in the CTMR that the notification by fax is provided for. But nothing was mentioned what date should be relevant. In the practice, our copying machine was working not only on working days, but also in the night, on Saturday, on Sunday. In consequence, the problem arises, if a notification arrives at Friday, at 11 in the night, what should be the relevant date. A German lawyer, normally, was used to receive such a document only on working days and he stamped: Arrived on Monday. As you know, lawyers always use a time limit for filing an appeal until the last moment. So, he filed the appeal at the last day. Therefore, it was relevant what was the starting point for the time limit. Was it Saturday? Or was it Monday? A decision of the Second Board says: The relevant date is the date of receipt of the decision by the fax device of the party irrespective of day or night, or working day or Sunday. It is a very clear solution. The Board found that it is impossible for Alicante to know what happens in Europe. In some countries we have holidays of the state, national festival days of the state. In some places we have holidays of regions, in some festival days of the town, in some holidays of the bar association. It seems impossible, to look in all the countries what festival days will here exist. Therefore, it was rectified not to come to another solution. In consequence, the rule was changed in 2005 by the Commission and then it has included what our jurisprudence had found. The new rule makes a clarification: The notification will be effective on the date on which the communication was received by the fax device of the recipient. So, you can see that in some cases we have developed the law.

Now, I will come to another very important problem. How to organize the Boards of Appeal for example? It was a very central question. You know the Boards are independent, not bound by any instruction. Nevertheless, the President of the office gave an order that every member of the Board should have a hierarchical superior, namely the Chairman of the Board. The Chairman of the Board should have a hierarchical superior, namely the Vice-President of the office. Two colleagues of the Boards said: No, we don't accept such an order. We want also oblige to use a clocking system. They had the only possibility, because the office was not able to change this order, to go to the Court of First Instance. In the ordered hearing following a proposal for a friendly settlement of the court, the office was able to change this order and instead of hierarchical superior the new formulation was "responsible for administrative matters". It's clear if I go on holidays, I must have some person to give my file to. You see, such kinds of struggles in the starting point of the Boards of Appeal show that it was very complicated to go on.

Let me go to the question of translations and the competence for translation. The OHIM is inclined not to have its own translation department, it must give all documents to the translation centre in Luxembourg. If we received the translation back, we should have a look on it. For example, I received a translation of a decision drafted by my Italian Chairman. The translation in German was not understandable. I thought, I have never been part of this decision. I could not understand any word and, therefore, I started on the weekend to retranslate it. The English style was a little bit an Italian variation with baroque wording. Nevertheless, people must understand it. However, it was impossible for a German lawyer to understand such a translation. I was inclined to retranslate it, but in a free way. The translation of the Luxemburg centre was not wrong, it followed very precise word for word what my Italian colleague had written, but it was not understandable. I must translate it in a free way that I could transport the relevant thinking and a German person could understand it. You see that is a very relevant point and it is also the problem of the law, it is also the problem of the judgment of the ECJ. We have in some cases differences in the translation. I remember that I was astonished about a decision. I went to my English colleague, he was very happy. Then ,we compared the English and the German versions and we found differences. The English version was right, correct, but the German version had some faults, but not really faults. It was not very perfect in the translation. Therefore, I always say to students and to people: If you are not very satisfied from the European Court, please go to the other versions of the languages, especially to the French version because it is the working language and then try to understand it and do not believe only the German version.

Therefore, it is very complicated, under such conditions to develop a common, uniform law. One thing for example was also surprising, as we started to create files. The registrar, who was a lawyer coming from France, said to me: I have two files, one official file and the other is a secret file. Some decisions of the board come into the secret file and other decisions into the official file. For example, if you have made a joint resolution of cases, he put this decision in the secret file and sent a letter to parties saying that it was decided to join the cases, but without any explanation why and what was the decision. Then, we had a long, long discussion with him and with the other members and he said that this would be the practice in France to have different files: One for the party and one only for the judges. We said, no we cannot follow these rules, we have one official file and it should include all the papers and decisions. You can see that the question of organization is also a question of following the law.

My last remark, how to write decisions. You will notice we have very different approaches in Europe. In England, it is more of a discussion style, an expertise style. In Germany, we are strongly educated to follow an order style to give the decision as starting point and then to explain the grounds as to why we have come to that decision according to the law and the arguments of the parties. In other countries, it was normally used to repeat the arguments of the parties and then come to the conclusion why you have decided in such a way. It was also within the OHIM a discussion which way we should follow. We tried to follow more or less the way of the European Court of Justice, but in some cases this was not so clear. Therefore, in the end, it was also a little bit a mixture between the expertise and the order style, "Entscheidungs-Stil". A further question was: Should we make a single decision for the single specific case or should we make a general decision. In Germany, normally, we make in decisions a quotation of the law, and then we develop a principle, a principle not only for the present case but a principle which should have value for hundreds of other similar cases. Then, we make a subsumption under this principle. In consequence, we have settled not only one case, we have settled all the similar cases and if anybody can read the decision, he will see how a similar case would be treated. But my English colleague said, no, we settle only this case, and I will not be bound tomorrow to come in a similar case to the same result. Therefore, it was very different to come here to a clear compromise and so we decided everybody should follow his own education and his own practice.

At last, I want to mention a question of culture, the practice of friendly settlements. In Germany we are used as judges to speak with the parties, with the lawyers to come to a friendly settlement. For example, in my Board now in the patent court, 75% of the cases will be closed by a friendly settlement. Before we set a date for an oral hearing, we inform the party what is the expected outcome of the case after reading the file and we inform about the problems, the open questions, the points of discussion and we propose a solution for a friendly settlement. After receiving our provisional outcome, the parties normally follow us. But this seems to me to be only a German habit. What I have seen and learned in Alicante, neither in the northern countries nor in the southern countries did such a practice exist. Therefore, my Italian chairman was shocked as I mentioned, that I made a telephone call with the lawyers of the case to ask for a friendly settlement, receiving the answer: Yes, we are expecting a proposal of the court. No, an Italian judge will never touch a telephone, it is absolutely unthinkable. You can imagine that we need, I would say, a long, long time to harmonize the practice in Europe.

Judicial (non)-Dialogue under the United Nations Convention on Contracts for the International Sale of Goods 1980

ALASTAIR MULLIS[1]

Ladies and gentlemen, good morning. Before I begin, can I perhaps just say thank you or add my note of thanks to Professor Baudenbacher for the warmth and generosity of the welcome that he has extended to me and all my colleagues. It has been a huge pleasure to be here. The other papers have all been of great interest. I am very grateful to you for inviting such stimulating participants, but also to my colleagues for the collegiality and geniality of your company. It has been an excellent occasion.

My topic today is judicial dialogue under the CISG. I was very struck yesterday by Professor Baudenbacher's classification of three different types of judicial dialogue, the first of which he described as mandatory, the second necessary and the third "it's a jolly good idea". So far as the United Nations Convention on International Sale of Goods (CISG) is concerned, it, of course, falls into the second category, not mandatory, but necessary. Unfortunately, the story I have to tell, as the title of my lecture indicates, is not one of dialogue, but non-dialogue. In this short paper, I examine the extent of this non-dialogue in cases on the CISG and then explore some of the reasons that have been offered for this lack of dialogue. Finally, I pose the question whether non-dialogue really matters and if it does what we should be doing about it.

Despite what both Professors Werro and Schanze say in their papers, many people would, and indeed have, claimed that the CISG has been one of the real successes or success-stories of international private law harmonization. It was, of course, itself a product of dialogue, a dialogue that began back in the 1920s under Ernst Rabel. Some 74 states have now ratified the Convention, including almost all the major trading nations in the world though with the notable exceptions of the United Kingdom and India. It has been extraordinarily influential in domestic law reform. Part of it has, in fact even found its way into English law, but only in respect of the CISG's remedial provisions that are now available under section 48A-F of the Sale of Goods Act 1979 to consumer buyers. All rather ironic given that the raison d'etre of the CISG was to provide a regime for international sales between commercial parties.

---

1 Professor at the University of East Anglia.

The dialogue that began in the 1920s has continued. There are many books and hundreds of articles on the CISG, dozens of conferences and symposia have been held on the subject. And there have been more than two and a half thousand reported decisions. It is, probably, the international private law convention about which there has been most dialogue.

Yet, it is, of course, the case that to create a harmonized law it is not sufficient simply to create and enact a uniform convention, because "even when outward uniformity is achieved [...], uniform application of the agreed rules is by no means guaranteed, as in practice different countries almost inevitably come to put different interpretations upon the same enacted words".[2] Drafters of conventions are of course aware of this potential problem and most modern conventions contain provisions designed to reduce the risk of divergent interpretations.[3] This is true of the CISG which provides in Article 7(1) that:

> *"In the interpretation of this Convention, regard is to be had to its international character and to the need to promote uniformity in its application and the observance of good faith in international trade."*

In essence, this has been said to require that the Convention must be interpreted autonomously and as an international instrument. Words or phrases in the CISG should not simply be regarded as having the same meaning as identical words or phrases that may exist in the domestic legal system.[4] They should instead be given a "CISG-meaning", based on the structure and the underlying policies of the Convention as well as on its drafting and negotiating history.[5]

The mandating of an autonomous interpretation should, of course, tend to uniformity but it will not guarantee it.[6] Recognizing this, the drafters added the obligation that in

---

2 Munday, Comment, *The Uniform Interpretation of International Conventions*, 27 INT'L & COMP. L.Q. 450 (1978).

3 See, for example, Article 4 of the Ottawa Convention on International Factoring: '(1) – In the interpretation of this Convention, regard is to be had to its object and purpose as set forth in the preamble, to its international character and to the need to promote uniformity in its application and the observance of good faith in international trade.' See too, the Cape Town Convention on International Interests in Mobile Equipment provides in Article 5: '(1) In the interpretation of this Convention, regard is to be had to its purposes as set forth in the preamble, to its international character and to the need to promote uniformity and predictability in its application.'

4 See, for example, John O. Honnold, *The Sales Convention in Action – Uniform International Words: Uniform Applications?*, 8 J.L. & COM. 207, 208 (1988), where the author states that "one threat to international uniformity in interpretation is a natural tendency to read the international text through the lenses of domestic law".

5 Mullis and Huber, *CISG: a new textbook for students and practitioners* (Sellier, 2007). Of course, this autonomous interpretation may lead to the result that the CISG-term actually has the same meaning as a corresponding domestic term. One should, however, not jump to that conclusion too easily, but only after a careful analysis. See in more detail Schlechtriem, in: Schlechtriem and Schwenzer, *Commentary*, *Art. 7 Nr. 10 ff.*

6 Ferrari, *"Tribunale di Vigevano: Specific Aspects of the CISG Uniformly Dealt With"*, (2001) 20 Journal of Law and Commerce 225, at 226.

interpreting the Convention regard is to be had to "the need to promote uniformity in international trade". This instruction has been interpreted in two ways. First, it is said that those to whom the task of interpreting and applying the Convention falls are under an obligation to adopt solutions, which are tenable on an international level, that is to say, "solutions, which can be taken into consideration in other Contracting States as well". Secondly, it has been said that, in applying the Convention, courts must take account of relevant foreign decisions.[7] By taking account of such decisions, it is argued, "it is entirely possible to render the terms of the CISG uniform by ensuring the autonomy of terms".

There have been differences of opinion as to what it means to say that account should be taken of foreign decisions with one commentator going as far as to argue that a "supranational stare decisis" should be applied thereby requiring domestic courts to follow the decisions of foreign courts.[8] However, this is not a view that has been taken by any court and it has been criticized by most scholars. The prevailing view is that when interpreting and applying the Convention, courts and arbitrators should, but are not obliged to, have regard to other court's interpretations of the Conventions, including courts from other jurisdictions. Moreover, decisions are of persuasive authority only. They represent a source of learning and practical application of the Convention from which another court can draw in support or rejection of particular interpretations or applications of the Conventions. But they are not in any respect binding.

What then is the record so far as the use of foreign decisions by courts applying or interpreting the CISG is concerned? That there have been cases in which courts have examined and commented on decisions of foreign courts is not in doubt. The UNCITRAL

7 See, for example, Andersen, *The Uniform International Sales Law and the Global Jurisconsultorium*, (2005) 24 Journal of Law and Commerce 159; 19. Eorsi, General Provisions, in International Sales, The United Nations Convention on Contracts for the International Sale of Goods, (Nina M. Galston & Hans Smit eds., 1984) at 2-1, 2-4 Cook The U.N. Convention on Contracts for the International Sale of Goods: A Mandate to Abandon Legal Ethnocentricity, 16 Journal of Law and commerce. 257, 261. Hackney, Is the United Nations Convention on the International Sale of Goods Achieving Uniformity? (2001) 61 Louisiana Law Review 473, at 478; Schlechtriem, in: Schlechtriem/Schwenzer, Commentary, Art. 7 Nr. 12.

8 DiMatteo, 'The CISG and the Presumption of Enforceability: Unintended Contractual Liability in International Business Dealings', (1997) 22 Yale International Law Journal. 111, 133. DiMatteo has subsequently explained that his use of the phrase supranational stare decisis 'may have been inappropriate. The use of the phrase was not meant to indicate that all foreign decisions, at whatever level of the judicial system and whatever the quality of the analysis, should be accepted as binding precedent. This is indicated by the fact that the full phrase used was "informal supranational stare decisis". The term informal highlights the point ... that because there is no supranational appellate process to speak of, binding precedent is nonsensical.' The point being made by Professor DiMatteo is that courts should (not must) follow well-reasoned foreign case law opinions; they are free to disregard foreign cases that demonstrate poor reasoning and those that fail to comply with CISG interpretive methodology. On this basis DiMatteo's position is not significantly different from the position taken by most scholars. See also Bonell, Article 7, in Commentary on the International Sales Law: The 1980 Vienna Sales Convention (Bianca & M.J. Bonell eds., 1987) at 91.

Digest, which contains a "synopsis of the relevant case law"[9] for each provision of the Convention, refers to a handful cases in which foreign decisions were referred to and points in particular to one Italian decision of 2002[10] in which 37 foreign court and arbitral awards were referred to. However, a review of CISG scholarship suggests that reference is very rare and rarer still is any real engagement with the reasoning of foreign courts. Although some have claimed that the position is now starting to change, the current position appears to be that, with very rare exceptions, courts do not refer to foreign decisions, notwithstanding the widely held view that they should.

The incidence of reference to foreign cases

For the purposes of this paper, I have examined in excess of 1000 decisions on the Pace University CISG Database from the United States, Canada, Australia, New Zealand, Germany, Austria, France, Switzerland, Italy, Spain and China.[11] While this is only about forty percent of the cases reported in the Database, the jurisdictions chosen represent a mix of common law and civil law jurisdictions all of which have been parties to the CISG for approximately twenty years. From this examination certain patterns have emerged. First, taken globally, the percentage of cases examined that refer to decision of foreign courts is very low, certainly below five percent. Moreover, in several of these decisions the reference was very superficial, consisting simply of a citation to a foreign case and a statement to the effect that the foreign court had interpreted the Convention in the same way that the instant court was doing.[12] Second, reference has increased since the 1990s but this is not entirely surprising as there were almost no examples of reference to foreign court decisions before 2000. Though reference has increased, it is difficult to identify any clear patterns or to be confident that today courts are any more ready to engage with foreign decisions than they were in the 1990s. Indeed, it is still common to read in American cases that 'case law interpreting and applying the CISG is sparse'.[13]

Third, perhaps somewhat surprisingly, the record of the common law jurisdictions of Canada, Australia, United States and New Zealand is no better than that of most of the

---

9 UNCITRAL, Digest of Case Law on the United Nations Convention on the International Sale of Goods (United Nations, 2009), at x, para 17.

10 Al Palazzo S.r.l. v. Bernardaud di Limoges S.A. 26 November 2002 District Court Rimini (Italy), available at http://cisgw3.law.pace.edu/cases/021126i3.html.

11 All decisions of Chinese courts and a selection of CIETAC cases.

12 See for example, Downs Investments v Perwaja Steel 17 November 2000 Supreme Court of Queensland (Australia), available at http://cisgw3.law.pace.edu/cases/001117a2.html; Gaec des Beauches v Teso Ten Elsen 23 October 1996 Appellate Court Grenoble (France)
available at: http://cisgw3.law.pace.edu/cases/961023f1.html; Zapatos Mediterraneos v Shoe Bizz 6 March 2002 District Court Hasselt (Belgium) available at http://cisgw3.law.pace.edu/cases/020306b1.html

13 For some of the more recent cases see, e.g., Miami Valley Paper, LLC v. Lebbing Engineering & Consulting GmbH 26 March 2009 Federal District Court [Ohio]; Hilaturas Miel, S.L. v Republic of Iraq 20 August 2008 Federal District Court [New York]; Macromex Srl. v Globex International, Inc 16 April 2008 Federal District Court [New York]; TeeVee Tunes, Inc. et al v Gerhard Schubert GmbH 23 August 2006 Federal District Court [New York]; Valero Marketing v Greeni Oy 4 April 2006 Federal District Court [New Jersey].

civil law jurisdictions surveyed and in fact it is substantially worse than Italy. Fourth, generalizing about civil law jurisdictions is more difficult. Thus, while in China, for example, there has been no reference to foreign decisions and very few in Austria and Switzerland, more can be found in German court decisions and considerably more in the decisions of the Italian courts.

In terms of the 'quality' of references, the picture is again a mixed one. As explained above, many references are very superficial with a decision (not necessarily the only available decision) referred to simply because it supports the decision and/or reasoning adopted by the instant court. Often there is a sense in such cases that the court had made up its mind and then happened to find or have referred to it a case that supported the opinion it had reached. Certainly, there is no real engagement in many cases with the foreign court's reasoning. So too, there are many examples, where the court and/or lawyers appear simply to have ignored a line of authority that takes a different approach from that taken by the instant court. That said, it is important to note that there are cases, and in this respect the Italian courts have led the way, in which the court has engaged in a real way with the relevant case law. Take, for example, the Tribunale di Padova's decision on the meaning of Article 78.[14] In dealing with this question, the court gave full application to the requirements set forth by CISG Article 7(1), acknowledging that "[i]n the interpretation of this Convention, regard is to be had to its international character and to the need to promote uniformity in its application and the observance of good faith in international trade." Indeed, almost twenty decisions from several jurisdictions were cited in construing the meaning of CISG Article 78. In addition, the court fully explained its reasoning, supporting it where appropriate with relevant case law. So too, while the American courts have not distinguished themselves in their reference to, and use of, foreign cases, and indeed have far too readily accepted the relevance of cases on the Uniform Commercial Code in interpreting the CISG[15], there are a couple of examples of excellent practice in their decisions. In this respect, Chicago Prime Packers, Inc. v. Northam Food Trading Co., et al[16] represents perhaps the highpoint of engagement by a United States Court, albeit that the court began its judgment repeating the statement that there are not many cases on the Convention. Seven foreign cases are referred to and properly analyzed for their relevance. A similar example can be found in Amco Ukrservice et al. v. American Meter Com-

14 31 March 2004 (Italy), available at <http://cisgw3.law.pace.edu/cases/040331i3.html>.

15 See, e.g., Chicago Prime Packers, Inc. v Northam Food Trading Co 23 May 2005 Federal Appellate Court [7th Circuit]: 'Many provisions of the UCC and the CISG are the same or similar, and "[c]aselaw interpreting analogous provisions of Article 2 of the [UCC], may inform a court where the language of the relevant CISG provision tracks that of the UCC.'; Genpharm Inc. v Pliva-Lachema A.S. 19 March 2005 Federal District Court [New York] available at: http://cisgw3.law.pace.edu/cases/050319u1.html; Schmitz-Werke v Rockland 21 June 2002 Federal Appellate Court [4th Circuit]; Raw Materials Inc. v Manfred Forberich GmbH & Co., KG 6 July 2004 Federal District Court available at http://cisgw3.law.pace.edu/cases/040706u1.html.

16 21 May 2004 Federal District Court, available at http://cisgw3.law.pace.edu/cases/040521u1.html.

pany[17] Beyond these cases, however, the record is not impressive and the overwhelming impression from the survey is that reference is very rare and where made frequently superficial. In the light of the requirement to have regard to the need for uniformity in interpreting the Convention, and the recognition that this means that regard be paid to what other courts have decided, the 'why?' question inevitably arises: Why do courts not refer to foreign court decisions? The next section of this paper will offer a number of possible answers to this question.

Reasons, why courts do not refer to decisions of foreign courts.

A. Inaccessibility of foreign decisions

A significant difficulty said to lie in the way of any lawyer or court that wants to consider relevant foreign decisions is the problem of identifying and interpreting them. 'The CISG is practiced in approximately 50 different languages with vastly different alphabets. The practitioners cannot be required to find all existing practice, let alone understand it.'[18] No lawyer would have the linguistic capacity to read all these languages, let alone get to grips with the different judicial systems within which these decisions were handed down. The sheer difficulty and expense of this task is as a consequence likely to deter all but the most intrepid.

While it is certainly true that the task facing a lawyer, who wants to take account of foreign decisions, is a significant one, it is also the case that the task has in many respects got easier over the last decade. Various universities have created web sites where, at no cost, foreign court decisions can be retrieved. Further, a significant number of these cases have now been translated into English. As many lawyers who practice international commercial law will, in addition, to their own language, be familiar with English this makes the task of identifying and interpreting easier. In addition, to the full reports available on various databases, UNCITRAL publishes a collection of abstracts of court decisions from all over the world dealing with UNCITRAL texts, among others the CISG, and the Centre for Comparative

---

17 29 March 2004 Federal District Court, available at http://cisgw3.law.pace.edu/cases/040329u1.html. See also Medical Marketing v Internazionale Medico Scientifica a U.S. federal court, for the purposes of reviewing an arbitral award, accepted the correctness of decision of the German Supreme Court on the meaning of article 35. In so doing, "it treated the CISG as a kind of international common law, the application and development of which is in the hands of the courts of all nations party to the Convention, which must therefore also give consideration to decisions made in other countries – in this case, 'the law as articulated by the German Supreme Court'". So too, in MCC-Marble Ceramic Center v. Ceramica Nuova D'Agostino the Federal Appellate Court for the 11th Circuit referred to other United States Court decisions on the CISG and importantly commented "Moreover, the parties have not cited us to any persuasive authority from the courts of other States Party to the CISG. Our own research uncovered a promising source for such decisions at <http://www.cisg.law.pace.edu>, but produced no cases that address the issue of parol evidence."

18 Andersen, "Furthering the Uniform Application of the CISG: Sources of Law on the Internet", (1998) 10 Pace International Law Review 403.

and Foreign Law Studies in Rome has developed UNILEX, a collection of case law and an international bibliography on the CISG, which aims at promoting the knowledge of foreign case law. An abstract or summary is, of course, never as good as the full decision, but it might be thought to be better than nothing. Accessing the cases is as a consequence easier than it once was.

In addition, to a more ready availability of reported decisions, summaries and abstracts, UNCITRAL also now publishes the UNCITRAL Case Digest.[19] The Digest is designed to present information on the interpretation of the Convention in a clear, concise and objective manner. In respect of each provision of the Convention, it indicates how courts have interpreted the rules, presenting both majority and minority or 'questionable' approaches where they exist. The Digest, the second edition of which was published in 2008, is undoubtedly of considerable assistance for anyone who wishes to identify relevant cases and trends in the case law and in these respects its succinct and clear language is likely to be of particular use for time pressed lawyers and courts. However, as Lookofsky has pointed out:

> *'Its virtues notwithstanding, the advent of the Digest hardly signals the kind of 'revolution' heralded by the birth of the Convention itself. Decision-makers who would honour the Art. 7(1) mandate need more than Digest access; they also need 'knowledge of how pertinent CISG issues have been handled by others, particularly courts and commentators representing different legal traditions'. Because the Digest is largely devoid of (critical) information about the ratio underlying foreign precedent, and since the views of CISG commentators are UN-taboo, the Digest cannot help us distinguish the wheat from the chaff (precedents which are persuasive from those which are not). For this reason, the Digest – however helpful as an information-organiser – provides practitioners with a cropped snapshot of the big picture, the overall status of (real) 'CISG law'*[20].

In short, the Digest does make things easier for lawyers and courts, and in particular it alerts them to trends and relevant cases. In that respect, it represents a stride forward towards the development of 'the "infrastructure" of the practice of the new international commercial law – resources that make it feasible (if not yet easy) to discover relevant foreign legal materials'.[21] However, it is not the panacea. If real uniformity is to

19 The background to and general approach of the Digest is described in the "Introduction to the Digest of case law on the United Nations Sales Convention", Document A/CN.9/562. The Digest itself is comprised of sections covering each of the subdivisions of the Convention (starting with this section, which covers the Convention as a whole, and including sections for each of the various clauses, Parts, Chapters and Sections described in paragraphs 2–7above, including the Preamble and the Witness clause), and each of the individual articles that comprise the Convention except for the individual articles in Part IV ("Final provisions", articles 89–101).

20 Lookofsky, Digesting CISG Case Law: How Much Regard Should We Have? 8 Vindobona Journal of International Commercial Law and Arbitration (2004) 181.

21 Flechtner, 'Recovering Attorneys' Fees as Damages under the U.N. Sales Convention: A Case Study on the New International Commercial Practice and the Role of Foreign Case Law in CISG Jurisprudence', (2002) 22 Northwestern Journal of Business Law & Policy 121, at 155.

be achieved, it requires active engagement with the full facts and reasoning of foreign cases and not just the digested snippets produced by UNCITRAL.[22]

B. Fundamental ignorance of the CISG

A second reason for the failure to refer to decisions of foreign courts, may simply be that those involved in CISG litigation are insufficiently well educated about the Convention, its rules and underlying principles. To put it differently, it is possible that there exists a lawyerly and judicial ignorance about the CISG that inhibits the proper interpretation of the Convention.

Nearly thirty years after the birth of the Convention, this may seem a somewhat surprising suggestion. While academic and professional ignorance may have been understandable in the early years of the Convention's existence, it surely cannot be the case today that lack of knowledge is a significant cause of a failure to have recourse to foreign cases. The last decade has seen a radical expansion in education about and knowledge of the CISG. Around the world, many universities offer courses that either focus exclusively on the Convention or teach it as part of a course on international trade law or contracts. Indeed, a survey by Fitzgerald of US law professors indicated that 78% addressed the CISG in their basic contracts courses and a remarkable 100% teaching a basic sales course address the CISG with the overwhelming majority incorporating detailed reference to at least part of the Convention.[23] There is also evidence from Ferrari's work on the impact of the CISG on national legal systems[24] to believe that the position is not significantly different in many other jurisdictions and it would appear therefore that those now leading universities should be well equipped to deal with the Convention.

However, the fact that the CISG is now being taught in universities does not necessarily mean that there is a high degree of familiarity with the Convention among practising lawyers and judges. In regard to this issue, Fitzgerald's research is particularly interesting in that it suggests a relatively low level of familiarity regarding the CISG among practitioners in the United States and an almost complete lack of knowledge among the judiciary with 82% of those who responded declaring that they were 'not at all familiar with the CISG'.[25] The conclusion Fitzgerald draws from this is that:

> *'These responses suggest that the CISG, in particular, continues to be misperceived as*

---

22 See generally, Fitzgerald, 'The International Contracting Practices Survey Project: An Empirical Study of the Utility of the United Nations Convention on the International Sale of Goods (CISG) and the UNIDROIT Principles of International Commercial Contracts to Practitioners, Jurists and Legal Academics in the United States' (2008) 27 Journal of Law and Commerce 1.

23 Ibid, at 20–21.

24 Franco Ferrari, The CISG and its Impact on National Legal Systems (Sellier, 2008).

25 Ibid, at 8.

> *a "foreign law" and of relatively little concern to U.S. practitioners and judges. Other commentators have anecdotally observed this manifested in two respects, either in a tendency to view the CISG as not being part of the contract law of the United States at all, or as being confined to federal law and of concern only in large international commercial contracts.'*[26]

Though, there is a lack of awareness in the United States and some other it appears that in this respect the United States is out of step with many other jurisdictions. According to Ferrari, though lawyers in Greece, Israel, and New Zealand, and to a smaller extent, Italy reported a relative lack of awareness of the CISG, lawyers in the remaining 18 states surveyed generally reported being aware of the CISG, with awareness in some states being extraordinarily high. It would seem to follow, therefore, that ignorance of the Convention, its rules and its principles, is not likely to be a significant cause of a failure to refer to foreign cases. Moreover, while it is concerning that a survey of lawyers and judges in the United States indicates a lack of knowledge about an important piece of legislation is concerning, it does not really explain why foreign cases are not more commonly referred to in that country. Even if there is a lack of knowledge among practitioners and judges generally and the CISG is occasionally misunderstood or overlooked, it is highly unlikely that litigators do so in court. Lawyers who conduct commercial litigation are in most jurisdictions from large specialized and experienced firms who very thoroughly check all the sources that may work to their client's advantage. It is hard to believe that they would not identify and use any material, including foreign cases if they thought them helpful. Moreover, it is hard to believe that they are not aware of the interpretative rules of the CISG. Blaming lack of reference to foreign cases on lawyerly and judicial ignorance is therefore, it is suggested, not particularly plausible.

C. Lawyerly hostility to 'foreign law'?

Even if it can no longer be said that there is widespread ignorance of the CISG, it is possible that lawyerly 'hostility' to 'foreign law', whether for reasons of national sovereignty[27] or because of the complexity of comparative research[28], means that lawyers and judges may be hesitant in identifying and selecting particular decisions from specific foreign jurisdictions. Empirical work by Siems on the citation patterns of the English Court of Appeal and the German Bundesgerichtshof has shown that while both courts do refer to decisions of foreign courts, and the English Court of Appeal does so regu-

26 Ibid, at 8.

27 Von Bar, 'Comparative Law of Obligations: Methodology and Epistemology' in Van Hoecke, M (ed) Epistemology and Methodology of Comparative Law (Oxford: Hart 2004) 123, 124–5

28 Markesinis, Comparative Law in the Courtroom and Classroom (Oxford: Hart 2003) 39, 61–2.

larly, citation of cases by courts of a different legal family is rare.[29] Given the narrowly national education of most lawyers this is not surprising. As Zimmermann has pointed out, legal education today tends to be almost exclusively national:

> *'The Law of a country came [during the nineteenth century] to be regarded as a characteristic expression of its national spirit. This view was bound to lead to the particularisation of legal science that is still with us today and it has set the legal science apart from almost all the other sciences taught at a modern university. There is no such subject as German chemistry or French medicine. But for the past hundred years or so there have been, in principle, as many legal systems (and consequently, legal sciences) as there are nation states. This is reflected in our modern law curricula and examination requirements, which are oriented almost exclusively toward the law of the respective countries for which they have been devised.'*[30]

Such an education, of course, risks the danger of inculcating a narrowly national frame for viewing legal rules. It may even cause, at worst, a 'hostility' towards, or scepticism about the value of, foreign case law. This scepticism is something from which even judges in the United States Supreme Court are not apparently immune. By way of example, Scalia J has commented that 'this Court ... should not impose foreign moods, fads, or fashions on Americans,' and the current Chief Justice Roberts is recorded as having said extra-judicially that 'in foreign law you can find anything you want. If you do not find it in the decisions of France or Italy, it is in the decisions of Somalia or Japan or Indonesia or wherever'.[31] While these views would not necessarily command widespread support, and they were made in the context of a debate focussed mainly on the permissibility of using foreign judgments in constitutional cases, they nevertheless raise a serious question about the frame of mind with which, even the very best lawyers, may approach a novel legal question.

The fact is that it is difficult for a person trained in one jurisdiction to understand fully decisions reached by courts in other jurisdictions. As a consequence, there is a natural tendency to fall back on our national legal understandings and education and not to

---

29 Siems, Citation Patterns of the German Federal Supreme Court and the Court of Appeal of England and Wales, available at SSRN: http://ssrn.com/abstract=1305185. These findings confirm earlier work by Markesinis and Fedtke (eds), Judicial Recourse to Foreign Law (2006); Fairgrieve, Andenas and Canivet (eds), Comparative Law Before the Courts (London BIICL 2004); Drobnig and Van Erp (eds), The Use of Comparative Law by Courts (London: Kluwer, 1999).

30 Lawrence v Texas 123 Ct 2472, 2495 (2003) (Scalia J) and Foster v Florida, 537 US 990 (2002) (Thomas J); similar Atkins v Virginia 536 US 304, 348 (2002) (Scalia J). More generally, see David Zaring, 'The Use of Foreign Decisions by Federal Courts: An Empirical Analysis', (2006) 3 Journal of Empirical Legal Studies 297.

31 Statement by the current Chief Justice Roberts during his confirmation hearings, September 2005, available at http://transcripts.cnn.com/TRANSCRIPTS/0509/13/se.04.html. It should be noted that Roberts was not discussing the interpretation of international treaties but the use of foreign judgments to shed light on US law. See also Roper v Simmons 543 US 551, 608 (2005) per Justices Scalia, Thomson, and Rehnquist ('to invoke alien law when it agrees with one's own thinking, and ignore it otherwise, is not reasoned decision-making').

look to systems that any good lawyer will realize he can at best have a partial understanding of. Roy Goode is surely right when he says:

> *'If the harmonization process is to have any hope of acceleration it is essential for law schools to reduce their preoccupation with national law and their assumption of its superiority over other legal systems and to revert at least in some degree to the internationalism of medieval law teaching. It is primarily by the spreading of awareness of foreign legal systems among our students that we can hope to accelerate the process of harmonization and to produce practitioners and judges of the future prepared to look beyond the horizon of their own legal system.'*[32]

The problem is that we are not yet at that point and until then a natural scepticism of what we do not know or understand is likely to mean recourse to foreign decisions will remain rare.

D. Limited number of relevant well-reasoned decisions

Perhaps one of the most significant difficulties in the way of a lawyer, particularly in the 1990s and early 2000s, was the relative paucity of relevant and well-reasoned decisions. There were, it is true some notable exceptions to this, but the earliest cases showed a pronounced tendency towards approaching the interpretation of the CISG with a domestic mind-frame. Consequently, many cases were not particularly persuasive or well reasoned.[33] Further, it of course took time for a significant body of case law to build up on the CISG and then to be reported and translated. Perhaps unsurprisingly, therefore, citation of foreign authorities was infrequent in the 1990s and early 2000s.

While the lack of well-reasoned decisions may offer some explanation of the infrequency of reference to foreign decisions in the 1990s and 2000s, it cannot do so today. A search of the Pace University database and/or the UNCITRAL digest reveals that, on almost every provision relevant authorities can be found. It remains true that some are better and more transparently reasoned than others, but it is no longer the case that relevant decisions cannot be found.

E. Cases are a common law fixation

A commonly expressed view is that only in the common law that cases matter. In the civil law what matters are the codes and the judge's role is to interpret these. Moreover, it is also emphasized that the binding force of precedent of the Common Law has no

32 Goode, 'Reflections on the Harmonization of Commercial Law,' in Commercial and Consumer Law – National and International Dimensions (Cranston and Goode, 1993) at 26.

33 See, for example, Delchi v Rotorex, 6 December 1995 Federal Appellate Court [2nd Circuit]: http://cisgw3.law.pace.edu/cases/951206u1.html.

equivalent in most civil law jurisdictions where decisions are only binding to the parties of a trial. If this view is correct then it would not perhaps be surprising to find that there were few references to cases in the judgments of civil law courts interpreting the Convention. So far as the common law courts are concerned, one would expect to find more references to, and engagement with, cases.

At least two responses can be made to this analysis. First, the empirical work by Siems referred to above indicates that the conventional view that case law does not matter in the civil law is simply wrong, at least so far as Germany is concerned. His work indicates that although citation of authorities by German courts is less frequent than is the case by English courts, citation is by no means rare and is indeed becoming more frequent. While similar empirical evidence is not available for other jurisdictions, Zweigert and Kotz have argued that in actual practice there is as much judge-made law in continental Europe as in England. To suggest, therefore, that it is only common law courts that are interested in cases is simply not accurate.

The second response that can be made is that there is simply no evidence from the CISG case law to suggest that civil law courts are any less prepared to engage with foreign case law than are the common law courts. In fact, the evidence suggests that the contrary is the case: civil law courts on average have referred to foreign cases more than common law courts.

Does it matter?

If it is accepted that citation of foreign authorities by courts is rare, a question arises whether that actually matters. The usual answer to this question would be that of course it does because without reference to foreign decisions, the goal of uniformity set out in Article 7(1) will not be met. The consequence of this will be that different jurisdictions will apply different 'texts' of the Convention leading inevitably to forum shopping and the undermining of the uniformity principle. There is a great deal of truth in this answer but, it is suggested, it should not be overstated. Thus far at least, there is no compelling evidence that the uniformity achieved by the creation of the CISG is in the process of being seriously undermined by the failure of courts to refer to foreign judicial decisions.[34] It is true that there have been some 'rogue' or just plain bad decisions, and that on some issues different approaches can be discerned in the reasoning of courts in different jurisdictions. These however represent the exception

34 See DiMatteo et al, "The Interpretive Turn in International Sales Law: An Analysis of Fifteen Years of CISG Jurisprudence", (2004) 34 Northwestern Journal of International Law and Business 299.

rather than the rule and are arguably inevitable in any legal system.[35] Further, and most importantly, any tendency towards a lack of uniformity is being checked by two factors. First, even though the courts have not referred to foreign court decisions, they have in a significant number of cases referred to and adopted the views expressed in the leading academic commentaries. This has had the effect of 'standardizing' the approach or principles to be applied to the determination of many questions and as a consequence where there are differences they exist in the result reached and not in the principles or rules applied. By way of example, the concept of 'fundamental breach', which is a pre-condition to the award of certain remedies, is susceptible of widely different interpretation. The commentaries, however, have articulated in a remarkably similar manner the factors that should be taken into account in determining whether there has been a fundamental breach and these factors have generally been adopted by courts when determining the fundamental breach issue.[36] It is true that different results have been reached by courts notwithstanding similar facts but this is, it is suggested, a consequence of the open-textured nature of the 'fundamental breach' question and not because they were applying different principles when interpreting the concept.

Second, even though the courts have not frequently referred to foreign cases, nevertheless, there are many examples of courts taking an international approach to the interpretation of the Convention.[37] Indeed, examples abound of sensitive interpretation of the CISG in light of its international nature. Thus in a decision of the Bundesgerichtshof[38] handed down in 2005 it was said:

> *'The provisions of the CISG are, therefore, generally autonomous, i.e., by themselves and within the overall context of the Convention, without recourse to the rules developed regarding the standards of the non-uniform national laws. Only insofar as can*

---

35 Di Matteo et al ("The Interpretive Turn in International Sales Law: An Analysis of Fifteen Years of CISG Jurisprudence", (2004) 34 Northwestern Journal of International Law and Business 299) commented (at 349) as follows on fifteen years of CISG case law: "A review of CISG jurisprudence is an enlightening experience in the creation and interpretation of a living commercial code. The extremes that are found in the national interpretation of any international convention are evidenced in CISG jurisprudence. At one extreme, some courts have largely ignored the CISG's mandate that interpretations are to be formulated with an eye toward the international character of the transaction and the need for uniformity of application. At the other extreme are courts, and more often arbitral panels, that have taken the above mandates seriously and have resisted the temptation of homeward trend interpretations. In the middle, are the majority of cases that have attempted to provide autonomous interpretations with various degrees of success."

36 See, for example, the recent decision of the Swiss Federal Supreme Court (18 May 2009 Bundesgericht , available at http://cisgw3.law.pace.edu/cases/090518s1.html. See also Mitias v. Solidea S.r.l. 11 December 2008 (Tribunale di Forli) available at http://cisgw3.law.pace.edu/cases/081211i3.html.

37 See, for example, Tribunale di Modena 9 December 2005 available at http://cisgw3.law.pace.edu/cases/051209i3.html; Oberster Gerichshof 23 May 2005, available at http://cisgw3.law.pace.edu/cases/050523a3.html; Bundesgerichtshof 2 March 2005, 25 February 2004, available at http://cisgw3.law.pace.edu/cases/050302g1.html; Tribunale di Padova available at http://cisgw3.law.pace.edu/cases/040225i3.html; Audiencia Provincial de Valencia 7 June 2003, available at http://cisgw3.law.pace.edu/cases/030607s4.html.

38 Bundesgerichtshof 2 March 2005, 25 February 2004, available at http://cisgw3.law.pace.edu/cases/050302g1.html.

> *be assumed that national rules are also recognized internationally – where, however, caution is advised – can they be considered within the framework of the CISG.'*

So too, the Austrian Oberster Gerichtshof[39] has said:

> *'The CISG creates substantive law … and is to be interpreted autonomously in accordance with CISG Art. 7. Therefore, discussions on the Austrian legal situation have to be omitted and it is to be primarily interpreted by its literal sense.'*

While adopting such an approach does not guarantee uniformity, it nevertheless goes some considerable way to achieving that end thereby lessening the need to refer to foreign cases.

While there is some truth in the claim that uniformity has generally been maintained, for several reasons it is argued that the continued failure of courts to refer to decisions of other jurisdictions is undermining the CISG's claim to be a truly global sales law and therefore it does matter. First, there are some provisions in respect of which at least two lines of authority have emerged and little attempt has been made to engage with the reasoning adopted by courts taking a different view. A good example of this can be seen in the way in which Article 78 has been applied.[40] Under Article 78, interest is payable on the price and any other sum that is in arrears. While it is accepted that this entitles a party to interest on damages, different approaches have been taken to the question of the relevant rate. Some courts have treated it as a matter governed by, but not expressly settled in, the Convention.[41] Others have treated it as not governed by the Convention,[42] and therefore subject to domestic law, and then gone on to identify a variety of different laws as potentially applicable to resolve the question. The rights and wrongs of the argument need not concern us. The concern I have with these decisions was the almost complete lack of engagement with what other courts were doing and saying on the issue. In an article written in 2004[43], Mazzotta noted that the issue of the relevant rate of interest had been considered in some 275 decisions. While there was reference to the academic literature in a significant number of cases, in only 3 or 4 cases did the courts make express reference to decisions of other courts and in only a single case, an Italian case, was the engagement real and substantial.

---

39 Oberster Gerichshof 23 May 2005, available at http://cisgw3.law.pace.edu/cases/050523a3.html.

40 See also, for example, articles 14 19, 39, 74, and 79. These provisions have all given rise to differences of judicial opinion. As with article 78, judicial engagement with different lines of reasoning has been almost non-existent.

41 San Lucio, S.r.l. et al. v Import & Storage Services, LLC et al. 15 April 2009 Federal District Court available at: http://cisgw3.law.pace.edu/cases/090415u1.html; District Court Ieper Belgium 29 January 2001 available at: http://cisgw3.law.pace.edu/cases/010129b1.html]; ICC Arbitration Case No. 6653 of 26 March 1993 available at: http://cisgw3.law.pace.edu/cases/936653i1.html.

42 See Appellate Court Stuttgart, Germany 28 February 2000 available at: http://cisgw3.law.pace.edu/cases/000228g1.html.

43 Mazzotta, 'CISG Article 78: Endless disagreement among commentators, much less among the courts', available at http://www.cisg.law.pace.edu/cisg/biblio/mazzotta78.html.

Second, a failure to engage with foreign decisions may, and has in many cases under the CISG, closed the decision maker's mind to a range of potential approaches and solutions that may be available to the instant case. Negative example of this can be seen in the way in which a number of courts and tribunals have approached their task. Thus, for example, the Russian courts have shown remarkable myopia when it comes to issues relating to Articles 12 and 14. So too, the decisions on Article 78 referred to above rarely show any evidence of knowledge that alternatives exist to the solution chosen by the court. The consequence may well be the choice of a sub-optimum solution.

Third, though it need not be so, a refusal to engage with foreign cases frequently evinces the same world view that leads to adoption of domestic legal understandings in interpreting the CISG – the so called homeward trend. Such a trend can be identified in the case law of many courts on important issues of principle. It would be easy in this regard to single out the American courts, not least, because of the far too common recourse to UCC case law in that jurisdiction in order to shed light on 'similar' provisions of the Convention.[44] However, even if American courts are the worst offenders they are not the only ones. Decisions exist in other jurisdictions that quite correctly have been criticized for a pronounced homeward trend. Thus, Mazzacano writing in 2006 spoke of the Canadian case law on the CISG: 'Most Canadian cases on the CISG have shared remarkable similarities with Brown & Root. As in Brown & Root, there have been no laudable efforts for proper CISG interpretation; indeed, most cases are, instead, lamentable.' Similar criticisms could be directed against the German and Austrian courts for their interpretation of reasonable time in Article 39.[45] A failure to engage with foreign case law almost inevitably exacerbates the homeward trend and risks undermining the uniformity of the CISG.

Finally, knowledge that courts do not have recourse to foreign decisions will inevitably weigh with lawyers when advising their clients on the appropriateness of choosing the CISG to govern their contract. When advising clients on an appropriate choice of law, predictability and certainty of the law is inevitably an important factor. Yet, if lawyers cannot be sure that courts around the world will have regard to what other courts have decided, the very certainty and predictability that uniform law promises threatens to be undermined. As a consequence when faced with a decision whether to advise their clients to choose the Convention or their own domestic law, with which inevitably they feel more comfortable, there is a serious danger that they will choose their own

44 See, for example, Macromex Srl. v Globex International, Inc 16 April 2008 Federal District Court; Hilaturas Miel, S.L. v Republic of Iraq 20 August 2008, Federal District Court; Miami Valley Paper, LLC v Lebbing Engineering & Consulting GmbH 26 March 2009 Federal District Court; Raw Materials Inc v Manfred Forberich GmbH & Co KG US District Court of Illinois, available at http://cisg3.law.pace.edu/cases/040706u1.html (see comment by Lookofsky and Flechtner, 'Nominating Manfred Forberich: The Worst CISG Decision in 25 Years?', 9 Vindobona Journal of International Commercial Law and Arbitation (2005/1) 199–208

45 Schwenzer, 'National Preconceptions that Endanger Uniformity', (2007) 19 Pace International Law Review 103. See also Italdecor SAS v Yiu Industries Milano, 20 March 1998, (Italy), available at http://cisgw3.law. pace.edu/cisg/wais/db/cases2/980320i3.html#ct.

law, or as in commodity sales, the law of another jurisdiction that has a reputation for predictability and certainty. Currently, parties do still appear to be excluding the CISG as a matter of course in certain types of transactions and it is suggested that one of the reasons for this is likely to be a perception of lack of certainty and predictability.

F. Conclusion

The continuing failure of courts to have recourse to foreign decisions is to be regretted. Not only is it the case that there are few good reasons why this should be so, but it is also the case, it is argued, that the failure to refer to foreign cases risks undermining the uniformity of the CISG, inevitably affects in a negative way lawyers' perceptions of the CISG and its suitability to govern all types of international sales contract. The decision maker is also denied, or deprives himself, of the full range of potential solutions to the problem thereby risking a failure to reach the best solution. Proper engagement with decisions of foreign courts must occur if these tendencies are to be avoided.

How then should this be achieved? The key lies in education. Law Schools need to ensure that the proper nature of the CISG as both an international convention and as part of the law of many jurisdictions is understood: The perception of its 'foreignness', in other words, needs to be dispelled. It is only by education that there will be proper engagement with foreign cases. This will take time, but it must occur if the CISG is to become a truly global sales law.

Dispute Resolution in the Shadow of Uniform Contract Law?[1]

ERICH SCHANZE[2]

I should like to extend my sincere thanks to Carl Baudenbacher and his assistants for being able to participate in this most stimulating conference, and to Franz Werro for his kind personal introduction. I have called my speech "Dispute Resolution in the Shadow of Uniform Contract Law?" The question mark indicates my basic doubts on the practical relevance of the current "offers" of uniform substantive contract laws for conflict resolution in the area of sizeable international business transactions. It is not by accident, nor is it a sign of ignorance, that the international drafting and arbitration practice is by and large disinterested in the present private law codification exercise.

It is an irony: The CISG, as the most prominent example of a uniform law, may be understood as the climax of comparative contract scholarship. Moreover, the ratification record seems to be impressive[3]. However, we are still confronted with routine abrogation in practice. Application of the uniform law comes largely by surprise. Alastair Mullis, in his previous presentation, has already indicated that the mere number of cases of "application" may be not relevant for claiming "success" if one takes a closer look at issues under decision. In short: For practical purposes of dispute resolution, the CISG or other new efforts of codifying substantive contract law rules are a failure, and failure story needs to be explained.

A. From "codification" of private law to discourses about "coding" for conflict prevention and conflict resolution of international business transactions

I do not want to be misunderstood. I will not talk about the relevance of uniform contract law projects for law teaching. For understanding the elements of substantive contract law in a teaching context it may still be useful having a comparative look at the current academic efforts of "codifying" the results of comparative contract law. My main point is, however, that even for purposes of teaching and a deeper theoretical

1 This is an edited version of my speech at the conference. The lecture style is maintained. Footnotes are only added where needed.

2 Professor emeritus at the Philipps University of Marburg, Professor at the University of Bergen, Permanent Guest Professor at the University of St. Gallen.

3 See I. Schwenzer (ed.), Schlechtriem / Schwenzer Commentary on the UN Convention of the International Sales of Goods, 3rd ed. 2010, 'Introduction', with complete references. The last important State joining the convention is Japan.

analysis, we should not be so much captured by "codification" of substantive law, but rather engage in a structured discourse about the present ways and means of "coding" international business transactions. "Coding" includes the professional context of legal language and the technical structure of legal process, comprising both substantive and procedural legal issues, plus extra-legal regulation in the form of international standards and ADR.[4]

We have, indeed, left the age of codification of a private law of transactions since a considerable time. Codification of private law, in the sense of organizing rules of substantive private law in a coherent legal text, which is passed as "law" in the national legislatures, is a historical movement within the broader process of the creation of Nation States. It is inspired by a long lasting effort of transferring, translating and adapting the institutions of Roman private law into the various national "legal systems". Thereby, the "national codifications" like the French Code Civil or the German BGB, and even the 19th century rules of English case law, have become part of the national languages and the fundamental national ideologies. It is one of the ethnocentric misunderstandings of the 20th century, and particularly the discipline of (European) comparative law, to assume, that this "codification movement" could be transferred to the global level. There is no common ideology, no common language, and there are obvious problems of legitimacy.

Moreover, the key matter of these codifications is "sales", as reflected in its most sophisticated codified variant, the CISG. At the turn to the 21st century, we could witness a fundamental shift in the modes of global production and interaction of business units. Even if we still speak in terms of "sale", we mean transfers of mixes of products and services, which cannot be captured in the old trading paradigm of spot transactions of moveable goods – the paradigm structuring the vision of Ernst Rabel in his celebrated "Law of Sales of Goods" from the 30s to the 50s of the 20th century.[5]

The astonishing success of the English common law in the area of business law, colonialism and language apart, is based on its modesty and relative but healthy "backwardness". English law, and its US offspring, never went deeply in the "typology" of contracts. The English sales law or the relevant rules in the Uniform Commercial Code never played a fundamental role in structuring legal rules, even in times when "sales" were the key transactions. More important: The common law jurisdictions never completed the division between substantive law and legal process. The practiced common law, with its reference to decided cases, retained the notion that private law rules do not come from heaven, but are results of constant compromise.

4 The concept of "coding" (instead of codification) is more fully developed in E. Schanze, International Standards – Functions and Links to Law, in: P. Nobel ed., International Standards and the Law, 84–103 at 101–103.

5 E. Rabel, Das Recht des Warenkaufs, vol. I, 1936, vol. II, 1958

B. Devitalization of substantive contract law

The overly ambitious natural law division between "rights" and "remedies" is not the only source of problems with uniform private contract law codification. In the last 50 years substantive contract law has been in a process of erosion. It is not by accident, that Grant Gilmore at Yale, as early as 1974, diagnosed the "death of contract law".[6] Patrick Atiyah, in England, has reformulated that phrase in 1979 as the "rise and fall of freedom of contract".[7] Both maintain, in essence, that "social functions" are replacing the "classical formalistic" concept of "liberal" contract law. Whatever one may think about the "progressive" tendencies in these observations, by hindsight, it is true that consumer law seems to have "consumed" large portions of "classical" contract law. Every teacher of contract law knows about the frustrations of finding neat examples for standard contracting problems outside the area of consumer law. Even business women and men may be consumers. Undoubtedly, the general rules of contract law, as "codified" today in the hornbooks on contract, have become truly "academic". With their 19th century cases (be they English, US, or German "Lehrbuchfälle") they have become a kind of "teaching folklore" in the law schools worldwide. The pretence of actuality is frequently achieved by changing the Chinese Ming vase in the old case to the sale of a used laptop. The sale of the new laptop would be covered by consumer law, anyhow. This mode of largely irrelevant, but vastly popular contract teaching includes regular attacks on "Victorian contract law", "formalism", "privity", and particularly, complaints about lacking "flexibility" and an absence of sensibility for fairness ("good guys stand for good faith, the others eat babies").

In this secular erosion process "classical" contract law was devitalised. Ironically, the irrelevance for the legal practice may be one of the main reasons, why the CISG, and in part, the ongoing European codification movement, have such a successful (ratification) record. These "codifications" have no grip; they do not hurt. It is "costless" ratifying them. The technical aspects are mysteries for the ratifying legislatures. The lobby is not interested.

Whereas classical contract law vanishes from mainstream practiced contract scene, it reappears in a different gown. In certain aspects it rises as part of a new contract theory, comprising the theory of incentive compatible contracts and a practice of operating with contract modules ("modularity"). The international arrangements are mainly produced and maintained in international law firms. They are as standardized as possible and as individualized as needed. Moreover, some questions of classical contract law return in variants of sector specific requirements. Key questions are "legality" (in view of existing specific regulation), "formation" (when is a specific deal a deal?), and "execution" (specification of indemnification, admission of efficient breaches, individual adaptation). All these questions cannot be answered anymore in terms of

6 G. Gilmore, The Death of Contract, 1974.
7 P. Atiyah, The Rise and Fall of Freedom of Contract, 1979.

one general rule. The central issues show up on a different level: Legal certainty and workability which are basically defined by the extent of coverage in the arrangement itself. Draftspersons routinely assume that "defaults" can be controlled by choice of a relevant national law plus an adequate dispute settlement mechanism, likely in the end: Arbitration. In this sense, legal language (typically: English) and elements of old (i.e. "classical") contract law form some pillars of the international transaction code. Other pillars are the modules, tested and changeable clauses, and international standards.[8] This code of practice and the associated legal discourse are structuring international contracting in various areas, including both drafting transactions and dispute resolution. The key reference is an internationally recognized existing code covering all kinds of specific transactions, not "new" codifications like CISG, or a future European contract law. Present business dispute resolution is not operating in the shadow of uniform contract law but is rather concerned with the improvement of standardized contract forms (modularity), the choice of relevant national laws, and the choice of competent conflict resolution bodies.

C. How different are national contract laws?

A main advantage of the choice of a uniform contract law seems to be the alignment of existing differences between the national laws. In a bilateral transaction no single party should have the claim to her own jurisdiction; only an "international" law will equalize national parochialism or market power. That is the received theory. Do business persons care? Or do they rather care for clear and functioning rules? In a recent lecture at the meeting of the German association of private law teachers 2009 the best noted German expert on sales laws, Ulrich Huber, stated one of the problems in a nutshell. For the case of non-delivery of marketable goods in kind, which is probably the most relevant case in international sales, German law answers: "specific performance", English law: "money damages", the CISG: "maybe either".[9]

To be sure: For almost all practical purposes (also in the practice of German courts) damages are the relevant remedy. This is not for praising the practicability of English law. It is an example of the comparative law cuckoo. Despite the "praesumtio similitudinis"[10], the famous presumption that, considering all substantive and procedural issues, all developed legal orders will largely reach the same result, it is clear that we, as teachers of comparative law, exaggerate the differences. The degree of sophistication of the CISG produces "self made" problems which are aggravated by different interpretations in the various national courts.

---

8 On modularity see E. Schanze, Legalism, Economism and Professional Attitudes Toward Institutional Design, Journal of Institutional and Theoretical Economics 149 (1993) 122–140.

9 U. Huber, Schadenersatz statt der Leistung, keynote lecture of the convention of the [German] Zivilrechtslehrervereinigung, Marburg, September 2009, to be published in: Archiv für die civilistische Praxis 210 (2010).

10 K. Zweigert, H. Kötz, An Introduction to Comparative Law 3rd ed (T.Weir transl.), 1998, 40.

One important recent tendency in the understanding of the law of obligations is the "common roots" argument advanced by Reinhard Zimmermann. If we would return to the beginning of the national codification movements, we would realize the similarities based on the technical references to Roman law.[11]

In these remarks I would like to move Zimmermann's argument to my own field of international business transactions. If we would not look for "codification", but rather engage ourselves in the preceding task of "coding", this time not in view of a later codification, but rather for capturing the present discourse elements of international business transactions, we would be closer together then by continuing the comparative law chase for the differences and the associated speculations how they came about. In this sense, the production and use of new "synthetic" codifications may be of little avail. Or, to use Savigny's felicitous phrase, our time may be not (or rather, no more?) ready for codification.

On the level of coding I should point to an inspiring set of literature which is currently derived from empirical studies of contract practice. This US literature published in leading law reviews is based on law and economics theory studying "default rules".[12] Not only does it provide insights in the present modes of contracting, particularly the modularized "clauses", but it also demonstrates a substantial international convergence in the styles, method, and drafting results. It also recognizes the shift in the modes of trading, investing and transacting from the 20th to the 21st century mentioned above.

D. Uniform laws as "clippings"

A major portion of the cases, which have been decided with reference to CISG, relates to disputes caused by the existence and possible application of the uniform law itself. In other words: In many ways the law does not settle the technical issues it is made for. This is a common feature of statutes which split a broader legal field. Important issues are e.g.

- Are the general convention requirements met?
- Was there a silent or explicit abrogation? Or choice of law?
- Was a "sales" transaction in the sense of CISG involved?
- Or a consumer transaction?
- Relevance of (national, supra-national) mandatory law?

---

11 R. Zimmermann, Das römisch-kanonische ius commune als Grundlage europäischer Rechtseinheit, Juristenzeitung 1992, 8; id., The Law of Obligations; Roman Foundations of the Civilian Tradition, 1990.

12 See the two seminal articles by R. Gilson, Value Creation by Business Lawyers: Legal Skills and Asset Pricing, Yale Law Journal 94 (1984), 239; I. Ayres and Robert Gertner, Filling Gaps in Incomplete Contracts: An Economic Theory of Default Rules, Yale Law Journal 99 (1989), 87, and numerous articles by leading US contract scholars like A. Schwartz, R. Scott and G. Miller and V. Goldberg.

The most difficult issues are those which involve the scope of the CISG. When does uniform law start? What are the "linkages" to standard matters of the "general part" of national laws, like earnestness, mistake, agency, transfer of ownership, backing-up arrangements and varieties of securitization? Even if the uniform law would be a "perfect" codification in its own realm, it would still carry the stigma of incompleteness, the associated generic maze of application, and the most difficult problem of aligning the uniform law with substantive national applicable law, including all kinds of ius cogens, and the relevant law of procedure. For these reasons draftspersons and judges do not like split regimes. They are interested in "whole" transactional regimes, not in legal clippings, dépeçage. This aversion leads to the choice of (possibly imperfect, but whole) national laws as defaults.

E. The awkward substantive/procedural law divide

Related to the problem of legal clippings is the more general issue of the divide between substantive law and procedure – and its variant: Rights or remedies. Of course, this is not only a problem of substantive uniform laws. The system of private international law is also working on the premise of the existence of "pure" private substantive national laws. International business parties and arbitrators are primarily interested in remedies, not in rights. This remedial aspect would be strengthened if the application of uniform laws could be coupled with a transnational commercial court system, including judges with a multi-language background trained in comparative law.

F. Functions of substantive legal rules in contract planning and dispute resolution

Substantive dispositive law (such as the CISG rules) contains valuable patterns of orientation for contract design. In this respect, it is rather more a "repertoire" for understanding characteristic contingencies than an order to be directly applied to individual transactions. There are obvious trade-offs between legal detail (which is normally achieved in a detailed written contract) and the generality of decision-making rules. As long as a uniform law serves as a set of default rules, there are still virtues in the simplicity of the legal text. But in some cases even a fuzziness of the legal text and difficulties in the interpretation are a basis for settlement. The already mentioned "application rules" aside, the CISG shows many traits of over-ambition. Less would be more. A cynic might remark that the CISG contains enough legal text and commentary for masking any result. I am referring to Ulrich Huber's observation, cited above. Complexity of the legal text and disputes between the commentators invite strategic action by counsel.

G. Curative and punitive avenues of contract litigation

Many contracts have a "biography". Contracts may also be part of the biography of the parties linked by a contract. Whereas in other areas of the law the determination of rights may be in foreground of litigation, contract litigation has two dimensions: a "curative" or a "punitive". An experienced judge or arbitrator will, from the outset, ask himself (and potentially the parties) this basic question: Is this "terminal" litigation, or do the parties want to co-operate in the future? If the parties are concerned about an ongoing relationship, the judge will try to remain on a "curative" avenue. She or he will not allow that the parties escalate conflicting views about facts, rights, and remedies. The perspectives have to be as simple as possible. The disclosure of facts and the prospect debating legal issues have to be a nightmare. However, if the litigation is terminal, it is difficult for a judge to avoid the "punitive" avenue, entering in all factual and legal aspects of the case.

Pure substantive sets of rules, including rules of application, like the CISG, do not capture this basic bifurcation. The rights-oriented codification does not serve the de-escalation motivation of the much needed curative avenue. This is one of the reasons for the rapid growth of a "private provision of law for global transactions":[13] Rules which are competing with the conventional public regimes, such as CISG. For reaching on-going co-operation, what I called the curative side, the parties are well advised to design ex ante-"conflict screening mechanisms",[14] starting from extra-legal settlement procedures, and only then, in a rigid time frame, entering into a possible "hot" phase of court proceedings.

H. Conclusion: farewell to illusions

Substantive contract laws, including synthetic "area" codifications like the CISG, have an orientation function, resembling historical monuments. They will, in their own right, remain a reference for the questions they address. They will also be useful in demonstrating the virtues of the declining craft of classical comparative lawyers and be of help, particularly in their linguistic aspects, for the daily routines of coding international transactions. Regarding the practical standards of application, there are obvious reasons for non-use, unless a matching court system, including a workable procedure and recognition of judgments, would be in place. Whether such a system is desirable

---

13 G. Hadfield, The Public and the Private in the Provision of Law for Global Transactions, in V. Gessner (ed.), Contractual Certainty in International Trade, 2009, 238–255; E. Schanze, International Standards (Fn. 3 above).

14 E. Schanze, Investitionsverträge im internationalen Wirtschaftsrecht, 1984; id., Regulation by Consensus: The Practice of International Investment Agreements, Journal of Institutional and Theoretical Economics 144(1988), 152–171.

remains an open question. I was slightly more optimistic in the past[15], but, currently, I do not see a massive demand from practice.

If such a system is under demand and seriously contemplated, it might be as well privately organized and might also provide for a set of contract forms and modules, which are closer to the practical needs than CISG, or a new uniform contract law codification. Partly, a "remedial" conflict resolution "system" is available, named commercial arbitration. I am not saying that commercial arbitration is the only solution. I hope that also the traditional court system will be prepared to engage in this exercise in the future.

Returning to the present, and my initial question: Does commercial arbitration, and even the existing commercial courts, need the CISG? In view of a functioning choice of complete national laws and existing private specific "legislation" within the drafted contracts or by reference to international standards, that question is rather to be answered in the negative.

Given this state of affairs, what should be the agenda for research concerning matters of contract and associated dispute resolution? In my view, it would be research in a "transactional perspective" of 21st century contracting – with a preference for simple default rules including "bright-line" rules against fraudulent practices and strong incentives for a reasonable formalization of arrangements. As lawyers we should return to a better understanding of the virtues of contract formality, a subject matter, which was neglected or even discarded in the 20th century. In essence: For purposes of designing "good" governance of international transactions, "good" law is both form and substance, and rather not, more substance than form. In the age of the new media there are speedier and less costly ways of formalization and modularization of arrangements. These may enhance legal certainty, and may leave matters of "flexibility" of contracts in the disposition of the parties, and not in the discretion of judges. The theoretical basis for understanding the law of international business transactions, comprising the quickly shrinking province of technical substantive sales law, should be the existing empirical contract research, inspired by the theory of incentive compatible contracts.

---

15 E. Schanze, New Directions for Contract Research, in B. Dahl and Ruth Nielsen (eds.), New Directions in Business Law Research, 1996, 61–72.

Discussion

FRANZ WERRO
We have now, as I believe, 15 minutes left to the discussion. Can I give you the floor Professor Rau?

ALAN RAU
I have two small points: The first is basically an elaboration of a point I think that Alastair already made, which is; There are different ways of ensuring collaboration. We know this from anti-trust law for example. You can accomplish coordination simply by parallel, simultaneous recourse to third sources (for example to "la doctrine" which is already very reach and voluminous). So, if German courts rely on Schlectreim and Belgian courts rely on Schlectreim, it does not really matter if German and Belgian courts rely on each other, you arrive at the same result. It would be unusual for them to rely on each other anyway, so, you are accomplishing the same result by the familiar resort to "la doctrine". I think you said that already, I am just sort of underlining the same point.

The second point is, I was a little surprised by the figures you cite about the teaching of the CISG in the United States. Using my own law school, which is relatively enlightened, as a representative sample, I think our Contracts classes refer to the CISG approximately 0% of the time and I think that is fairly common. I think it is fairly unknown. I think if the Vis Arbitration Moot in Vienna has any function at all (about which I am fairly sceptical anyway), but if it has any function at all it might be in sensitizing students, particularly American students, to the existence of the CISG and to its importance.

ALASTAIR MULLIS
I guess I was also slightly surprised to read the statistics, but that seems to have been Fitzgerald's research revealed.

As I said this was an article by Peter Fitzgerald entitled "The International Contracting Practices Survey Project: An Empirical Study of the Value and Utility of the United Nation's Convention on the International Sale of Goods (CISG) and the Unidroit Principles of International Commercial Contracts to Practitioners, Jurists, and Legal Academics in the United States ". I have to say I found the statistic regarding contract courses (78%) very surprising. I am somewhat sceptical about it. With regard to sale courses, it seemed to me to be less surprising that the CISG was mentioned in all such courses. How anybody today could teach a class in the United States on sales without referring to the Vienna Sales Convention or CISG seems to me to be extraordinary.

ALAN RAU
That is true. On the other hand, the free standing Sales course itself is about to disappear or more properly, has already effectively disappeared in many places.

ALASTAIR MULLIS
So, it is subsumed under IBT?

ALAN RAU
No, it is just simply disappeared. Yes, I know I share your incredulity, but there you are.

CARL BAUDENBACHER
Thank you. Well, on the Vienna Sales Convention, obviously, there is some disappointment. I could sense it at least. But let me ask President Bender a question concerning the area of intellectual property law; I very much enjoyed your presentation based on your experience in Alicante and it showed the tremendous difficulties even if you have, not only uniform law, but Community supranational law in form of a regulation. But if we talk, and I am asking you now as a German High Court judge, about the European Patent Convention, interpretation of the European Patent Convention or interpretation of the Paris or the Bern Convention; is there something going on? Do you look at how high courts in other countries give interpretation to key notions?

ACHIM BENDER
It is a little bit different. I think my experience in relation to the trade mark law, which is not so complicated in comparison with patent law, has shown that we need some time for the development of a common law in Europe. Therefore, I am now not pressing the European Commission to come in short time to a compromise in relation to the Community Patent system because we have the good functioning EPO system. The situation is different to the trade mark sector. In the field of patent law, we should settle the principal conflict, which is the problem of the languages. In relation to the Community Trade Mark we have twenty-three languages, but we have only to translate the list of goods and services. However, in patent law, if you have to translate a description of the patent then it will be very complicated to have too many languages. The next principal conflict is the question of the courts. Who will take over the control and what kind of experience should the judges have? I think we should have a very qualified panel to be in a good position in relation to the international competition. In Germany, for example, we have technical judges in the Federal Patent Court who are able to understand the specific material, for example chemists or engineers. Only one jurist is sitting in the panel. Therefore, I think we should not go to hurry. Before making faults we should discuss that issue deeply and find a very solid solution. At the

moment, it seems to me that the reform procedure is sleeping. I do not want to wake it up because we have at the moment no clear solution for the future.

CHRISTOPH PAULUS

Thank you very much. I found this panel extremely interesting and I am a little bit sorry to hear so many lawyers and not one linguist, because those guys who are doing this law and language thing, they are discussing this problem: The text is an individual in itself and the recipient is a different thing. That is your entire problem.

In sight of this extreme position of these linguists saying that the text says nothing and the recipient says everything, in sight of this extreme position, does it not give at least some comfort that you all come to the conclusion that the system does not work very well, but at least it does work to a certain degree? Would that be a level of where you all could find some comfort?

ALASTAIR MULLIS

Yes, but I do not want to give the impression that I think that the CISG has been a failure, because I think in many respects it is actually a considerable success. Certainly, if somebody like Professor Schwenzer was here, she would present, no doubt a very convincing case in its support. I guess I am also interested to what extent is the CISG different from other international conventions, for example we have a number of experts here on the New York Convention. Is it the case that courts interpreting the New York Convention never refer to decisions of other courts? I do not know. But, that Convention seems to work well. The Uniform Customs and Practice on Documentary Credits are a rather different type of creature but very few credits will be issued that do not include reference to them. Do courts interpreting provisions of the UCP refer to decisions of other foreign courts when interpreting the UCP? I have rarely seen such reference. Nevertheless, the UCP seems to work well in practice perhaps because of the involvement of the ICC's Banking Commission. Ultimately, in most cases, some harmonization is probably better than none. I guess we have a responsibility to keep worrying away at it in the direction that Mr. Tercier has suggested.

GUEST

If I may pick up the last sentence. We must take care of that. Could it not be that you all have been a little bit misled by the general topic of this conference, the dialogue between courts? In your field, there is quite clearly no dialogue or at least extremely little between the courts. Should that missing dialogue not be replaced by the dialogue of the "we's" of the international conferences?

ERICH SCHANZE

I would answer that question in a different way. The "substrate" of CISG is lawyer's law. Thereby, I mean it is something which is more or less a base structure in which lawyers are trained in the law schools, and it is also a subject of a limited practical legal discourse. Every national law has a complete set of functioning sales laws. The deeper question is: Does the English Sales of Goods Act work? Does the US Uniform Commercial Code work? Ironically, you can also answer both questions in the negative. To put it bluntly: The codified sales acts do not "work" because they do not matter. There is a broad consensus about the underlying legal rules, which is captured a little bit by American contract teaching. In the US national law schools you study neither Massachusetts contract law, nor do you "compare" the relevant 50 jurisdictions, nor are you exposed more intensively to the codification of the UCC. You study the basic structure of contract law. Here, we are not talking about a potential judicial dialogue about interpretations of different or identical codified rules, or even new legal problems. Rather, it is a dialogue about generally accepted deep structures of a key legal area: Contract law. In this field it is not really essential for judges to entertain a judicial dialogue for looking at other jurisdictions and to learn from other decisions. In present times, the intricacies of "different" contract laws are rather a hobby of the comparative law professors. "Unification" has become obsolescent for purposes of practical application because there is a broad consensus in this area. This also reduces the relevance of choice of law issues in practice, if there is not some strategic element involved. Every good arbitrator knows that. It is standard practice looking at the CISG or other potentially applicable national contract laws from the angle of the contract law you know best. This is, obviously, a different instance of "judicial dialogue".

FRANZ WERRO

If I may briefly intervene, I would like to ask you a question. I am intrigued by the way in which you seem to want to make the point that substantive classical contract law, as it is taught, is actually no longer relevant. You seem to consider instead that there are private competing orders that are much more successful because they grasp the reality of contract law practice much better. What I do not understand, in this account, is the framework, the conceptual and intellectual on which these private competing orders are founded. Is classical contract law no longer the basis of these private competing orders?

ERICH SCHANZE

The simple answer is that we have long left the straight jacket of "sales". The key achievement of the 19th century was the possibility of freely negotiating legally enforceable relationships of all sorts of transactions without looking to a sale or a work contract, and so forth. This is really the hallmark of liberal contract law. But it destroyed contract law as a closed set of substantive institutions. We have moved away from a world of sales to a world of services and "hybrid" transactions. Today's contract law is not a set of "contract types", but rather a repertoire or tool box of "modules", schemes and clauses which are used and refined in the drafting routines. The CISG may still be a useful teaching tool in the law schools, as a sort of enacted "basic" contract law, but it hardly serves as a key reference for drafting or adjudicating business transactions in 21st century.

ACHIM BENDER
I am not so pessimistic. As I was going from the German Federal Patent Court to Alicante, in 1997 it was the practice of the Court to make references in the decisions only to the German Federal Supreme Court. After ten years of European development and judgment in Luxembourg in relation to trade mark issues, coming back from Alicante in 2007, I was astonished, that nothing had changed in that respect. After such a long area of European jurisprudence in the harmonized trade mark law, my German colleagues continued only making references to the national Supreme Court. Now, I try to bring European fresh air in the German decision making procedure and I train my colleagues to make firstly reference to the European Court of Justice. Only if the European Court had not solved the case, then we make references to the German Supreme Court. Now, I see more and more that the German jurisprudence goes in that direction. If you have a look to the judgment of the German Supreme Court, you will see a clear change of the habit. The new judgments of the Supreme Court are firstly grounded by the jurisprudence of the European Court. Therefore, it needs some time, but the habit is changing and national judges will be able to take over international decisions. However, I think it is not a process of our generation, it is a process of the youth. I hope that the young students will learn other legal systems and will be trained to work with international law and international judgment.

FRANZ WERRO
Sorry for not paying attention to the whole room, it is a little difficult visually. Mr. Planzer was first and then you, Professor Larsen, and I will remember you in a minute.

SIMON PLANZER
Thank you very much for your presentations. And thank you indeed for your presentation, Professor Mullis; you have analyzed a great number of cases. You mention that there is hardly any engagement in judicial dialogue, which comes quite as a frustration to us. But it would appear to be the truth. The way to remedy this situation, you suggest, would be through law schools that educate people truly internationally. Frankly, I wonder whether things might not have been easier in the Middle Ages than nowadays. In the Middle Ages, people from all over Europe went to northern Italy, later on also to other places, to study Roman law and Canon law. Consequently, they would bring home a common heritage – ius commune – and implement it in their home country. But what are we supposed to do nowadays? Are we supposed to study thirty or forty different national laws in order to be prepared for the challenge?

ALASTAIR MULLIS
That is a very nice question. I think there are various scholars who would take issue with you about the Middle Ages and the extent to which there was a common legal education at that time. But let us assume that that is the case. I guess in terms of education one of the things that I think is amazing that has happened over the last twenty five or thirty years is of course the growth of the Erasmus programmes. These offer the opportunity for students to travel to other countries to be exposed to education in

other countries. Personally, I would make participation on one of these programmes compulsory for all those who want to practice law. That would not be very popular in England, of course because, it would require people to speak another language. I would also like to see students being introduced to how foreign legal systems deal with common legal problems as part of their mainstream legal education. In other words, they should be taught comparative contracts, torts etc. Comparative law should not be a stand-alone minority pursuit. I think in the long run, it would make them better lawyers. Do I think it is likely to happen in my lifetime? No.

LARS BAY LARSEN

In a sense I want to repeat and perhaps develop a remark I made yesterday. I understand perfectly well how for scholars it is so tempting to focus on the explicit references in judgments, because it is empirical. You can find the quotations or, you can identify the lack of quotations or lack of references in various courts' judgments. You should, however, be very careful not to let this mislead you to say, "since here is no explicit reference, consequently there has been no judicial dialogue". Sometimes it may even work exactly the opposite way around precisely because the relationships between some of our various national or regional or international courts are so delicate and not strictly hierarchical. It is a very delicate matter to express such a relationship, to make a clear reference and leave an impression of a perhaps more binding source of inspiration than it is from a strictly constitutional point of view. In fact you protect your ability to seek inspiration where inspiration can be found precisely by not bringing it out in the full broad transparent daylight by making an explicit reference. But certainly both national and international courts do seek inspiration by each other, even though it rarely produces an explicit reference in the end.

FRANZ WERRO

This reminds me of Professor Riesenfeld's remark in Berkeley. One day he told me: "you know, when I was drafting legislation for Minnesota, I would never say where it was from. It was obviously inspired by German law but saying it would have been to give it the kiss of death."

MR. BURKE

It is just this study of contract law I find very interesting and when you say that it has been almost deconstructed and become very, very modular, there is no question that that is the case and everybody is looking for a standard clause. But one of the things, when you are in practice and particularly when you are dealing with multi-jurisdictional contracts, there is no standard and you have to be so incredibly careful when you draft something like an arbitration clause and the first thing that will happen when something has gone wrong, where is the contract, what does it say and most importantly what is the applicable law to resolving the dispute. If you do not have a very sound and solid basis in your own domestic contract law, you cannot actually endeavour in any way to apply any logic whatsoever to resolving the dispute. You may not understand it or you may not understand the theoretical underpinning of contract laws in other countries, but you will have at least some concept. I mean also my experience of studying the CISG was that it was a fantastic thing to study but it was terribly complicated and it was complicated not by the fact that it in itself is a difficult document, but how, and I studied it with fifteen other nationalities. There was absolutely no agreement whatsoever on what the provisions meant if you applied it in a certain way and I think that that is where the academic discussion comes in and why it is very, very useful.

FRANZ WERRO

Thank you very much indeed. Unfortunately, the time has come to take a break. I want to thank you very much for this lively discussion.

Focus: International Bankruptcy Law

Introduction

DANIEL HUNKELER[1]

Preamble

Thank you very much, Professor Baudenbacher, for the introduction and for the flattering words. Dear colleagues, ladies and gentlemen, dear students, although icy temperatures prevail outside, I warmly welcome you to our fourth panel dealing with a judicial dialogue in international bankruptcy law. We are very pleased that you expressed your interest in the topic and that you are joining our conference on this Friday afternoon. Indeed, international bankruptcy law has become more and more important, especially nowadays in the light of a worldwide economic crisis, and it is becoming even more important that a judicial dialogue, meaning the communication between courts in the field of international bankruptcy law, takes place; the dialogue ought not only be held in international bankruptcy law, but, of course, also in international reorganization law. This panel will deal with both fields of law on behalf of their importance and actuality.

Let me introduce the three speakers of today's panel in the sequence in which they will hold their speeches after my introduction. First of all, Professor Christoph Paulus sitting on my left-hand side. Professor Paulus is from the Humboldt University. He has studied in Munich and Berkeley. He has been Professor for civil law, procedural law, bankruptcy law and ancient legal history at the Humboldt University in Berlin since 1994 and he has been the Dean of the mentioned University since 2008. Before that, he was an associate Professor at the Universities of Augsburg, Berlin, Heidelberg and Saarbrücken and visited several universities including the University of Bocconi. Furthermore, he consulted the German government, the World Bank and the International Monetary Fund.

The second speaker of today's panel is Professor Jay Westbrook sitting on my right-hand side. Professor Westbrook is from the University of Texas, Austin. He holds the Benno C. Schmidt chair of business law at the University of Texas, Austin, where he also studied law. He is the grand and great old man of American scholars in the field of bankruptcy law. He also teaches and writes on commercial law and international business litigation. He used to practice in Washington D.C. in a major law firm. Professor Westbrook visited as professor the Harvard Law School and the University of London. Among many other functions, he consulted the International Monetary Fund and the World Bank.

---

1 Partner at Schumacher Baur Huerlimann, Zurich.

Last but not least, I would like to introduce Mr. Adam Goodison. Mr. Goodison works as a barrister in London in the firm Gray's Inn. He studied at the Durnam University and visited the bar school in London. He was called to the bar in 1999 and was elected as a member of the bar council. Adam Goodison is specialized in bankruptcy and reorganization law. He has gained a broad practice since he has been called to the bar and has been more or less very active in these fields of law. He has taken part at big restructuring cases, notably BCCI and TXU.

As you can see, we have got worldwide known experts in today's panel and I am very glad and I am looking forward to interesting speeches and interesting discussions.

A. Introduction

I would like to give you an introduction on today's topic before we start with the main speeches. I would like to start off with a general short introduction on insolvency litigation in an international context. I would like to talk about why a dialogue between courts in international bankruptcy law is nowadays becoming increasingly important, which problems we face in this regard and how these problems can be addressed.

More than ever in the so-called period of globalization companies develop economic activities worldwide. Their assets are not concentrated in only one country, but are spread all over the world. If it comes to a breakdown like the one we had experienced in the banking sector recently, the existing assets of bankrupt debtors must be liquidated in order to satisfy the creditors. The liquidation procedure should be adjusted to maximize the revenue for the creditors. In the case of international companies, the economic entities are legally located in different countries, (e.g. parent company in one country and subsidiary companies in other countries), the assets are not concentrated in only one country and the creditors live in different countries. It is obvious that transaction costs on one hand and procedural costs on the other hand are higher compared to national bankruptcy cases. Normally, there are several procedures in different countries and not just the one. In the end, creditors of an international acting debtor get less, as a general rule, than creditors of a small local debtor in case of a bankruptcy. Usually, an international debtor is bigger and its insolvency causes more damages to its creditors. That makes efficient procedures in international insolvency cases particularly important. Efficient procedures in reorganization cases are even more important: Successful reorganization presupposes a quick acting and an effective cooperation of the different players, especially, of the courts as well as of the debtor's management, the trustees appointed by the courts and also by the lawyers involved.

B. Approach

In what follows, I will focus on the cooperation between courts in different sovereign nations. In my opinion, such cooperation is the most important approach in order to make procedures in insolvency cases more efficient, because in the end, courts are the institutions which have to deal with bankruptcy cases and which have to make important decisions.

In the past, courts applied to the "first-to-judgment rule" or the "anti-suit injunction" in order to determine the optimal forum for multinational cases. A modern approach is judicial negotiation (interaction between courts). I will discuss this approach in conjunction with insolvency proceedings.

C. Categories of international insolvency cases

Before I elaborate on this, let me make some remarks regarding international insolvency cases in general:

If lawsuits involve many of the same parties as well as many of the same claims and are pending in courts of two or more sovereign nations, we have a situation of so-called "parallel litigation". In insolvency cases we can distinguish subcategories of "parallel litigation", namely "parallel proceedings" and "parallel claims" cases.

"Parallel proceedings" are situations, in which courts in two different countries have to deal, separately and independent from each other, with a complete insolvency proceeding related to the same debtor (e.g. parent and subsidiary).

In "parallel claims"-cases, only one insolvency is pending and a local court would dismiss or stay a claim against the insolvent debtor in favour of the foreign insolvency court that was charged with resolving all such claims.

In my opinion, judicial negotiation is an approach to deal with cases of both categories in a pragmatic way. Nevertheless, it might be more important for parallel proceedings. That is why judicial negotiation seems to be more developed in such cases.

Hereinafter, I will commence with more rudimental forms of judicial negotiation explaining "parallel claims"-cases, and are going to finish off with more progressive forms by explaining "parallel proceedings". I will give some examples for both categories by summarizing court decisions taken mainly in the United States of America and in England, for – as you will see at the end of my speech – Switzerland has no considerable precedents in this field of law. The examples mentioned by me are discussed more detailed in an article of Professor Jay Westbrook, member of our today's panel, in the

Texas International Law Journal. I will keep my remarks short, but in case of any interest, the article in the Texas International Law Journal can be consulted.

D. "Parallel claims" cases

In "parallel claims"-cases, non-insolvency courts have to decide whether they dismiss or stay a claim they are confronted with, assuming the foreign insolvency court will act properly and fairly, or whether they proceed. It is obvious that such a situation needs cooperation. From my point of view, the conditional dismissal or stay as a possible approach in such situations can be considered as a first step to cooperation between courts. In the Blanco litigation for example, a company from Venezuela filed a lawsuit against a Venezuelan development bank in New York. The plaintiff company went bankrupt in Venezuela and trustees were appointed to control the company. The control was taken from the shareholders. The trustees sought dismissal of the New York suit. The shareholders, however, did not support this decision and intervened in the New York action, arguing they could not get justice in the Venezuelan courts and the trustees being hostile and unfair to them. The suit was dismissed (from the second court) under the condition that the Venezuelan bankruptcy court appoints a new co-trustee acceptable to the shareholders, otherwise the suit could be reopened in the U.S. In this case, it is interesting that the U.S. court somehow intervened in the foreign court proceeding (namely in the Venezuelan insolvency proceeding), taking all aspects of the case into consideration. This example shows how a court can determine the decision of the court of another country.

E. "Parallel proceedings"

In "parallel proceedings" courts used to follow the "grab rule": They sold the entire debtor's property within their territorial sovereignty under local law. Unfortunately, they did not think about the other courts involved. It is obvious, therefore, that this procedure used to cause losses for the creditors. Nowadays, courts started to use alternative procedures:

In the case *In re Inverworld* the debtor defrauded hundred millions of Dollars from the investors. Cases against the parent company and subsidiaries were pending in Texas (U.S.), the Cayman Islands and England. In Texas, because the main office was there, in the Cayman Islands and England because transactions had been processed through subsidiaries located there. In addition, the contracts with investors as well as the contracts between companies had different and conflicting choice of law and choice of forum clauses. In order to avoid extremely expensive litigation in three national courts, and in order to avoid conflicting decisions, the representatives of the parties created protocols which were accepted by every court involved. The English insolvency proceeding was dismissed under conditions (conditions regarding the treatment of claimants therein and allocation of functions among the two remaining courts), while the remaining courts established a division of competences (the U.S. court was to resolve the outstanding legal and factual issues relating to entitlements as among various classes of investors, while the Cayman Islands court was to oversee the administration of the distribution of proceeds to claimants). To counter parallel litigation, each court had to respect the other court's action as binding. In the end, a worldwide settlement was reached, which saved a lot of money.

In the famous case In re Maxwell Communication Cooperation (1994 – 1996) similar protocols led to a good solution. In this case there were two parallel proceedings, a Chapter 11 reorganization proceeding under the U.S. Bankruptcy Code in the U.S. and an administration case and reorganization proceeding in London. As it was a multinational reorganization case, there were an operating protocol at the beginning and a distribution agreement at the end of the case. A special examiner, appointed by the U.S. court, created an operating protocol together with the London administrators to establish a cooperative administration. Later on a combined plan in order to distribute the debtor's assets was approved by the two courts. It was the first successful distribution plan adopted on a worldwide basis.

F. Direct communication

Also the UNCITRAL model law on cross-border insolvency stipulates direct communication between courts. We will hear about this later on. There are certainly a lot of questions around direct communication, which have not been solved yet, namely, how courts should communicate. From a technological point of view there are a lot of possibilities. In U.S.-Canadian insolvency cases, the courts even used joint video and telephonic hearings. There are also other difficulties, such as the language used for communication.

G. Conclusion

The few examples just mentioned show that there is international cooperation between courts in the field of insolvency law. Although no procedural questions have been answered yet, the existence of cooperating courts and of direct communication between courts and the acceptance of these circumstances as a principle is an important step towards more efficient results in international insolvency cases.

H. Situation in Switzerland

To finish off with, let us shortly look at the situation in Switzerland. Unfortunately, Switzerland has no considerable legal basis for judicial negotiation in insolvency cases.

We have not adopted the UNCITRAL model law on cross-border insolvency, and as non-members of the European Union the European Ordinance Nr. 1346/2000 of May 29 2000 unifying the international bankruptcy law between the member states does not apply. Swiss courts rarely cooperate with foreign courts because they fear that even giving information to foreign authorities without sufficient legal basis could be considered as an official secret injury punished by law. Therefore, as an important first step, Swiss law must be changed in order to provide for judicial negotiation in insolvency cases.

The Swiss Supreme Court had to decide the following case in the insolvency and reorganization procedure of the national Swiss airline "Swissair" recently: At the time the insolvency (reorganization) procedure of "Swissair" was pending in Switzerland. Lawsuits of the two Belgian creditors (namely of the national airline "Sabena" and of the Belgian State) against "Swissair" were pending at courts in Belgium for breach of contract. These creditors also filed their claims in the Swiss insolvency procedure. When the insolvency administrators in Switzerland and the Swiss courts had to decide over the acceptance of the claims of the creditors filed in the Swiss insolvency procedure, the two Belgian creditors applied for a stay of the decision in Switzerland until the lawsuits were decided by the Belgian courts. The Swiss Supreme Court, however, ruled that such a stay does not apply and that the stay would only be granted if the lawsuits were pending in Switzerland in front of Swiss courts. There was no proper cooperation. The Swiss insolvency administrators refused recognition of the claims of the Belgian creditors in the Swiss insolvency procedure and as a consequence these creditors were forced to cease appeal against the decision of the Swiss insolvency administrators and thereby to file new – and expensive – actions against the estate of Swissair in Switzerland.

Unfortunately, cooperation between Swiss and foreign courts is at the very beginning. An exception to this exists with regard to banks, which are under the supervision of the Swiss Financial Market Supervisory Authority FINMA. The FINMA has broad powers to intervene if banks are facing insolvency or already are insolvent. In such cases the FINMA is empowered to cooperate to a large extent with foreign courts. But with regard to other debtors there are neither precedents nor legal foundations for such an approach. I am glad to welcome our colleagues from abroad here in St. Gallen and I am happy to have the opportunity of considering their inputs. I think this dialogue is a first step to a creation of a more pragmatic law in Switzerland. At least there is cooperation even in Switzerland. In the light of the given legal situation it is also very important for foreign debtors as well as for foreign creditors, judges and lawyers to deal with lawyers in Switzerland, who are flexible and creative. Thank you very much ladies and gentlemen for your attention. Now, I would like to give the word to Professor Paulus.

A German's Thoughts on a Dialogue between Courts in Borders Crossing Insolvency Proceedings

CHRISTOPH G. PAULUS[1]

Unlike in almost all other areas of law, dialogue between courts or judges means not only taking into account of the others' judgments, but nothing less than, for instance, picking up the telephone and calling the colleague.[2] Cooperation and coordination of parallel insolvency proceedings has evolved in the last decade or so to somewhat like a key concept in modern international insolvency law.[3] This has to do with the evolution of the universality principle, which replaces more and more those jurisdictions that adhere to the territoriality principle. However, this evolution has not yet reached such a level of uniformity – not even in such a closely connected area as the European Union – that it were feasible to deal with any debtor's insolvency in just one proceeding under the guidance of only one insolvency law (i.e. lex concursus). Instead, universality is usually applied in a modified version – i.e. by at least offering exceptions to the general applicability of the lex concursus plus the possibility to open secondary proceedings. In the latter case, i.e. when a single debtor's insolvency is dealt with in more than one proceeding, the deficiencies of the territoriality principle with its multiple proceedings is if not avoided then at least mitigated by obligating the participating parties to cooperate and communicate and, thereby, to coordinate those parallel proceedings.

The European paradigm for this modern approach is art. 31 EIR[4] which, however, imposes respective duties just on the administrators – not also on the judges. In contrast, art. 25 of the UNCITRAL model law on cross-border insolvency addresses explicitly

---

1 Professor at Humboldt University, Berlin.

2 As happened, e.g., in the case of Amtsgericht München, NZI 2007, 495; with comments by Paulus, Die EuInsVO – wo geht die Reise hin?, NZI 2008, 1, 6.

3 See just Wessels/Markell/Kilborn, *International Cooperation in Bankruptcy and Insolvency Matters*, 2009; Paulus in: Westbrook/Booth/Paulus/Rajak, A Global View of Business Insolvency Systems (forthcoming 2010).

4 Cf. Ehricke, ZIP 2007, 2395; Omar, *Cooperation and Communication in the UNCITRAL Model Law*, Eurofenix Spring 2006, 18; Paulus, Judicial Cooperation in Cross-Border Insolvencies, available at: http://siteresources.worldbank.org/GILD/Resources/GJF2006JudicialCooperationinInsolvency_PaulusEN.pdf.; Vallender, Gerichtliche Kommunikation und Kooperation bei grenzüberschreitenden Insolvenzverfahren im Anwendungsbereich der EuInsVO – eine neue Herausforderung für die Insolvenzerichte, KTS 2008, 59; Wessels/Virgós, European Communication & Cooperation Guidelines for Cross-border Insolvency, 2007; Westbrook, International Judicial Negotiation, Texas Judicial Negotiation, Texas Int'l Law Journal 38, 2003, 567; idem, The Duty to Seek Cooperation in Multinational Insolvency Cases, in: Peter/Jeandin/Kilborn (Hrsg.), The Challenges of Insolvency Law Reform in the 21st Century, 2006 S. 361.

the courts as coordinators and even communicators (as an entitlement). Some member states of the EIR – such as Austria – include their judges into the obligation scheme by listing them in Annex C of the Regulation which contains the list of what this state declares to be a "liquidator" pursuant to art. 2 lit. b) EIR; in these cases, the courts of such member state are subject to art. 31's EIR obligations. This is not true, however, for Germany; there, the judges still are – with a few exceptions[5] – extremely reluctant to any such involvement. It might be an interesting question to search for where this attitude comes from and whether or not such attitude can (or should respectively) be upheld in the future.

A. The role of the judiciary in historical perspective and evolution

The self-image of the German judiciary has been ever since the early 19th century subject to an intense and still today ongoing debate.[6] The today often quoted description of the judge having been for a long time nothing, but the mouth-piece of the statue (taken from Montesquieu: «la bouche de la loi»[7]) has probably always been misunderstood.[8] For quite some time, this phrase was used, for instance, on purpose in order to persuade the rulers that the shift from being servant of these rulers to becoming servants of the law was completely un-dangerous and safe.

In the 19th century,[9] the characterization of the judiciary shifted from the keeper of the traditional class order to the servant of the late absolutistic principalities and to the servant of the civil society. In its first role, the judiciary was seen as the defender of the feudal hierarchy and social structure of the Ancien régime. However, both the enlightened modern rulers (they abolished the age-old so called Patrimonialgerichtsbarkeit, i.e. the nobility's private jurisdiction and court-apparatus) and the bourgeoisie opposed this concept and developed their own understanding. But finally, at the end of the 19th century, the judge again was understood as being the servant of the monarchistic state. The discussion about this characterization was accompanied by a similarly intense debate about the relationship between the statute and the judicial decision. Whereas around 1875 the tendency prevailed that the legislator presents not more than a theoretical pattern which in each individual case needs the practical individualization through the court's decision in order to become „the applicable law", a turnaround began with the enactment of the Bürgerliches Gesetzbuch (BGB = Civil

5 See footnote 1 supra.
6 See only Ogorek (ed.), Aufklärung über Justiz I, 2008.
7 De l'Esprit des Lois, I, XI, VI, 57.
8 See Ogorek, Die erstaunliche Karriere des ‚Subsumtionsmodells' oder wozu braucht der Jurist Geschichte?, in: Ogorek (supra in footnote 5), p. 93.
9 Cf. Falk, Von Dienern des Staates und von anderen Richtern. Zum Selbstverständnis der deutschen Richterschaft im 19. Jahrhundert, in: Gouron/Mayali/Padoa Schippoa/Simon (eds.), Europäische und amerikanische Richterbilder, 1996, p. 251 ff.

Law Code).[10] Despite the efforts of Ehrlich's so called „Freirechtsschule" – seeing the judge as the real legislator by attributing him the freedom to interpret the statute according to his own understanding)[11] – the mainstream went back and characterized the judge as the servant of the state and its power.

The conservatism of the judiciary in general (with some remarkable exceptions, of course) caused after the lost World War I that the Weimarer Republic's efforts to establish democracy was widely ignored if not thwarted by many judges and their decisions.[12] Instead, the „Führer" as a newly legitimized kind of monarch was hailed and supported by all kinds of methodological hotchpotch. The overarching commonality was, however, that the judiciary[13] again defined its own role as being servant of the political power if not the „Führer" alone. In the former GDR, this self-image was replaced by serving the party of the workers' class, whereas in the newly established BRD the judiciary began to see itself briefly as the keeper of the ethical order (in what is nowadays called the period of the natural justice's renaissance = Naturrechtsrenaissance) before it turned into the keeper of the constitution. The most recent emanation of this struggle for an appropriate self-understanding is the former Supreme Court's president's comparison of the judge as someone who interprets the statutory law like a musician the notes.[14]

Needless to say, that this short description of a long errantry for one's own positioning in the legal culture is somewhat misleading in that it describes the historical development only in broadest terms without doing justice to many differing and sometimes even opposing tendencies. However, for the present purposes even this sketchy description will suffice to make the point that Germany's judges, during the last 200 years (and longer), had always been closely connected with the state power. Their self-image was always defined by a sometimes more sometimes less intense interrelationship with the legislator – what always mattered was the question of how closely the judges would have to stick to the statutes' wordings and ideas. In contrast, the interrelationship with the parties was, if at all, defined in a reflex to those prevalent questions.

Two examples will clarify the issue, both are taken from civil procedure law and, thus, from the judges' original playing field. The first refers to questions of the place of ju-

10 For this development see Ogorek, Richterkönig oder Subsumtionsautomat?, 1986, p. 197 – 279.

11 About this school and its founder Ehrlich see Vogl, Soziale Gesetzgebungspolitik, freie Rechtsfindung und soziologische Rechtswissenschaft bei Eugen Ehrlich, 2002.

12 For this, see Drosdeck, Richterbilder und richterliches Selbstverständnis in der Weimarer Republik, in: Gouron et al. (as in the previous footnote), p. 293 ff.

13 This is true not only for the judiciary. My former teacher and friend, Prof. S. Riesenfeld, told me that Prof. Kohlrausch from the then Friedrich-Wilhelms-Universität at Berlin (nowadays Humboldt-Universität) inculcated his students that „wir Juristen sitzen nur auf dem Kutschbock! Wir fahren dorthin, wohin die Herrschaft befiehlt!" (We lawyers are sitting just on the coach box. We are driving where the master orders us to go to).

14 Hirsch, Auf dem Weg zum Richterstaat?, JZ 2007, p. 853 ff.; Rüthers, Hatte die Rechtsperversion in den deutschen Diktaturen ein Gesicht?, JZ 2007, p. 556 ff.; idem, Fortgesetzter Blindflug oder Methodendämmerung der Justiz? Zur Auslegungspraxis der obersten Bundesgerichte, JZ 2008, p. 446 ff.

risdictions, the second to the model of knowledge distribution within a procedure. As to the jurisdiction issue, it is a well-known fact that the continental law approach is almost contrary to that of the common law world in that it strives for utmost ex ante-clarity and predictability. Whereas the English or US-judges have no problems in handling the vagueness of a "forum non conveniens" which ultimately leads to the (hopefully) better suited court dealing with the case, do their continental counterparts ask for the legislator's utmost precision. This discrepancy in legal understanding,[15] but also self-esteem, cannot be better pinned down than by the ECJ's decision called "Owusu".[16] The English court had asked whether or not it would be allowed to refer the case to Jamaica as the better suited place of jurisdiction on the basis of "forum non conveniens". After all, the plaintiff was an English citizen, but had had an accident in Jamaica where all the relevant evidentiary circumstances could have been directly checked; therefore, four out of six defendants were domiciled in Jamaica. However, the plaintiff pleaded for the applicability of art. 2 of the (then) European Convention on Jurisdiction and the Recognition and Enforcement of Judgments and the ECJ followed his argumentation. There is hardly any stronger opposition imaginable against such judicial freedom.

The facts of the second example are taken from the International Law Association's report (2008) on International Commercial Arbitration: "Both common and civil law are in agreement that facts are to be pleaded and proven by the parties and that courts in general should decide on proven facts and should not make inquiries as to issues not raised by the parties. The legal traditions, however, diverge as to causes of action and the status of law in civil litigation. In the common law, the parties are to indicate the cause of action and to assist the court in applying the law by giving the legal arguments that support the relief sought. On the other hand, many civil law countries have a tradition where the maxim iura novit curia applies under which the court is assumed to know the law and where the parties have only to prove the facts supporting their claim and identify the relief they seek. Courts may then identify the cause of action and apply the law to make a decision. In this respect, courts are authorized to recharacterize facts (since characterization is a legal process), in certain cases may modify the cause of action if the claim would fail under the cause of action identified by a party but not under a different cause of action and substitute its legal reasoning for that of the parties."[17] This description, again, could not be clearer in showing the procedural barriers in the civil law tradition against communication even between the judges and the parties – let alone with third parties.

15 For another striking example see the contribution of Prof. Chalas in this volume.
16 European Court of Justice, Owusu v Jackson et al., dec. from 1.3.2005 – C 281/02, EuZW 2005, 345.
17 Text by Friedman/Radicati di Brozolo/De Ly, p. 852.

B. The role of the judge in bankruptcy proceedings – earlier and today

Having come to this conclusion so far, it is now essential to clarify a judge's role in an insolvency proceeding – again, in its historical development.[18] Here, I can be briefer – since there is a clear tendency from the almost exclusively court-driven "Gantprocess" in the 19th century to the increased creditors' autonomy in the modern Insolvency Ordinance (Insolvenzordnung) from 1999. The dominating role of the judge in that "Gantprocess" was a relict of the enormous influence of Salgado de Somoza's treatise "Labyrinthus creditorum concurrentium ad litem per debitorem communem inter illos causatam", 1651, in Germany.[19] However, the Bankruptcy Ordinance (Konkursordnung) from 1877 did away with this court-centration and assigned many of the previous court-tasks to the creditors and the administrator respectively. Moreover, the bankruptcy judge's role was restricted to a supervisory task with only very limited competence to decide about litigious issues; in other words, there was almost no vis attractiva concursus. What started already in the Bankruptcy Ordinance was amplified in the Insolvency Ordinance. Here, the creditors play an even bigger role in the course of the proceedings;[20] thereby leaving the judge even less space for action.

To be sure, this restricted function would absolutely be tolerable in liquidation proceedings. After all, in very simplified and condensed words, what is needed in this type of proceeding is a good salesperson. Of course, this is more often than not a highly complicated task with innumerable pitfalls which make the job difficult enough. But, generally speaking, the complexity of these tasks is less than the ones in reorganization proceedings. As my colleague, Prof. Flessner, puts it: "Que cosa può fare il diritto fallimentare per la conservazione delle imprese in crisi? Salvare un'impresa dal fallimento richiede solitamente un combinazione di misure organizzative, commerciali, finanziarie e giuridiche. Il processo fallimentare risponde solo delle misure giuridiche."[21] In fact, the Insolvency Ordinance addresses only legal measures and ignores the organizational, commercial, and financial ones. But they are essential when it comes to a debtor's reorganization; what is required there is an

---

18 See A. Meier, Die Geschichte des deutschen Konkursrechts, insbesondere die Entstehung der Reichskonkursordnung von 1877, 2003.

19 About author, book and its influence, see Forster, Konkurs als Verfahren, 2008; Smid, Auf der „spanischen Straße" in das Labyrinth des Konkurses, Festschrift für G. Fischer, 2008, p. 489 ff.; Uhlenbruck, Zur Geschichte des Konkurses, DZWIR 2007, p. 1, 3; K.Schmidt, Labyrinthus creditorum – Gesellschaftsrechtliche Haftung im Insolvenzverfahren nach §§ 92, 93 InsO –, Zeitschrift für Unternehmens- und Gesellschaftsrecht (ZGR), 1996, p. 209 ff.; Hanisch, Bemerkungen zur Geschichte des internationalen Insolvenzrechts Festschrift Merz, 1992, p. 165 ff.; Walder, Francisco de Samoza's „Labyrinthus creditorum concurrentium", Zeitschrift für Schweizerisches Recht 1964, p. 239 ff.

20 Cf. Hänel, Gläubigerautonomie und das Insolvenzplanverfahren, 2000; Riedemann, Zur Entwicklung des Konkursrechts seit Inkrafttreten der Konkursordnung unter dem Aspekt der Gläubigerautonomie, 2004; Beissenhirtz, Gläubigerautonomie in der Insolvenz, Festschrift E. Braun, 2007, p. 183 ff.

21 Flessner, La Conservazione delle imprese attraverso il diritto fallimentare. Un sguardo di diritto comparato, In: Il Diritto Fallimentare 2009, 1, 3.

entrepreneur. The differences between these two ideal administrator types causes by itself enormous problems in establishing the new type of proceeding – this is true at least for Germany.

The new approach towards a debtor's insolvency requires, however, a different reaction of the supervising judge, too. It is one thing to control the legality of a sale and another one to control the legality of an ongoing business. Not only that the judge is, generally speaking, unfamiliar with the latter task; he is also more at risk since continuation of a business is more complex, is longer lasting, and is harder to supervise due to the diversity of the abovementioned facets. In sum, what is needed in a reorganization proceeding is a judge with a solid understanding of how management and business works in daily life. This is to say, that parallel to the need of a new type of insolvency administrator there is also a need for a new type of insolvency judge – at least in reorganization cases. The changed circumstances of how the debtor's estate is dealt with in the latter scenario make it advisable if not necessary to communicate with the stakeholders; this is just one more example for Maine's observation that things tend to move from status to contract.[22]

C. Universalism as a managing task

A similar increase of complexity is inevitably connected with the increased existence and importance of cross-border insolvency cases. This is not just because there is another set of rules to be taken into account; it is also due to the fact that insolvency law constitutes something like a meta-level of the entire domestic law. Since insolvency law is so closely intertwined with all sorts of other regulatory fields such as tax law, secured transaction law, unfair competition law, environment protection law, etc. – including even the soft law of Corporate Governance recommendations –, the need of respecting an additional insolvency law means to respect this entire universe. After the preceding observations, it is needless to state that this complexity is even graver when the respective insolvency is a reorganization case. But even in plain liquidation settings, cross-border cases are regularly much more complicated and more complex than their purely domestic counterparts. Their handling requires a multi-dimensional attention and awareness of the acting administrators which goes well beyond the abovementioned salespersons' skills. In particular, when the original singular insolvency proceeding is split up into more than one proceeding through the opening of secondary proceedings managerial capacity is indispensable. Arrt. 31 ff. EIR, accordingly, impose duties of team-working on the administrators.

22 To be sure – "contract" is here to be understood as "entering into communication". For Maine's dictum see: Ancient Law, its connection with the early history of society and its relation to modern ideas, with an introduction and notes by Sir Frederick Pollock, 4th American from the 10th London edition; Chapter V, p. 165.

This exclusive reference to the administrator brings me back to my initial remarks about the self-image of the German judiciary. Since the judge is not addressed in Art. 31 EIR as communicating party, many judges see this as their clear exemption from any such duty. To be sure, there are remarkable counter-examples. But these are individual cases; they depend on the individual judge's mentality and understanding and, thus, cannot be generalized. Quite to the contrary, the majority still hides behind those methodological "obstacles" such as a law which keeps silence about the judge as addressee of a communication duty.

Up to this point, the preceding deliberations are more or less descriptive. Their conclusion is that a long lasting tradition of self-definition and self-orientation has concentrated almost exclusively on the judges' role with respect to the state and its legislative powers. What was never really discussed was the judges' relationship to other, let alone to foreign judges. They could, for centuries, be approached only through the help of the state and its diplomatic channels. Moreover, the preceding observations have shown that, at least in Germany, the changed demands of the modern insolvency law have not yet fully reached the relevant actors' awareness. In particular, the need for a more active role of the judge is a telling example of the general trend "from status to contract" which is a step still to be pursued. Finally, the complexity of modern cross-border insolvency cases must lead to the same conclusion as to the judge's involvement in the contractual, i.e. communicative, behavior. Since this alone helps to reduce the complexities of the respective cases. The latter, however, is already a normative recommendation! It is to be hoped that this message will be recognized and accepted by the addressees of the presented thoughts.

International Bankruptcy Law

JAY WESTBROOK[1]

I want to begin by thanking Carl and his whole staff that has produced such a marvellous conference, intellectually and logistically. It has been delightful. On the other hand, it is rather cruel to the audience to bring in the bankruptcy people after lunch on the last day. I was reminded of standing up in the Delaware Equity Court, which is where all the great corporate cases are decided in the United States, to argue a case. I got no more than my name out, before the judge said, "You are a professor, aren't you?" And I said "Yes.". He said, "Can I go to sleep now?" I said, "Well judge, the students usually give me five minutes." He replied, "Alright, I will give you five minutes." I must tell you, I won the case.

You have already heard two excellent presentations on why the insolvency area is one in which this business of international communication among courts and even directly between courts has developed more rapidly. I will talk about some bankruptcy cases as we go along. But I want to emphasize that this is also happening outside of bankruptcy, although more slowly, more tentatively, and less often. I may even proselytize a little bit and urge my colleagues in other areas of civil litigation to consider that this sort of contact among courts is an important and increasingly a necessary way for international litigation to be managed effectively for the benefit of the parties. My title here is "International Judicial Negotiation" and negotiation, of course, always involves communication. But communication also has a virtue in and of itself. Thus, although this talk is about judicial negotiation, it is also about judicial communication. Whenever I say to judges, you are engaged in negotiation, they always bridle and say, "No, I am a judge, I do not negotiate with people, I decide the case." But certainly in the international context judges who are responsible and helpful to the parties must negotiate, meaning, they must be prepared to cooperate with each other. And human cooperation inevitably involves some level of negotiation. So, that is a large part of my topic today as well.

This cooperation can happen and communication can happen in many different ways. Everyone is familiar with the formal letter of request process. That sort of thing is certainly common. But more and more, there are informal conversations, informal letters and even telephone calls as Christoph described a few minutes ago. As mentioned by Daniel, in US and Canadian insolvency cases it has become relatively routine to have joint hearings, either on the telephone or video hearings between the courts. And finally, there are protocols, actual agreements, as in the case Daniel described, and I will talk some more about that later.

---

1 Benno C. Schmidt Chair of Business Law Professor at the University of Texas at Austin School of Law.

Perhaps the ultimate example of multi-national litigation at the moment is Flashlines. I think we are going to hear more about that later, but here you have the case of a crash in the Red Sea of an Egyptian aircraft. You have parallel cases in France and California. The California case is dismissed for forum non conveniens, which we will learn more about shortly, conditioned on the French court taking jurisdiction. Then, France refuses to take jurisdiction, then that is reversed on appeal and it is now pending. But this is an extraordinary case. And a classic example I would want to argue of cases where everyone would have been better served had there been a level of communication between courts, rather than each of them acting in their own narrow procedural universes without regard to what was happening in the other countries.

As Daniel mentioned, I wrote an article back in 2003 about this subject of judicial communication and negotiation and what I hope to do today is to give you a little bit of an update in terms of recent cases and also a little survey that I have done, that I hope you will find interesting in that regard. There are a couple of recent articles that will give you many of the relevant citations and you might want to take a look at them if you have a chance.

Daniel has already covered beautifully the argument that I made in that 2003 article, but I will emphasize that insolvency is an area in which this has been most developed, because bankruptcy is an operation on a living patient. As Christoph pointed out, we are trying very frequently to save a business; maybe for the owners, maybe it will be sold, but we are trying to save the going concern value of the business. We know that if we auction it off, we will lose that value. So, it is an operation on a living patient. Justice Farley in Canada is one of the leading judges in this whole area and much involved in judicial communication. He said regular civil litigation is autopsy law. Five years ago something bad happened and now we are deciding who has to pay for it. But bankruptcy law increasingly, nowadays, is a living case all over the world at a single time in which value will be gained or lost in six months or a year or less.

And finally, we have had a little discussion of the model law as promulgated by UNCITRAL in 1997. It has now been adopted by 18 countries including a number of the major commercial countries of the world. In Articles 15 and 25 to 27, it explicitly authorizes direct communication between insolvency administrators and also between courts, so that in a civil law country in particular, the judge has an authorization in the statute to communicate directly with other judges if the judge is so inclined.

To summarize over all, negotiation means communication plus conditionality, that is to say, one court either takes or is prepared to take an action conditioned on some action or step that another court might take. It does not have to mean a formal agreement. It does not have to mean an agreement signed with ribbons and feathers, as we say. That sort of thing is increasingly happening. But it includes also implicit agreements, agreements that are implicit in an action taken that is conditioned on an action by the other court.

Communication is important in itself. It is particularly important because it informs the other court. It informs the other court about the law in our jurisdiction. It informs the other court about the state of the proceeding in our jurisdiction. It is important because it provides an opportunity for the other court to know what we intend to do here. As in Christoph's example, we may advise that we intend to open a case by Monday. It is enormously helpful for the judges in each court to know these things in real time rather than at some later time. I emphasize that is not only in insolvency cases. We live in a world, a remarkable world, in which all of us can be in email communication with an enormous number of people, hundreds of millions of people in an instant. All of us can pick up the phone if we can afford to do it and call around the world. And increasingly rates have come down so we can afford to do it. We live in a world too in which hundreds of millions or even billions of Dollars or Euros or whatever can be transferred very quickly from one country to another. We live in a world moving too fast for letters of request or the process of issuing an opinion and six months later you will enforce it or you will not. In all civil litigation, these traditional procedures are simply no longer adequate to the task presented us by a globalizing world.

Finally before I plunge into more details I want to make this larger point. This business of cooperation, communication and negotiation, is part of a much larger subject that I hope all of you will think about. That subject is this: What is the optimal forum for the resolution of a particular judicial dispute? In what country, in what court on the face of the globe, do we find the best place, the most sensible place, the most cost effective place, the fairest place to resolve this litigation? Traditionally, we have proceeded as if the other litigation did not exist. Bankruptcy makes it almost impossible for us to do that. It forces us as a necessity to begin to communicate and to try to decide which court perhaps ought to be the primary court in resolving this set of difficulties. I would suggest to you that addressing this question is the direction we should be going in civil litigation generally. Where is the best place for this matter to be resolved?

Inverworld is a case that has already been described to you, a classic instance, perhaps *the* classic instance of communication and cooperation. There a protocol was made among three different countries. Each country gave its approval, each court's approval expressly conditioned upon the actions taken by the other two courts. So, this was the classic three way negotiation among courts.

Federal Mogul is going to be discussed later by Adam. It is a limited success in this area, but nonetheless one in which a protocol was agreed in an enormous multibillion dollar transnational case in which everyone agreed that the protocol saved a lot of time and money, even though ultimately some aspects of the resolution were not agreed. He will tell you more about all of that.

Flashlines I have already mentioned. We will hear more on that later. But it is a recent conditional-dismissal case. It is a case in which an Anglo-American court, in this case the California court, dismisses a case for forum non conveniens, but on the condition that there is an adequate forum available elsewhere. In this case the only adequate forum was held to be France. So that if the French forum turned out for whatever reason not to be available to these plaintiffs, whose loved one had been injured in the Red Sea crash, then they could come back to the court and say, no, we could not get into the French court. Please reopen the case here in California. So, this is a conditional dismissal, conditioned upon the French court being prepared to take jurisdiction. In my view this is classic judicial negotiation. You will hear more about how that came out as we go along.

Another case goes beyond a forum non conveniens with a dismissal conditioned on jurisdiction in the other country. The case involved IP litigation in the United States and Canada. The condition was not only that the Quebec court take jurisdiction. The US judge said, if the Quebec court does not take jurisdiction or fails to act within four years, I will reopen the case here in the United States. So, in effect the US court was saying, as long as you proceed and resolve this case in a timely way, fine, I am happy for you to have the jurisdiction, but otherwise, I will return to the fray and I will take it up and I will resolve it. This is a classic conditional dismissal. It is a classic negotiation among courts.

Now, we move from negotiation to simple communication. A classic case is Cenargo and I take it Adam is going to mention this, but he suggested I should go ahead and talk about it. Briefly, in Cenargo we had a clash of injunctions. It was a Chapter 11 bankruptcy case filed in the United States. There was an administration, also a reorganization case, filed in England. The US judge took the position that the filing of the English case violated the automatic stay or moratorium of the American court. The American court claims a world wide jurisdiction over the debtor's property (as most bankruptcy courts do) and therefore was going to hold the English lawyers in contempt. The English court was, of course, much put out by this proposition and therefore it issued an injunction forbidding anyone from going to court in the United States on pain of contempt. Everyone was walking a tight rope above the lions and tigers, obviously a deplorable situation to say the least.

How was it resolved? It was resolved by the lawyers persuading both judges, the English judge and the American judge, to get on the telephone together, which they did, with the lawyers, I should say, on the phone at the same time and with a transcript taken of the conversation. The judges were able to ease their way around this very awkward, prickly situation and arrive at an agreement in the course of which things sorted themselves out. The case went forward in the UK as it should have done all along because it was a UK based case and nobody went to jail, best of all from the lawyers point of view. This is a classic case where I think only direct communication could have solved this case short of serious embarrassment and serious loss for everyone concerned, including the courts and the lawyers.

More recent cases: Golden Honey involved Israel and the US. Here is a classic case where communication would have done an enormous amount of good. The US court was hesitant to recognize an Israeli receivership because it did not think the Israeli receivership was a collective proceeding within the meaning of the model law, which is now part of American law. The Israeli court was not sure about the scope of the American automatic stay. The consequence was that both courts once again enjoined each other. I do not know the outcome of that one. It was a classic instance where had the judges been on the telephone together or even exchanged informal letters, but in real time by fax or by email, they could have informed each other of the state of the law in their own jurisdictions, no more than that, and found, I suspect, some accommodation.

The Harms case in the UK, which also involved the US, is another very interesting case. It was a UK administration. While the administration was pending an attachment was obtained in New York against various funds of the debtor that were in New York. The UK court then issued an anti-suit injunction against the attachments in the US, thus freezing them. In that situation, the Harms court then published an opinion, which it said was designed to explain its action to the US court. It says this explicitly in the opinion: This is designed to explain to the US court why we would reluctantly issue an injunction against the US case going forward. As it turned out, the US court accepted the resolution. Once again, nobody went to jail and it was a happy result. But, it seems to me clear that, rather than publishing an opinion, which was only issued some time later, it would have been much better for this matter to be resolved by some direct communication. The answer may be that there was informal communication, that it simply is not reflected in the reported cases and that only the litigants know that that happened. It is a classic instance where communication was the best answer, but may not have been reflected fully in the official reports.

I want to tell you briefly about a survey that I took. This does not pretend to be great empirical work. I have done a fair amount of more rigorous empirical work. This is not statistically reliable but it is suggestive and interesting I hope. I surveyed the members of the International Insolvency Institute, who are about 275 very distinguished lawyers who are interested in international insolvency. I got a response rate of about 25% which believe it or not in the survey business is quite a good return.

About 81% of the respondents had knowledge of parallel litigation in bankruptcy. My first question inquired if there had been direct communication between courts or administrators in the cases you know about. Seventy-one percent of them said yes, which seems to me is very striking. Ninety-three percent of the lawyers reported this communication resulted in some cooperation. So, in the great majority of cases this communication had a positive effect. Sixty percent reported good cooperation, not just some cooperation, but good cooperation. Again, I do not pretend there is scientific accuracy here, but I think it is very suggestive and very positive.

I also asked about a lesser form of direct communication, between lawyers and accountants. Seventy-six percent of the respondents knew of this sort of communication. Ninety-seven percent reported some cooperation, but only twenty-six percent said it was good cooperation. So, to the extent one might rely on these figures, which one should not, nonetheless it suggests that direct communication between courts and administrators may be superior to mere communication between the professionals involved. At least this possibility is worthy of further research.

Finally, what about protocols? Protocols are essentially agreements the lawyers work out that then are approved by each of the courts involved. How many of these responding lawyers knew about cases with achieved protocols? The answer was only six percent. So, as important as these protocols may be, it seems that such formal agreements were obtained in relatively few cases. Six percent of the lawyers said people tried to achieve such protocols but were not successful. So, that is some measure how far we still have to go in these cooperative efforts.

My conclusions from the survey are, first a surprising number of these cases resulted in or included direct communication between administrators and courts. This is much more than I would have guessed. It is very encouraging to me. Secondly, I have noticed, since I wrote my original article, that there are fewer cases that talk about direct communication, that talk about what amounts to judicial negotiation. I speculate that the lack of reported cases might arise, paradoxically, because there is more of it going on. Perhaps it is going on informally. It is going on by telephone. It is going on in ways that are beneath the radar, as we say, of the normal legal methods of reporting and therefore we may actually have more such communication than we have had up to now.

Just one final point: Adam is going to talk about Justice Richards hesitating about judicial communication in the Federal Mogul case. I think that maybe in the question period, if we have time, we can talk about possible solutions for the problems that he saw.

Thank you very much for your attention, late in an afternoon with a subject that is as seemingly dry as bankruptcy.

International Bankruptcy Law: Judicial Dialogue. An English Perspective.

ADAM GOODISON[1]

This brief article looks at processes, both statutory and pursuant to the inherent jurisdiction of the English High Court, where judicial dialogue is possible and/or has taken place in practice. Insolvency law provides one of the best examples of local courts showing a willingness to cooperate and work with each other to achieve common objectives. Statute law, both local and on a European basis by Directive has given statutory teeth to what previously in England was often done pursuant to the inherent jurisdiction of the court.

First to statute. The Insolvency Act 1986, section 426 (4) provides: "*The courts having jurisdiction in relation to insolvency law in any part of the United Kingdom shall assist the courts having the corresponding jurisdiction in … any relevant country or territory.*"

Section 426 (5) provides: "*For the purposes of subsection (4) a request made to a court in any part of the United Kingdom by a court … in a relevant country or territory is authority for the court to which the request is made to apply, in relation to any matters specified in the request, the insolvency law which is applicable by either court in relation to comparable matters falling within its jurisdiction. In exercising its discretion under this subsection, a court shall have regard in particular to the rules of private international law.*"

Relevant countries or territories are the Channel Islands, Isle of Man, Anguilla, Australia, the Bahamas, Bermuda, Botswana, Canada, Cayman Islands, Falkland Islands, Gibraltar, Hong Kong, Republic of Ireland, Montserrat, New Zealand, St Helena, Turks and Caicos Islands, Tuvalu and the Virgin Islands, Malaysia, South Africa, Brunei.

There was no precursor in Companies Act 1948 (repealed and replaced by the Companies Act 1985, and now the Companies Act 2006). Provision was made however for letters of request in section 122 Bankruptcy Act 1914 regarding "*every British court*" regarding orders of the court seeking aid.

1 Barrister at Law, Grays Inn, London.

Next, to give some practical examples of where letters of request have been used, and the purpose of their use.

Re HIH *Casualty and General Insurance Ltd* [2008] 1 WLR 852 (UKHL) concerned 4 insurance companies which were in liquidation in Australia pursuant to Australian winding up orders. There were English provisional liquidations also in place (which are commonly used in England as regards insurance companies because it avoids the need to have a creditors meeting which would be required in liquidation, and thus avoids the need to assess the values of policyholders of which there may be many thousands). By an Australian letter of request, the Australian Court requested the remission of assets held in England to Australian liquidators for distribution. The Australian scheme for distribution in insolvency was different to English distribution rules in that in Australia preference was given to insurance creditors to prejudice of other creditors. The English House of Lords (the highest English Court, now replaced by the UK Supreme Court) decided that the request should be complied with and the assets should be remitted and paid to Australia despite the differing distribution processes under the two laws. Their Lordships' opinion held that the mere fact that under the insolvency laws applicable in Australia there would be a significant class of preferential creditors whose debts would not have priority under English law was insufficient reason to refuse to remit the assets, and that there was nothing unacceptably discriminatory or unfair about the Australian insolvency scheme in relation to preferential creditors which would justify an English court refusing to exercise its discretion to remit. Accordingly it was appropriate to order remission of the assets to Australia for distribution by the Australian liquidators in accordance with Australian law.

Re Bank of Credit and Commerce International SA (No 10) [1997] Ch 213 concerned the Luxembourg incorporated BCCI SA. There were principal winding up proceedings in Luxembourg, and an ancillary winding up in England. The liquidators had procured the BCCI companies to enter pooling agreements and agreements between liquidators that the liquidation worldwide should be a joint enterprise with all creditors wherever situated receiving the same level of dividend from a central pool. However, the English rules of liquidation set off were different to Luxembourg rules of set off. Therefore the English liquidators asked the English Court whether the English liquidators should remit assets to Luxembourg only after allowing for English set off rights, or whether Luxembourg set off rights applied. *Sir Richard Scott* V-C held that the ancillary nature of the English liquidation did not relieve the English Court of the obligation to apply English insolvency law and that there was no power to disapply rule 4.90 of the Insolvency Rules (the mandatory set off rule) and accordingly English set off should take effect before any remission of assets to Luxembourg. Thus creditors with set off rights were protected under English local law.

There is also an inherent jurisdiction of the English Court pursuant to which it is willing to issue letters of request. In *Re Nortel Networks* SA [2009] BCC 343 there were insolvency proceedings in Canada, the USA and England. The English Administrators requested the English Court to send letters of request (under the inherent jurisdiction of the court) to the courts of a number of EU Member States asking those courts to put in place arrangements under which the Joint Administrators would be given notice of any request or application for the opening of secondary proceedings under the EC Insolvency Proceedings Regulation in those local jurisdictions. The purpose of the letter was so that the Joint Administrators would be able to explain to any EU Member State court why the local opening of any such proceedings would not be in the interests of creditors. The judge said *"It seems to me highly desirable that the assistance of the foreign courts specified in the schedule to the draft order should be sought with a view to enabling the joint administrators to be heard prior to the opening of any secondary insolvency proceedings in these jurisdictions and I will therefore authorise the sending of appropriate letters of request to the judicial authorities in those states."*

The examples of judges actually speaking to one another from differing jurisdictions are few – and in fact amount to only one example so far. *Re Cenargo* took place in the English High Court, Chancery Division in January/February 2003. The group was an international shipping group. The English Judge, Mr Justice Lightman appointed provisional liquidators over Cenargo. Judge Drain in the USA granted Chapter 11 relief and founded jurisdiction in the USA on the basis of a bank account opened by Cenargo management to found jurisdiction in the USA (somewhat artificially). A telephone conversation was organised between the two judges to establish which jurisdiction should take control, and which jurisdiction was in truth the most appropriate jurisdiction for the insolvency proceedings. It soon became apparent to both judges that England was the appropriate jurisdiction and the New York proceedings fell away.

An invitation to talk was made in another English case, but turned down. *Re T&N Limited* [2004] EWHC 2878 (Ch) (David Richards J) concerned T&N and its subsidiaries which were subject to parallel proceedings in England (consisting of administration insolvency proceedings) and in the USA (where the proceedings were chapter 11 proceedings). Massive scale asbestos claims had led to the insolvencies. In the USA there was a proposed reorganization plan promulgated, which would have been binding under US law if supported by the creditors and confirmed by the US Court.

The US plan proponents applied to the English Court for an order for direct communication between the two courts. There was serious divisions among creditor groups as to the terms of the US reorganization plan. Important UK based creditors (including the trustees of the T&N pension scheme and UK based asbestos claimants) objected to the plan – which could only be enforceable in England through company voluntary arrangements or schemes of arrangement (pursuant to which claims can be compromised and then be statutorily enforced if the requisite majorities of creditors are achieved).

One of the fundamental issues on which the parties were divided was how to make an appropriate estimate of current and future asbestos claims. The judge commented: *"The purpose of the Plan Proponents' present application is to initiate a direct communication between the US Court and this court regarding the process for an estimation of the aggregate amount of current and future asbestos personal injury claims against the UK debtors and the purposes for which such determination should be used."*

The plan proponents emphasized to the English Court that they were not seeking a direction that the decision of one court would be binding on the other. They said that the aim of the communication was to identify the issues which were relevant to both jurisdictions and to ensure that the process in one court or another to estimate asbestos claims was, to the maximum extent possible, likely to be recognized and given effect to by the other court.

The administrators made clear to the Judge that they strongly opposed the direction to communicate. The Judge commented: *"They do not oppose a communication to the US Court which identifies and explains issues of English law and procedure which would arise in an assessment of the likely level of admissible asbestos claims in an English winding up of the relevant companies. They do however oppose any communication between the courts which is designed to ensure so far as possible that the process in the US Court led to a decision likely to be recognised as being recognised as binding by this Court."*

In his decision, the highly experienced Judge, Mr Justice David Richards, said as follows:

"The problem is that it is these highly controversial issues, including the issue of whether the decision of the US Court should be binding on the administrators, which are liable to be the subject of application to this court. In these circumstances it would not in my view be appropriate for me to discuss those issues, with a view to finding or laying the ground for a common or binding resolution, with the US Court. If any constructive step were to come out of it, it is liable to have the effect of pre-empting to some extent the later proceedings on those issues in this Court. There would exist, as it seems to me, a real risk of prejudging those proceedings or appearing to do so. Even a general discussion with the US Court on these issues carries these risks."

"At root I do not consider it appropriate for this Court to enter into substantive discussions with the US Court on matters of controversy between the parties which may come before the Court for decision. As and when appropriate, the Court should hear argument on the relevant issues and give its judgment on them.

In the light of that judgment, inter Court communications may be appropriate."

"In adopting this approach, I am not seeking to nullify the process of inter court communications before they have even started. That is not my intention. As I have said more than once already, I support the view that inter court communications can have a vital role to play in major cross border insolvencies such as these ... But in considering an application for inter court communications the court must necessarily proceed on a case by case basis, balancing the

desirability of inter court communications against other relevant factors. The circumstances of this particular application have led me to conclude that a direct inter court discussion of the issues would not be appropriate at this stage."

Statute law continued to march. In force since 4 April 2006 in England are the Cross Border Insolvency Regulations 2006 which enact the UNCITRAL Model Law on Insolvency in its UK version: see Schedule 1, CBIR. By Schedule 1, Article 25 cooperation and direct communication between a court of Great Britain and foreign courts or foreign representatives is provided for.

"1. *In matters referred to in paragraph 1 of article 1, the court may cooperate to the maximum extent possible with foreign courts or foreign representatives, either directly or through a British insolvency officeholder."*

"2. *The court is entitled to communicate directly with, or to request information or assistance directly from foreign courts or foreign representatives."*

So when, as a matter of practice, will judicial communication occur? At an INSOL conference in Cape Town in March 2007 there was a panel discussion between 4 judges from England, Australia, Bermuda and US. On that occasion Mr Justice Lightman suggested that direct judicial communication should occur only:

- Where the communication is necessary;
- Where there are sufficient procedural safeguards in place to ensure that parties have an opportunity to be heard on the application to communicate and (if appropriate) to attend the occasion on which the communication takes place; and
- On matters which do not concern the substantive merits of any dispute.

The English Judges, in terms of due process, need to take account of the provisions of the Human Rights Act 1998 (which enacted the European Convention on Human Rights into UK law) and in particular Article 6 which provides: "*In the determination of his civil rights and obligations … everyone is entitled to a fair and public hearing within a reasonable time by an independent and impartial tribunal established by law.*"

It is a genuine pleasure to come to St Gallen with warm greetings from London, and news from the rather distant shores somewhere off the north west of Europe.

Discussion

DANIEL HUNKELER

Thank you very much, Adam, for this remarkable, interesting and riving speech. We have fifteen more minutes and I ask you, dear colleagues, ladies and gentlemen, do you have any questions? Please ask your questions.

CARL BAUDENBACHER

Well, first of all, I am impressed by this panel. I had heard Jay Westbrook speaking on the subject a couple of years ago in Texas and there seems to be an unbelievable development going on, unbelievable from the perspective of those who are not involved in bankruptcy proceedings. Many things struck me: First of all, judges picking up the phone. In an international courts context that is virtually the worst thing you can do because if a judge, who is sitting on an international court picks up the phone, the suspicion will be that he will call his own government. So it is a fine line you are walking here. Now, Adam said that a judge may pick up the phone or not. It could also amount to a violation of the right to a fair trial. I would like to hear more on that. Whether it should only happen under the strict conditions which have been formulated or whether there are judges who feel free to do that.

The second point I would like to take up is the idea of the best place judge. I think that is an idea which we see also in other fields. I recall that when the Council passed Regulation 1/2003, the so-called Modernisation Regulation in competition law, the number of competition law enforcers was multiplied. Now we have 28 competition law enforcers in the European Union and three in the EFTA States belonging to the European Economic Area. The ones in the Union form the so-called European Competition Network. If you have a cartel which extends to more than one member state, the case is assigned to the best placed competition authority. That seems to be exactly the same concept. And that is probably a concept which we will also see in other fields.

ADAM GOODISON

I have probably said enough, I thought it would be quite interesting too. I think all I have said regards the English judges is that they are very procedure driven. The first instance judge is always thinking about what the Court of Appeal might be thinking and if you are a litigator and you are going to lose, you want to lose in the most spectacular way possible. You really want the first instance judge to start abusing you and abusing your client because you have a green card as regards the Court of Appeal. The clever first instance judges are very aware of process and that is why they are very cautious about it. You see it in a number of instances, you see it particularly that the English Court is able under our procedural rules to make orders entirely of its own motion, but English judges very rarely do it because of the dangers involved. I had a case where actually the judge fell madly in love with one of the litigants. It was a very, very glamorous American woman and he dismissed her original case on her pleading entirely but then, in the last four pages of his judgment, he made up a brand new case for her, which nobody had ever argued and, of course, the Court of Appeal decided that his judgment should be overturned. So, I think that explains a bit more of the background as to why the English judges are very cautious. But I am interested to hear what Christoph and Jay think.

CHRISTOPH PAULUS

There is an additional facet to that, it is a complication in insolvency law: The position of the role of the insolvency judge is defined in the particular system. This refers to the so called "vis attractiva concursus". This means that the insolvency judge is deciding everything, i.e. on all substantive issues as well; prototype of this system is the USA. On the other side of the spectrum, you have the German model where the insolvency judge is just a supervising authority, deciding almost no substantive question. Disputes in this respect are to be decided by the particular courts which are already in existence. So, that is a different approach and that is why for the German judge, as well as for many continental European judges, communication would be much easier since as long as you do not have "vis attractiva concursus" you are not in danger to prejudice yourself for a future decision.

JAY WESTBROOK

Responding directly to your point, Carl, about the concern about a judge picking up the phone, although it also goes to why Judge Richards declined to do in Federal Mogul. First of all, the American Law Institute as part of its trans-national insolvency project, which was devoted to try and to find methods of cooperation within NAFTA on these insolvency matters, included an appendix of guidelines which was adopted by the American Law Institute. It has now also been adopted by the International Insolvency Institute. It has been translated into about thirty different languages and has been adopted by a number of courts. So, one solution to this problem is to adopt guidelines of this sort which provide no such call is made until everyone involved has been notified and, has an appropriate opportunity to comment. People have an opportunity to participate in this sort of communication in the sense of at least listening to what is said and so forth. So the procedural protections are very important, but they are also achievable.

Secondly, I would say with respect to something like the Federal Mogul situation, a telephone call like that or perhaps an exchange of letters or whatever; it is much like the visit of a Prime Minister, you know, to sign a new trade agreement. I mean, it is not done without preparation, without the lawyers, if their doing their jobs, having prepared a sort of agenda, making sure that certain subjects are out of bounds, and so forth all that can be done, all that is being done even as we sit here today in these large multinational insolvencies, especially within North America. So, yes these are serious problems but they are absolutely addressable and the pay off for addressing them is resolving these questions in real time. I have great respect for Justice Richards. I want to emphazise that, I do not think he is anti-internationalist at all, he is certainly not a parochial judge; but nonetheless the effect of his unwillingness to communicate (whatever the lawyers maybe should have done in that case and perhaps did not do), the effect of that is that the American Court then has to come up with a plan. The plan has to go over to the British Court. The British Court has to say, no, no, no that will not do, try again. This is an incredibly time consuming effort which may well make it impossible for the parties to agree, hold on to their financing, and otherwise put together a very complex international transaction within a realistic time frame. Therefore, it may lead to results much less valuable to creditors and others than would have been possible had it been possible to do things in a more direct and more immediate way. So, recognizing all the difficulties, they should be overcome if possible.

DANIEL HUNKELER
Thank you. We have two more additional remarks from the public, first Professor Nobel and then Professor Schanze.

PETER NOBEL
Yes, I think there is quite a lot of discussion and also dialogue going on at this time in and around bankruptcy law with the large financial institutions presenting a systemic risk. I think now people worldwide try to design rules, techniques of cooperation, joint action for winding up in emergency cases. What do you expect from these endeavours which are an everyday reality? I read practically every day in the paper about new designs for insolvency procedures for these large institutions, international burden sharing and so on.

CHRISTOPH PAULUS
This is a very valid observation, of course, and I am quoting from the paper which I have not presented to you but in order to make the reading for you afterwards easier and nicer; a colleague of mine, Professor *Flessner*, he has rightfully pointed out that in order to rescue (and we are talking about rescuing when we are talking about systemic crisis) systemic relevant banks, then we need organizational, commercial, financial, and juridical measures. However, the law addresses only juridical measures. The point he is making in this context is that we are talking here about a management task. It is not done by deciding something; it is something which can be done only by means of communication. People have to cooperate. They have to share forces in order to get their thing through. The judge, in these areas, is not only an observer anymore who gives his yes or no. He has to involve him or herself.

PETER NOBEL
If I may add something, in Switzerland in banking cases it is not the judge anymore. This system has been changed. It is actually supervised by the FINMA which makes all the decisions. It is a management task, you know, and the legislature has seen this and

has taken the necessary arrangements. The judges are basically excluded in the field of bank bankruptcies.

JAY WESTBROOK
The banking problem is a special one and in most countries has separate systems as you suggest.

PETER NOBEL
Very important.

JAY WESTBROOK
Incredibly important, unbelievably important, maybe the most important, but it is generally done with much more involvement of regulators, I am sorry to say, regarding tax payer money and so forth and so on. And there it seems to me that the regulators do communicate with each other pretty constantly and informally. But at the same time we also have, because of this crisis, a number of large multi-national companies in serious trouble. And because it is a systemic crisis, in many cases these are not bankruptcies because the companies have failing businesses, it is because of the credit, the lack of availability of credit in the current atmosphere. So, you really have companies that it would be a crime not to rescue because they are really perfectly viable businesses, but they need time and opportunity to negotiate with their creditors. Insolvency proceedings can do that. Again if they are multinational companies it is difficult to negotiate those agreements without knowing that the courts will be able to work together in order to keep all of these companies going while they go through that process.

ERICH SCHANZE
It is interesting that you talk about judicial dialogue in this situation. Obviously, there is "judicial dialogue" for the refinement of certain rules, and "judicial dialogue" for coping with the administration of new legal problems. In the first variant, judicial dialogue is about consensus building with respect to different the interpretations of certain rules, say of the CISG or in EV regulations. This is more a matter of professional sophistication – and can be done in a very relaxed fashion. What is happening between the judges and administrators concerned with complex international insolvency issues is obviously a dialogue for the alignment of competencies and proper legal process, also issues of the effectiveness of procedure. These are dramatic, very fundamental problems, indeed, which can only be resolved quickly by picking up the phone. Who will get the job? How can we both speed up a procedure? How can we accomplish the essential objectives of doing justice to all affected parties? What are the limits of parochialism? We may need different rules for these two games of judicial dialogue. Or am I wrong? Maybe, I am simply missing the point.

ADAM GOODISON
No, I think that is right. I think what is illustrated by these insolvency cases is that judicial dialogue can only go so far because you can either talk about it in terms of talking to each other about process, about management, about managing issues. But once you drill down into essentially conflict of law issues, each local jurisdiction is going to be applying its local law.

ERICH SCHANZE
May I just add one question? What are the incentives for the officials of engaging in these discourses?

CHRISTOPH PAULUS
As to the first question: This case which I mentioned, the BenQ case, a certain interpretation of Article 3 Paragraph 1 of the European Insolvency Regulation was of relevance. Here, the German judge called his Dutch colleague and told him: I leave it to you, to your Dutch decision on interpretation where the main case shall be opened. As to the second question, it is the efficiency thing. It is where do the creditors get the best outcome. In order to improve that you have this communication and for that reason they enter into it.

DANIEL HUNKELER
We are quickly running out of time. Alberto please, and then a short question of Mr. Steinbrück.

ALBERTO ALEMANNO
Thank you Daniel. I was also very intrigued by the opening statement by Professor Paulus saying that insolvency law is much ahead of any other area of law in terms of dialogue. I think that you have been showing us – and also your comment, Erich, really confirmed that – that the reasons behind this phenomenon are the following: the dialogue in insolvency is a sort of need, is a sort of conflict of law tool. In sum, it is a recipe for efficiency. So, if you do not do this, you do not really move and you do not come out with solutions. Instead, in international courts, judicial dialogue is a sort of luxury, it is not a need, but a mere possibility. It is something you can do. You can get better solutions but is about refinement of rules as you said correctly. So, we are really talking about two different methological ideas probably.

BEN STEINBRÜCK
My question goes in the same direction. Apparently, jurisdiction in insolvency law does not really matter whereas in other areas of European procedure law, for example, in arbitration, it matters a lot. English Courts do not want an Italian Court to say whether an English arbitration clause is valid or not because they are afraid that the Italian court will get it horribly wrong. If English Courts then have to recognize the judgment by the Italian Courts on the merits they might invoke the public policy arguing that there is a valid English arbitration agreement, so they do not recognize this

judgment. So, my question is this: Does the substantive insolvency law matter so little in this field that it is not important which court renders the judgment?

JAY WESTBROOK

Well, that is an excellent question and one of the things that is characteristic of insolvency law, is that choice of law and choice of forum are intimately connected. More so perhaps than in any area of the law. So, to some extent if one adopts rules out of necessity, I agree entirely with that, that tends to focus jurisdiction and administration in a particular primary court that has the tendency also to make that court's laws crucial in the resolution of various issues. Not all issues by any means, but many issues. So, yes there is a close connection. But it is a connection that is increasingly recognized and accepted around the world. It is a sort of choice of law rule, if you will, that is tied to choice of forum because of the nature of insolvency as Professor Paulus described earlier. So, that is the best answer to your question. I think that would be my response to your question.

CHRISTOPH PAULUS

You remember the tourism which he has described? We have it not only on the level of private persons, we have it also to a certain degree on the level of enterprises, which are moving from Germany to England in order to get privileges and the advantage of the English insolvency law. We have a kind of bankruptcy tourism now and in so far substantive law matters, of course.

DANIEL HUNKELER

Dear Colleagues, I thank you very much for participating so actively. It was a very interesting discussion. A lot of issues, of course, still remain; they may give us an opportunity for a later discussion.

Keynote

The Flash Airlines Case: Transatlantic Ping Pong or Judicial Cooperation?

CHRISTELLE CHALAS[1]

Introduction

In the absence of a universal jurisdiction treaty, the only way to solve problems of competing jurisdictions is negotiation or at least cooperation between courts in multinational cases. The objective of such cooperation would be to determine the optimal forum for each case. The question is whether such cross-border judicial cooperation can be practically set in place? It is a matter of fact that public authorities have difficulties with the idea of cooperating with each other: Not only do linguistic barriers at times make communication difficult, but the main obstacle to cooperation is the absence of a sufficient level of mutual trust.

Cooperation becomes even more difficult when the case is linked to two juridical cultures that bear different approaches to treat the question of jurisdiction: While the common law courts enjoy discretion to exercise or not the jurisdiction they are vested with, a civil law court by contrast must accept jurisdiction according to mandatory legal rules. At first glance, the common law concept of flexible jurisdiction appears to be more apt to cooperation with foreign courts than the mandatory system of civil law[2]. Indeed, the common law court's discretion could be exercised in a cooperative way[3].

The "Flash Airlines" Case, originating from a tragic airplane accident in Egypt involving many French passengers, addresses the specific issue of judicial cooperation in the two legal cultures. After presenting the facts of the case and the various procedural steps it went through (A), we will try to answer the delicate question of whether the U.S. American and the French court involved in this cross-border litigation entered into a process of judicial cooperation (B). The answer is not clear and reveals the extreme difficulty of building international judicial cooperation in litigation, in particular in fields such as torts, where strong economic interests are at stake.

---

1 Lecturer at the University Paris 8.

2 See P. Schlosser, *Jurisdiction and International Judicial and Administrative Co-operation*, Collected Courses of The Hague Academy of International Law, 2000, t. 284, p. 27.

3 Ibid.

A. The case (facts and procedure)

I. The accident

In January 2004, a Boeing 737 crashed in the Red Sea off the coast of Egypt a few minutes after leaving Sharm-El-Sheikh for Paris. All of the 135 passengers, most of whom were French, and the 13 crew members, died. Among the victims were Philippe Fouchard, a French leading scholar in arbitration and private international law, and many members of his family. The airline company (Flash Airlines) was Egyptian and so was its insurer. The aircraft had been owned by the Californian International Lease Finance Corporation (ILFC). This company had leased the aircraft to Flash Airlines in 2001. Boeing, as the manufacturer of the aircraft as well as its subcontractors or suppliers (Honeywell International and Parker Hannifin) were U.S. American.

In December 2004, 488 plaintiffs brought legal proceedings in France against Flash Airlines and its insurer under the Warsaw Convention. Almost simultaneously, in January 2005, 150 plaintiffs sued the U.S. parties before the District Court of the Central District of California. They alleged strict liability, negligence and breach of warranty against the mentioned U.S. corporations. Flash Airlines and its insurer were not subject to jurisdiction in the United States.

II. The Californian Procedure

The U.S. American defendants filed a joint motion to dismiss on the grounds of forum non conveniens. Forum non conveniens is a common law doctrine, which allows the court to decline jurisdiction and dismiss the case when it thinks that a foreign court would be more appropriate to deal with it[4]. The defendants argued that France was a more appropriate forum for the product liability action.

To succeed, the defendants had to show that there was an adequate alternative forum (1) and that the balance of private and public interest factors favoured dismissal (2).

(1) To satisfy the adequacy requirement, the defendants first had to prove that the French courts would assume jurisdiction over the plaintiff's claim. Not surprisingly, both parties submitted contradicting evidence in support of their respective position. Nevertheless, the Californian court thought that there was a reasonable basis for con-

4 The US Supreme Court laid the foundations of the forum non conveniens doctrine for federal courts in its 1947 ruling in *Gulf Oil Corp. v Gilbert* (330. US. 501 (1947)). The modern liberal version of the U.S. forum non conveniens doctrine, was set in 1981 by the Supreme Court in *Piper Aircraft v Reyno* (454. US. 235 (1981)). For a study on the doctrine of forum non conveniens (in French langage), see Christelle Chalas, L'exercice discrétionnaire de la competence juridictionnelle en droit international privé, PUAM, 2000; A. Nuyts, L'exception De Forum Non Conveniens (Etude de Droit International Privé), Bruylant, 2003.

cluding that French courts would be able to exercise jurisdiction over the plaintiffs' claims. This statement was reached by the Californian court mainly because the defendant agreed, as a condition of dismissal, to submit to the jurisdiction of a French court in action re-filed by plaintiff there and to toll any statutes of limitations that might apply. But, since the possibility remained that French courts would refuse jurisdiction, the Californian court conditioned its order of dismissal upon the French court's assumption of jurisdiction over the plaintiff's claim.

(2) The next question for the Californian court was whether the French forum was also a more convenient one. This would be the case, if the public and private interests weighed in favour of France. The court applied the criteria of the U.S. Supreme Court's Gulf Oil ruling, which are: "ease of access to sources of proof; compulsory process to obtain the attendance of hostile witnesses, and the cost of transporting friendly witnesses; and other problems that interfere with an expeditious trial" (Gulf Oil v Gilbert, 330 US. 501, 508 (1947)).

First, regarding the ease of access to sources of proof, the Court found that most of the evidence, in particular the witnesses and various documents pertaining to the victims, was located outside of the United States and was more easily accessible in France. It also noted that only one piece of the wreckage of the plane was actually located in the United States and that the evidence to be supplied by the Californian-based lessee ILFC – a 700 pages document relating to the accident – was minimal and easily transportable to France. On the contrary, the court thought that the evidence located in France would be difficult, if not impossible to obtain in California.

Second, regarding the attendance of witnesses, the court underlined that because most of the victim witnesses resided in France, it was unlikely that the court could be able to compel them to testify. And, if they were willing to testify voluntarily, the cost of their travel to the court district would be too great. Accordingly, the Court concluded that this factor also weighed in favour of dismissal.

Third, regarding the expeditiousness of trial, the Court noted that Flash Airlines could not be compelled to appear as a defendant in the United States while the plaintiffs' claim against the U.S. American defendants could be brought in France. Since in France an action was already pending against Flash Airlines and its insurer under the Warsaw Convention, the Californian Court held it would be more convenient to resolve all claims involving all defendants in France.

While private interest factors seemed to favour litigation in France, the Court went on to check the public interest factors, and again it analysed the criteria set by the Gulf Oil ruling, which are: court congestion, the local interest in resolving the controversy, and the preference for having a forum apply a law with which it is familiar (Gulf Oil, 330 US at. 508).

As regards court congestion, courts in Paris seem to be as busy as in California. The Court found that this factor was neutral and did not favour dismissal.

The Court commented that France had a greater interest in hearing the case, first because most of the victims were French. Second, it would be in France's interest to ensure that the heirs and beneficiaries were compensated fairly. The Court recognized that the United States had an interest in ensuring that products manufactured by the United States companies were safe. However, it held that California's interest in this action was minimal since it consisted solely of the fact that ILFC, who leased the aircraft to Flash Airlines two years before the crash, was headquartered in California.

Finally, the court came to the conclusion that a foreign law (either French or Egyptian law) would apply, and found that also this factor weighed in favour of dismissal.

For all these reasons, the Californian court granted defendants' motion to dismiss the action under two conditions, one that the defendants agreed to submit to the jurisdiction of a French court, and two that a French court would accept jurisdiction over the claim.

This second condition represented quite a challenge for the plaintiffs and raised intricate legal questions for the French Courts.

III. The French Procedure

In August 2005, a group of 281 plaintiffs, sued the U.S. parties in front of a French Court, but petitioned to obtain a judgment declining jurisdiction.

The difficulty here is that this kind of declaratory relief has traditionally been unavailable under French civil procedure. According to the French Code of Civil Procedure, the issue of jurisdiction is a means of defence and not of action (art. 75 NCPC). What follows is the inadmissibility of a claimant's challenge of jurisdiction of the court to which the claimant submits the case. Without surprise, this very conclusion was reached by the French court of first instance in June 2006[5].

The plaintiffs then appealed to the Paris Court of Appeal which, quite surprisingly and stirring controversies, admitted the petition and ruled on its jurisdiction[6]. The reasoning that evoked the particular judiciary context is of great interest to our subject:

---

5 TGI de Bobigny, the 27th of June 2006.

6 Paris Court of Appeal, the 6th of March 2008, n°06-15786. For commentaries of this decision in French language see: Patrick Courbe, Dalloz 2008, p. 1452; I. Gallmeister, Dalloz 2008, p. 852; G. Cuniberti, Journal du droit international (Clunet) 2008, p. 27.

First, it underlined that the plaintiffs' exercise of rights was impeded by the fact that the forum non conveniens exception was available in California, while French Courts were bound by French rules on jurisdiction, meaning that courts had no discretion to decide that a foreign forum was more appropriate.

The French Court also noted that the American Court had not yet solved the problem of international jurisdiction but that it had simply decided not to exercise its own jurisdiction. The French Court considered that the U.S. Court had materially transferred the case. The Court went on saying that the U.S. Court, by making its dismissal conditional upon the French's Court acceptance of jurisdiction, had invited the French judge to rule on international jurisdiction in this case. Remarkably enough, the Court of Appeal notes that the French judge "cannot be the only one to be excluded from the debate concerning his own jurisdiction since the question arises in a context of mutual trust which leads to international cooperation and coordination of different juridical systems".

For that reason, the Court came to the conclusion that the action seeking a declaratory relief on jurisdiction was admissible.

This first and most controversial step being made, the Court still had to examine if it had jurisdiction over the case. The final answer was that it did not. Even though, this aspect of the French Court decision could also be discussed, it is of less interest to our concern.

What is interesting is that despite saying that French Courts had no legal possibility to decide which forum was more convenient, the court insisted, in an obiter dictum that the U.S. American Court and not French Courts was the most appropriate forum. Not only that, the French Court openly contradicted the U.S. court's findings almost on each count:

- First, the Court did not consider the action brought by the plaintiffs against Flash Airlines and its insurer under the Warsaw Convention to be linked to the action in product liability against the U.S. parties. The Court concluded that the risk of inconsistent judgments between France and California did not exist.

- The Court also found that most of the evidence was located in the United States and referred to the necessity to hear U.S. witnesses for the liability action, to evidence relating to the aircraft (manufacture, tests, and certification), and to the location of a part of the wreckage in the hands of the U.S. National Transport Safety Board.

- Finally, the Court also referred to the availability of pre-trial discovery in the United States, concluding that U.S. American judges had more power to investigate the facts relating to the defendant's liability.

With its reasoning the Court of Appeal attempted to send back the case to the United States. Whether this can be considered judicial cooperation is the question we will address in an instant. But before, for the sake of completeness, a few words on the last procedural step that was made following this remarkable judgment.

The French Cour de Cassation was seized by the defendants and it reversed and set aside the aforementioned judgment[7]. It did so, however, on a mere technicality of the French civil procedure, and therefore left the main question, namely concerning the admissibility of declaratory relief, unanswered. It held that no appeal was allowed from the Court of first instance to the Paris Court of Appeal because the former had not ruled on its jurisdiction but only on the admissibility of the jurisdictional challenge. The Cour de Cassation held that no appeal could be lodged against such a decision under French civil procedure (according to articles 544, 545 of CPC). Now, the case is pending in the court of first instance in Bobigny.

B. The question of the judicial cooperation

This dramatic case raises the question whether the Paris Court of Appeal and the Californian Court entered into a process of judicial cooperation. It seems to me that the answer depends on what we mean by "cooperation" between courts: Do we mean a mere interaction, or a real negotiation under conditions of mutual trust or something in between? Professor Schlosser makes a further distinction between passive and active judicial cooperation[8]. Now, where can we place Flash Airlines? There are good arguments to see the forum non conveniens doctrine as an expression of "the will to cooperate" (A), but, forum non conveniens is seldom exercised in a co-operative manner (B). The Flash Airlines case illustrates this duality very well. Nevertheless, I would not exclude that forum non conveniens could become an instrument of international judicial cooperation provided that its use is regulated internationally, ideally by way of international conventions (C).

I. The Forum non conveniens doctrine as a "will to cooperate"

A part of the academic literature presents the forum non conveniens doctrine as a typical instrument of international cooperation between courts. Some describe it as "a less tangible form of judicial assistance"[9]. According to Professor Schlosser, forum non conveniens is a good example of "deliberate judicial passivity as an expression of

7 Cour de cassation, 2ème chambre civile, the 30th of April 2009, n°08-14.883, Bulletin des arrêts de la Cour de cassation.

8 "Jurisdiction and International Judicial and Administrative Co-operation", Collected Courses of the Hague Academy of International Law, 2000, t. 284, p. 29.

9 Bermann, in Goldsmith (ed.), International Dispute Resolution. The Regulation of Forum Selection (Irvington, NY, 1997) 99.

the will to co-operate"[10]. By declining to exercise their jurisdiction, the common law courts recognise the judicial activity of the foreign courts and decide to give them priority because they appear to be more appropriate to deal with the matter. This form of cooperation is normally passive because it consists in a mere abstention of a judge in favour of another judge (there is no active consulting with the other judge).

However, conditional dismissal brings co-operation one step further (as in our case). Professor Schlosser sees such practice as "the most intensive and highly interesting manner of co-operating among courts in the context of forum non conveniens"[11]. Under a conditional dismissal the local judge does not simply refuse the case, but contributes to the finding of the appropriate forum by imposing conditions upon the defendant. These conditions mainly serve to facilitate proceedings in front of the alternative forum. The non-compliance with the undertakings made by the defendant vis-à-vis the court can go as far as allowing the plaintiffs to re-file the proceedings before the court having declined its jurisdiction.

In his article on "International Judicial Negotiation"[12], Professor Westbrook considers bankruptcy and forum non conveniens to be the two leading examples of the growing phenomenon of international judicial negotiation.

To some extent, the Flash Airlines case illustrates these arguments. It is true that the decision of the Californian court does not contain an explicit offer to cooperate with the French court, but that makes the answer of the Paris Court of Appeal even more extraordinary. As we have already seen, the terms used by the Court are unequivocal: the conditional dismissal of the Californian court was interpreted as a clear "invitation" to the French court to enter "into a process of international judicial cooperation and coordination of juridical systems". These are not only words, since the court took the risk to rule contra legem by admitting the plaintiffs to challenge its jurisdiction by way of action.

The openness of the Paris Court of Appeal cannot be denied in this case. Indeed, it would have been much simpler to ignore the Californian "invitation" and state, just as the judge of first instance did, the inadmissibility of the plaintiff's action. Neither have the judges of the Cour de Cassation demonstrated anything close to a trans-national judicial cooperation. It is also striking to see the Paris Court of Appeal entering into a kind of forum non conveniens analysis despite its non-existence in French law. One could think that the Paris Court of Appeal wanted to give a fully relevant answer to the U.S. American judge and in order to do so, went as far as adopting its own specific approach to international jurisdiction.

---

10 Op.cit., p. 381.
11 Op.cit., p. 66.
12 38 Texas International Law Journal, 2003, p. 567.

All these aspects of the French judgment make it tempting to conclude, like some scholars actually did, that the Paris Court of Appeal had entered into judicial cooperation and displayed mutual trust. Unfortunately, other aspects of the judgment seem to contradict this optimistic conclusion.

II. The exercise of discretion under forum non conveniens: «le dialogue de sourds»

In French language we have this expression: «le dialogue de sourds» – which means "dialogue between the deaf", and I believe it fits quite well to describe the situation here.

Naturally, we cannot say for sure what the judges of the Paris Court of Appeal bore in mind when they rendered their unusual judgment. It seems to me, however, that if there was a negotiation, it occurred more likely between each party and its respective national judge (2°) rather than between the French and the U.S. judges (1°).

1°) I see two principal aspects of the French court's judgment that speak against the asserted judicial cooperation.
First, we can see quite clearly that the French Court is aware of its lacking discretionary powers in comparison with its U.S. homologue. When the Court states that, I quote, "the French judge cannot be the only one to be excluded from the debate on jurisdiction", it expresses its regret that a U.S. American Court could decide better than the French Court on the French Court's own jurisdiction. Furthermore, in saying that the plaintiffs' exercise of rights was impeded by the fact that the forum non conveniens exception was available in California but not in France, the French Court also appears to be upset by the procedural inequality between the plaintiff and the defendants. Indeed this leads to the paradoxical result that not the plaintiffs but the defendants hold the keys to choose the competent forum! In other words, what we have here is a case of defendant's forum shopping. In my opinion, the French Court's statements demonstrate that cooperation is difficult when the cooperating parties do not have equal powers; in our case, when the courts and then the parties are not equally equipped with procedural tools.

Second, although cooperation does not mean that you have to agree on everything, refuting every single point of your adversary does not reveal a very cooperative posture. When the Court of Appeal, surprisingly enough, tries to justify that it is not the appropriate forum for the case (which was useless because it lacked jurisdiction) it goes on, as we have seen, contradicting the findings of the U.S. American court in almost all respects.

2°) Our opinion is that the negotiation rather took place between each court and its respective national party than between the courts.

The truth is that it is extremely difficult, if not impossible, to appreciate the sincerity of a judicial dialogue between courts in forum non conveniens cases. The debates this doctrine give rise to and are always more or less "polluted" by the economic interests of the parties. Put briefly, forum non conveniens is very often an "outcome determinative"[13]. Everyone knows that victims in tort cases are better compensated in the United States than anywhere else in the world. After all, the French Court of Appeal would not be the first one in the world to try to send its nationals in a US forum hoping for better compensation[14]. Would that be cooperation?

Although, according to Professor Schlosser, conditional dismissal might be a very sophisticated form of international judicial cooperation, I believe that it most of all permits bargains between U.S. American defendants and their national judge: It was the defendants who offered to submit to the court's conditions in exchange for dismissal. In our case, it looks as if the defendants were ready to submit to French jurisdiction at any cost only for the sake of avoiding U.S. American justice. In other cases we have seen that U.S. American defendants were even willing to acknowledge liability in front of the foreign forum as the price for the U.S. court's dismissal.

In conclusion, I think it is difficult to speak of international judicial cooperation in this case. The Californian Court unilaterally dismissed the case like all U.S. American Courts do when an accident occurs abroad and the case is brought by a foreign plaintiff against a U.S. defendant. The Californian decision is by no way extraordinary. It is telling that the case did not arouse much academic interest on the other side of the Atlantic – in fact it was not even commented in U.S. academic literature. The French Court of Appeal's reaction is, by contrast, remarkable. Maybe the will to cooperate was there, but the result and the motivation of the French decision tell that this cooperative will was quickly overwhelmed by the very sensitive conflict between the parties.

Now, do the foregoing comments imply that forum non conveniens can never be an instrument of international judicial dialogue? I do not think so. However, the weaknesses of forum of non conveniens must be addressed, which can be best achieved by way of international conventions that seek to establish mutual trust.

13 This expression is used by Professor David. W. Robertson in "Forum Non Conveniens in America and in England: A Rather Fantastic Fiction", 103. L. Q. Rev. 398, p.420 (1987).

14 A tragic example of this approach is the Bhopal case, resulting from the biggest industrial accident of the XX° century in India: the Indian government preferred to finance the proceedings of the heirs of the victims in New York than to give the Indian justice the means to compensate them properly.

III. Forum non conveniens and the need for regulation by way of international conventions

Forum non conveniens has become a somewhat automatic defence against foreign plaintiffs in transnational liability actions. It is conventionally used as the principal weapon against forum shopping in the USA. One of the most recent doctrinal developments is that a court may conduct a forum non conveniens analysis without even first establishing personal jurisdiction over the defendant and subject-matter jurisdiction over the claim[15].

Far from spreading the spirit of cooperation in international litigation, the modern practice of forum non conveniens has prompted brutal retaliations in some foreign countries. To counter the systematic dismissals against foreign plaintiffs by U.S. courts, some South and Central American states have enacted Discrimatory Foreign Laws (DFLs) against U.S. defendants. For example, Guatemalan legislation[16] renders Guatemalan courts unavailable once a lawsuit is filed in a foreign court in order to prevent dismissals by U.S. courts pursuant to a forum non conveniens analysis. In other words, Guatemala will not accept jurisdiction once a lawsuit has been dismissed in the United States. The idea is that since there will be no alternative forum, the US court will be pressured to assume jurisdiction if it wants to avoid a denial of access to justice.

Further, many will find it difficult to speak of forum non conveniens as a means of judicial cooperation, when the memory of the Union Carbide dismissal by the U.S. Court of Appeals for the Second Circuit is still alive. We all cannot turn a blind eye on the fact that most of the victims of one of the worst industrial disasters in the world still have not received any remedy despite the fact that Indian courts were deemed to be an adequate alternative forum. Professor David Robertson has demonstrated that in many cases involving foreign plaintiffs and U.S. defendants, forum non conveniens is equivalent to dismissal on the merits because the claim is never heard again in any court[17]. Based on Robertson's study, another scholar has noted, "Although courts and commentators routinely discuss forum non conveniens as if the issue at stake were a choice between two competing jurisdictions, in fact the usual choice is between litigating in the United States or not at all"[18].

---

15 See *Sinochem Int'l Co v Malay Int'l Shipping Corp.*, 127 S. Ct. 1184, 1188 (2007) ("[A] court need not to resolve whether it has authority to adjudicate the cause (subject-matter jurisdictions) or personal jurisdiction over the defendant if it determines that, in any event, a foreign tribunal is plainly more suitable arbiter of the merits of the case").

16 Ley de Defensa de Derechos Procesuales de Nacionales y Residentes (Guatemala's Law for the Defense of Procedural Rights of Nationals and Residents), art. 2, May, 14, 1997 (Guat). Another prominent example is the Law 364 in Nicaragua.

17 David. W. Robertson, "Forum Non Conveniens in America and in England: A Rather Fantastic Fiction", 103. L. Q. Rev. 398, 409, 418–420 (1987)

18 Laurel E. Miller, Comment, Forum Non Conveniens and State Control of Foreign Plaintiff Access to US Courts in International Torts Actions, 58. U. Chi.L.Rev. 1369, 1388 (1991).

However, all these are abuses that we could prevent. In fact, three European Conventions show that a restricted forum non conveniens clause can be used in a genuinely cooperative manner. Take for example the 1996 Hague Convention in Respect of Parental Responsibility and Measures for the Protection of Children (art. 8 and 9)[19], the 2000 Hague Convention on the International Protection of Adults (art. 8) and the 2003 Brussels Regulation on Divorce matters and matters of Parental Responsibility (art. 15)[20]. These texts organise a mechanism of "transfer of actions" between courts

19 Article 8

1 By way of exception, the authority of a Contracting State having jurisdiction under Article 5 or 6, if it considers that the authority of another Contracting State would be better placed in the particular case to assess the best interests of the child, may either

– request that other authority, directly or with the assistance of the Central Authority of its State, to assume jurisdiction to take such measures of protection as it considers to be necessary, or

– suspend consideration of the case and invite the parties to introduce such a request before the authority of that other State.

2 The Contracting States whose authorities may be addressed as provided in the preceding paragraph are

a a State of which the child is a national,

b a State in which property of the child is located,

c a State whose authorities are seised of an application for divorce or legal separation of the child's parents, or for annulment of their marriage,

d a State with which the child has a substantial connection.

3 The authorities concerned may proceed to an exchange of views.

4 The authority addressed as provided in paragraph 1 may assume jurisdiction, in place of the authority having jurisdiction under Article 5 or 6, if it considers that this is in the child's best interests.

Article 9

1 If the authorities of a Contracting State referred to in Article 8, paragraph 2, consider that they are better placed in the particular case to assess the child's best interests, they may either

– request the competent authority of the Contracting State of the habitual residence of the child, directly or with the assistance of the Central Authority of that State, that they be authorised to exercise jurisdiction to take the measures of protection which they consider to be necessary, or

– invite the parties to introduce such a request before the authority of the Contracting State of the habitual residence of the child.

2 The authorities concerned may proceed to an exchange of views.

3 The authority initiating the request may exercise jurisdiction in place of the authority of the Contracting State of the habitual residence of the child only if the latter authority has accepted the request.

20 Transfer to a court better placed to hear the case:

1. By way of exception, the courts of a Member State having jurisdiction as to the substance of the matter may, if they consider that a court of another Member State, with which the child has a particular connection, would be better placed to hear the case, or a specific part thereof, and where this is in the best interests of the child:

(a) stay the case or the part thereof in question and invite the parties to introduce a request before the court of that other Member State in accordance with paragraph 4; or

(b) request a court of another Member State to assume jurisdiction in accordance with paragraph 5.

2. Paragraph 1 shall apply:

(a) upon application from a party; or

(b) of the court's own motion; or

(c) upon application from a court of another Member State with which the child has a particular connection, in accordance with paragraph 3.

A transfer made of the court's own motion or by application of a court of another Member State must be accepted by at least one of the parties.

when the court of a Member/Contracting State having normal jurisdiction considers that the authority of another Member/Contracting State would be better placed in the particular case to assess the best interests of the child or the adult. The very interesting thing about these rules are the procedural safeguards that ensure an effective and secure use of this mechanism: transfer is exceptional; the courts to which the case can be transferred are limited; the two concerned courts have to agree on the transfer and may proceed to an exchange of views; there is no dismissal of the case but only a stay of proceedings to await the answer of the receiving court; in the case of the mentioned Brussels Regulation, this answer has to come in the short mandatory delay of six weeks.

Of course, the use of the forum non conveniens doctrine is very particular in this context because its unique objective is "to assess the best interests of the child". One may think that this kind of litigation is less controversial between the parties than tort liability and, for that reason, seems to offer an inherent barrier against abuse. However, such argumentation is questionable, if we take into account that battles between parents for child custody can sometimes become quite vicious.

In my opinion, even in fields with as much economic impact as in tort law, a well conceived clause of forum non conveniens could provide a useful form of international judicial cooperation. First of all, its use should be only exceptional and that could only be ensured if very restricted conditions were imposed upon the court wishing to waive its obligation to exercise its jurisdiction. A good example of a carefully drafted clause can be found in the defunct Hague Judgments Convention. This ambitious scheme

---

3. The child shall be considered to have a particular connection to a Member State as mentioned in paragraph 1, if that Member State:
(a) has become the habitual residence of the child after the court referred to in paragraph 1 was seised; or
(b) is the former habitual residence of the child; or
(c) is the place of the child's nationality; or
(d) is the habitual residence of a holder of parental responsibility; or
(e) is the place where property of the child is located and the case concerns measures for the protection of the child relating to the administration, conservation or disposal of this property.
4. The court of the Member State having jurisdiction as to the substance of the matter shall set a time limit by which the courts of that other Member State shall be seised in accordance with paragraph 1.
5. The courts of that other Member State may, where due to the specific circumstances of the case, this is in the best interests of the child, accept jurisdiction within six weeks of their seisure in accordance with paragraph 1(a) or 1(b). In this case, the court first seised shall decline jurisdiction. Otherwise, the court first seised shall continue to exercise jurisdiction in accordance with Articles 8 to 14.
6. The courts shall cooperate for the purposes of this Article, either directly or through the central authorities designated pursuant to Article 53.

which attempted to replicate the success of the 1968 Brussels Convention on a global scale, provided a watered-down version of the forum non conveniens doctrine[21].

However, most important of all is the procedural regime of the exception and in this respect the Hague Convention was not ambitious enough. The dialogue between courts should not remain silent like in the Flash Airlines Case. With modern communication tools, the time has now come for the courts to talk with each other over national borders.

First, in order to avoid denial of justice, it is crucial for the dismissing court to be certain that an alternative forum is actually available to the plaintiff. A court should not waive its obligation to exercise its jurisdiction, unless it has assurance that another forum has jurisdiction over the case. This sine qua non condition would obstruct the U.S. American practice of conditioning dismissal upon a defendant's agreement to submit to the jurisdiction of the foreign court (like in the Flash Airline Case).

Second, it is not sufficient that a court wishing to waive its jurisdiction first suspends its proceedings and then declines to exercise jurisdiction once the other court exercises jurisdiction (which was by the way the solution of the defunct Hague Convention). Of course, a stay of proceedings is always better than a dismissal, but even better is a "transfer of the case" between courts that necessarily involves an active and direct dialogue. The European texts provide a good source of inspiration in this respect. We could also mention the "Leuven /London Principles on Declining and Referring Jurisdiction in Civil and Commercial Matters" adopted by The International Law Association in 2000. These principles provide a very relevant scheme for referral of matters between courts and full support should be given to such courageous proposals (that, however, presuppose a sufficient level of trust between judicial authorities).

---

21 Article 22 Exceptional circumstances for declining jurisdiction

1. In exceptional circumstances, when the jurisdiction of the court seised is not founded on an exclusive choice of court agreement valid under Article 4, or on Article 7, 8 or 12, the court may, on application by a party, suspend its proceedings if in that case it is clearly inappropriate for that court to exercise jurisdiction and if a court of another State has jurisdiction and is clearly more appropriate to resolve the dispute. Such application must be made no later than at the time of the first defence on the merits.

2. The court shall take into account, in particular –

a) any inconvenience to the parties in view of their habitual residence;

b) the nature and location of the evidence, including documents and witnesses, and the procedures for obtaining such evidence;

c) applicable limitation or prescription periods;

d) the possibility of obtaining recognition and enforcement of any decision on the merits.

3. In deciding whether to suspend the proceedings, a court shall not discriminate on the basis of the nationality or habitual residence of the parties.

4. If the court decides to suspend its proceedings under paragraph 1, it may order the defendant to provide security sufficient to satisfy any decision of the other court on the merits.

5. When the court has suspended its proceedings under paragraph 1,

a) it shall decline to exercise jurisdiction if the court of the other State exercises jurisdiction, or if the plaintiff does not bring the proceedings in that State within the time specified by the court; or

b) it shall proceed with the case if the court of the other State decides not to exercise jurisdiction.

Discussion

CARL BAUDENBACHER

Thank you very much, Christelle. That has been a wonderful finale.

ALAN RAU

This is really fascinating. Unfortunately, nothing is more opaque than the procedure of another system and so what I want to say will undoubtedly sound naïve to you, in which case I do hope you will set me straight. It seems to me that the problem, here, stems from what strikes me as the incoherent distinction and dichotomy in French law between defences and causes of action, between sword and shield. Suppose, for example, that the Tribunal of First Instance had been able to consider the jurisdictional challenge on a declaratory basis, on the request for a declaratory judgment as to whether there is jurisdiction, without worrying about whether it was a defence or a cause of action. We have a live controversy. The controversy is the same no matter whether it is an affirmative cause of action, or a defense, and, it should not matter who gets to the court house first. We would have an immediate answer to the American court and then the French litigation could proceed immediately if there was jurisdiction under the French understanding of jurisdiction. So, a lot of the problem, I think, stems from that. Now, from one point of view then, one framework would be to say that part of the problem, I think, results from a rather outdated conceptual framework of civil procedure, but another way of looking at it might be that the French Courts seem to be showing a rather touching concern and solicitude for French plaintiffs, to enable them to avoid having to appear in French Courts and to save them the absolute right of every Frenchman to appear in an American Court. That is a little strange. If that is the real engine that is driving this machine, I have a little bit of difficulty finding sympathy for it.

CHRISTELLE CHALAS

I think you might be right with regard to the French Court's efforts to help the plaintiffs and that's also what I suggested in my presentation. The French Court would not be the first one in the world to try to do that. What is really the French Court's intention? It is difficult to say. It may appear to us that the court is trying to help French plaintiffs, but can we be sure? I do not know. As I have said in my contribution, some French scholars even wrote that it was an amazingly cooperative judgment and evidence for an open-minded approach to transnational issues. To follow up on your first point, I do not think that the problem of this case really lies in procedural conceptions of French law. In my opinion, it may be that France simply did not have jurisdiction in this case. I did not develop this question in my presentation, but, indeed the Flash

Airlines Case would present very complex questions with respect to the jurisdiction of French Courts. So, maybe what should have happened in order to avoid this trouble is that the American Court had made sure that the French Court would assume jurisdiction over the case. Sure, they had contradicting evidence about this issue and it even mentioned that there would still be a chance that the French Court would decline its jurisdiction over the case. We see that the question of jurisdiction was substantively controversial and not much of a formal issue of available actions and defences in French civil procedure.

ALAN RAU
If you had a mechanism by which the French Courts could immediately on the request of a plaintiff decide yes or no, up or down, whether we have jurisdiction, the American Court would have its answer immediately.

CHRISTELLE CHALAS
Ok, we could have had an answer, perhaps six months before, but would it not have been better to have it in California already?

BEN STEINBRÜCK
I have got a remark on European law. The concept of forum non conveniens is a one-way street in your case. American Courts are allowed to stay their proceedings in favour of a more appropriate place, but French Courts as a member of the European Union are not allowed to do so. If this is a tort claim before the French Courts and they would have jurisdiction under a jurisdictional head of the Brussels Regulation, European law would forbid them to apply this concept as the ECJ has ruled in Owusu. In this case, the English courts tried to refer their case to Jamaica because an accident had happened there and they thought it should be heard overseas, but the European Court said no, since the defendants were domiciled in England. So, it had to be heard in an English Court. So this concept is, I think, very interesting from a conceptual point of view in the future but, as the way the law stands now, French Courts just would not be allowed to do it. It is now discussed in the Heidelberg report whether disputes that actually relate to third countries, non-European countries, should be excluded from the rigid rule that says that you always apply the European jurisdictional heads under the Regulation. If I understand you correctly, if there would be a tort claim jurisdiction in France, this would have to be exercised.

CHRISTELLE CHALAS
Yes, of course. There is absolute absence of flexibility and discretion not only inside the Brussels Regulation, but also within French law on international jurisdiction, where the rules are largely mandatory. However, in this case, it could very well be that jurisdiction could not be based on a heading of the Brussels Regulation because the defendants were not domiciled in the EU and that is the condition of the Regulation's applicability. This is the reason why the Court of Appeal's decision is so striking: Despite admitting that forum non conveniens does not exist under French law and saying

that French Courts do not have jurisdiction, the court goes on, and in fact, enters into a sort of forum non conveniens analysis. That is why this decision raises so many questions that one could almost believe the Court wanted to favour its nationals by sending them back to the United States.

BEN STEINBRÜCK
This was not a tort claim in the French Court, right? The claimant asked for a declaration that the French courts did not have jurisdiction? So it did not fall under the Regulation. I think that is the important difference, that you did not have a tort claim in the French courts.

CHRISTELLE CHALAS
No, of course not, initially, it was not a tort claim. But today, after the Cour de Cassation's decision, the plaintiffs are again in front of the judge of first instance and they have to argue on the merits. Now, let us imagine that there is an appeal against the judgment of the court of first instance and jurisdiction is challenged again. What would happen then? There is a problem here. The result could be very dramatic because then the plaintiffs might end up without any judicial remedy. Could they in such a case go back the United States?

BEN STEINBRÜCK
I understood you correctly. They stayed on the condition that the other court accepts its jurisdiction. Since the other court did not accept it, they will hear the case.

CHRISTELLE CHALAS
Yes, perhaps. But there is case law on forum non conveniens, in which the American courts checked whether the decision of not admitting jurisdiction was obtained in good faith. And that could be discussed here, because, as you maybe know, Article 14 of the French civil code grants a privilege of jurisdiction to French plaintiffs and here we are dealing with two hundred French plaintiffs. So, would the American Court, being aware of this privilege, find it a proper decision of a French Court to decline jurisdiction over two hundred French plaintiffs? I am not sure. I hope that all this will not happen and that the case stays in France, where the parties argue on the merits and receive a final decision as they deserve it. Still, it is not excluded that the worst could happen in this case. Rather than talking about cooperation, we could be confronted with a denial of justice.

JAY WESTBROOK
I liked your talk very much. I have a comment and a question. The comment is, I am no defender of the US doctrine of forum non conveniens, believe me. It produces perverse results, there is no question about that. But there are other cases, for example, in which foreign non conveniens, for example, has its uses. There was a trade mark suit going on in Japan. The American party tried to bring an American suit to pre-empt the suit that was happening in Japan. It was over the defendant's use of the trade mark

in Japan. Obviously, the case should be in Japan, but the Americans said, well, but the case in Japan goes on and on and it is never resolved. So, the US Court said, well, we think it should be in Japan. We defer to the Japanese Court. We dismiss, but if you come back in two years or so and nothing has been done in Japan, then we will consider re-opening it. Well, this is a very different case from something like Flashlights. That is just a comment.

Secondly I have just a question on French procedure. Could or does the French Court routinely decide on its own jurisdiction regardless of the parties? That is, we have a doctrine that says the US court must be satisfied of its jurisdiction, whether or not the parties raise it. I was curious about French jurisdiction.

CHRISTELLE CHALAS
Can you please repeat the question again? Just to be sure.

JAY WESTBROOK
In the US, if the parties come before the court, even though both of them say: "Fine judge, you have jurisdiction", The judge has an obligation to understand that the court has jurisdiction or dismiss the case, even if the parties do not argue lack of jurisdiction, subject matter jurisdiction correct. So, in that case, does a similar situation exist in France?

CHRISTELLE CHALAS
No, not according to the Brussels Regulation, because – outside areas of exclusive jurisdiction – entering an appearance without contesting jurisdiction provides a basis for jurisdiction. Now, in French domestic law on international jurisdiction, if the defendant does not contest jurisdiction, the court still has a faculty to declare itself not competent. So, in this respect, there is no mandatory rule and the judge can ex officio decide or not on jurisdiction. However, to go back to our initial debate, if a party wants to contest jurisdiction, it has to be the defendant. It cannot be the plaintiff. The wisdom goes that if you size a court, it is not for challenging jurisdiction, it is for receiving justice. That is how it works.

DANIEL HUNKELER
Listening to this highly interesting speech and this highly interesting case, leads me to a new definition of forum non conveniens. An example for forum non conveniens can be judges – being normal human beings – who sometimes just do not want to work.

CHRISTELLE CHALAS
Do you mean that the French judges did not want to work on this?

DANIEL HUNKELER
I did not say which judges.

CARL BAUDENBACHER
If I may add one remark here: Richard Posner wrote an article under the beautiful title "What do judges maximize?" And he gave the answer, "the same as everybody else, their own utility". The question is then, what is a judge's utility? And he named a couple of utilities, for instance, prestige, power, influence, reputation, being promoted to a higher court, not being annulled by a higher court and he added two things, moonlighting and if moonlighting is not possible, leisure.

ALBERTO ALEMANNO
Thank you. Looking into the future, at the end of your presentation you seemed to suggest that in order to avoid a situation like the one you just described, a possible solution would be to agree through a convention on a forum non conveniens at world-wide level. Which would be the incentives to do so? Why states around the globe should do so, when in reality some member states have it today, like the US, and they like to use it? Some of the states are stuck because they cannot use it, like in Europe. So, why should they agree on a standardised forum non conveniens?

CHRISTELLE CHALAS
Because, if you think about, it is a wonderful mechanism to resolve recurrent problems that we have been discussing for years now, which are parallel litigation, competing jurisdictions and this forum shopping problem. I think the civil law tradition has evolved quite much in this respect. For example, we find a very good forum non conveniens clause in the Brussels II Regulation after all. We find another example in the defunct Hague convention, which provided a watered down version for forum non conveniens, but still a forum non conveniens clause. I think we had a very good draft, except maybe for the procedural regime which to my concern was not strict enough. The negotiations showed at least how common law and civil law countries could meet and agree on a forum non conveniens clause, something which would have been highly improbable only fifteen years ago. And here, don't you think that the Court of Appeal is sorry not to have this mechanism and is actually jealous about the American Court's procedural tools? Maybe this is what its obiter dictum wanted to say, "Look, we can do it too. We can also figure out where it is more convenient to raise evidence." The Court might have wanted to demonstrate its readiness. And maybe, in fact, we are ready for an international rule of forum non conveniens.

CARL BAUDENBACHER
Ok, thank you very much once more Christelle.

Closing Remarks

CARL BAUDENBACHER[1]

The programme now foresees that I make some concluding remarks. I think we had two very fruitful days. We started yesterday morning with my little introduction. I suggested that there should be a triad consisting of prescribed, necessary and voluntary judicial dialogue. On the necessary, I forgot to mention that in the new Lugano Convention, there has been an important change because the dialogue is no longer one sided now, as it was in reality in the past. The courts in the EFTA countries would follow the ECJ, but now there is a provision in the protocol calling on the ECJ also to take into account the decisions of the EFTA countries courts. In fact earlier, this year for the first time, the European Court of Justice made reference to a judgement of the Swiss Supreme Court under the Lugano Convention. This was deemed to be a revolutionary step.

We then had the first speech by Ulrich Haltern. He used a contextual approach vis-à-vis judicial dialogue and he in particular concentrated and focused on the difficulties of certain American judges to participate in this conversation. He made reference to the specific history, the difference in history between the U.S. and Europe and the different beliefs. I think it was a very good launch for the conference.

The first panel dealt with the relationship between the European Court of Justice, the Court of Human Rights in Strasbourg and the WTO. As far as Strasbourg and Luxembourg are concerned, Peer Lorenzen and Lars Bay Larsen demonstrated that there is a very intensive dialogue in what has been called the horizontal relationship, although there are certain judicial conflicts. But there is also a vertical dimension, that became rather clear in particular in the Bosphorus case. We will see whether, after the entry into force of the Lisbon Treaty, the European Union will join the Human Rights Convention. I suppose so, but it may not happen tomorrow. We then had the outlook to the WTO by Alberto Alemanno, who used the example of the recognition of the precautionary principle and showed that not only the WTO played a role there and my own court, the EFTA Court, and the ECJ and the Court of First Instance but also the Commission, which is a hybrid as you all know. It is unparalleled in legal history, I think, to have such an institution like the Commission.

The second panel's subject was arbitration and it became clear that there are many dialogues going on in the framework of the appointment of the arbitrators, within the tribunal, with the parties, with the experts, with the state judge. Ben Steinbrück made

---

1 President of the EFTA Court, Luxembourg, Professor at the University of St. Gallen, Director of the Institute of European and International Business Law, St. Gallen.

it clear that reference to earlier case law is quite frequent in investment cases and in sports cases, but less common in commercial cases.

Keynote speaker Professor Pierre Tercier addressed the privatization of international disputes, but also warned and said there may be *a retour du juge*, not least in view of the actual crisis. He also described a market on which state judges and arbitrators are actors, but he opposed total delocalization and emphasized the important role of the state judge.

Professor Marco Bronckers this morning spoke on the role of dialogue in the relationship between the European Court of Justice and international courts. He made three suggestions at the end of his speech: Firstly, that as a lawyer you have to improve your toolbox; in big cases, it is no more good enough to plead the precedents from your own jurisdiction, you have to use a global view. Secondly, that you should not overstate your case. This is psychology and certain lawyers do overstate. And they may pay. No, they do not pay, but their clients pay. And thirdly, he said, think strategically. Again, you need to have a big case in order to be able to think strategically and I was very impressed by the suggestion that you may go to the WTO first if you have a case there and then try the ECJ to acknowledge some kind of hidden or indirect effect. It is not dialogue as such, it is a dialogue of those who have their eyes open but they do not make it visible in the judgement.

On the third panel on uniform law, I think there was general agreement that under the Vienna Sales Convention there is little dialogue. Professor Mullis made this excellent research, looked into all these cases and the result is obviously not very encouraging. Erich Schanze said even, it doesn't matter. It is more of an academic exercise, but it is of little practical utility. In IP law, we heard that, for instance in Germany, things have changed, that German Courts are much more open-minded than they used to be some twenty years ago.

Now, as far as relevance of dialogue is concerned, the opposite holds true in bankruptcy law. I think you can say that bankruptcy law judges are the front runners of the whole movement. But what they do is not only dialogue, it is cooperation, it is negotiation, it is communication. I noticed that all of the speakers said that they were dealing with a dry subject but they were all particularly witty. Probably, there was a correlation.

Finally, we had Christelle Chalas' beautiful final presentation on this airline case and the further elaboration on whether the forum non conveniens as a judicial, as a legal figure, could be another point for judicial dialogue.

My final point is that I would like to thank our speakers, those who have chaired the panels, but also the participants, the practitioners and students from all over Europe who have come here to St. Gallen. Lastly I have to thank my team. I just mention two of them, Benjamin Rhyner who was responsible for a lot of work behind the scenes and then, in particular, Simon Planzer who right now is writing his doctoral thesis at Harvard. We were always in contact via email and telephone. He did an outstanding job. I have been to many conferences and I have hosted many conferences, I have never seen so much pre-conference email exchange among the panellists and the chairpersons of the panels, and Simon was relentless. Even if things had been made rather clear, he insisted on fine-tuning and I think it shows at the end of the day. It was a very good conference not least because of that. I think he deserves applause.

Now, I wish you all a good trip home and I hope to see you on another occasion.